Praise for

WE'LL BE BACK

"Slaps you upside the head, whether he's talking about parallels with Roman history, why a free people needs to be an armed people, or the critical importance of God-given rights."

—*Dan Bongino,* national radio host and author

"A guided tour of disasters and decline, yet Kurt Schlichter still leads us to that shining city on the hill. It's exciting, thought-provoking, and funny too."

—*David Limbaugh,* author

"America is being fundamentally transformed into a commie craphole, and Schlichter has the fighting spirit and the plan to stop it. No bowties and no pearl-clutching, it's a manual for the based Right."

—*Jim Hanson,* former Special Forces operator and author

"Kurt Schlichter gives you exactly what you expect: something to think about, something to get furious about, and something to laugh about."

—*Buck Sexton,* national radio host and intelligence analyst

"Kurt Schlichter pulls no punches as he exposes the dark goals and ruthless tactics of the Democrat/Communists destroying America— and he does it with his usual crisp insight, ferocious truth-telling, and sharp wit."

—*Monica Crowley,* host of *The Monica Crowley Podcast* and former assistant secretary of the treasury

"America's headed for a showdown, and Kurt pulls no punches talking about a national divorce, Chinese domination, and even civil war.... Pretty good, for an Army guy."

—*Jesse Kelly,* national radio host and Marine

"Certain to be banned by Biden's Ministry of Truth, a delicious stew of facts, experience, wisdom, and incisive spit-take inducing humor. If you want to have hope for America's return to respectability after the humiliating Biden years, this incisive and often hilarious analysis will lift your spirit—unless you are a Bulwark or a Dispatch fan, of course, in which case it will make you flounce around the room with your hands on your hips and your knees held tightly together while you roll your eyes and exclaim, 'Why can't we all just get along?'"

   —*Nick Searcy,* Hollywood acting legend

"Kurt Schlichter, Colonel K to American patriots, is a man who uniquely understands what happened to America in 2016. In *We'll Be Back*, he tells you the future of the America First movement and your role in it. Read it, share it, and act now."

   —*Sebastian Gorka,* national radio host and author

"Takes the reader on a provocative yet well-researched journey to the place we find ourselves today in American politics. He rightly points at our cultural curators as the root of the rot in American politics and our culture yet finds a way to be aspirational about the future."

   —*Salena Zito,* journalist and author

"With the same spirited and combative style of the legendary Andrew Breitbart, Kurt takes the fight directly to the enemies of our country's sacred values, principles, and institutions. When you're not laughing your ass off, you'll be grabbing your torch and pitchfork ready to storm the castle. Piss off a commie, buy this book."

   —*Larry O'Connor,* radio host and columnist

WE'LL BE BACK

KURT SCHLICHTER

WE'LL BE BACK

THE FALL AND RISE OF AMERICA

Regnery Publishing
WASHINGTON, D.C.

Regnery® is a registered trademark and its colophon is a trademark of Salem Communications Holding Corporation

Cataloging-in-Publication data on file with the Library of Congress

ISBN: 978-1-68451-330-7
eISBN: 978-1-68451-343-7

LCCN: 2022937288

Published in the United States by
Regnery Publishing
A Division of Salem Media Group
Washington, D.C.
www.Regnery.com

Manufactured in the United States of America

10 9 8 7 6 5 4 3 2 1

Books are available in quantity for promotional or premium use. For information on discounts and terms, please visit our website: www.Regnery.com.

To Lieutenant Commander Stephen L. Schlichter,
United States Navy

A great father and American patriot

CONTENTS

FOREWORD

In Combined Arms Staff Service School, called CAS3 (but pronounced "CAS-cubed"), they taught us senior captains about briefings. Briefing is what staff officers do. They brief the boss, the commander, so he can make a reasoned decision and capably execute it. We were taught that in a briefing, you tell them what you are going to tell them, then tell them, then tell them what you told them. So, let me do the part about telling you what I am going to tell you right here.

I am going to tell you about where America is now, and about how we are at a perilous crossroads. Just a couple of decades ago, we were great, untouchable, indisputably more powerful than any other nation in human history, and yet today, America is broken, exhausted, and morally bankrupt, and its citizens are at each other's throats. The choices we make in the coming years will determine whether we slide further down the slippery slope into chaos, conflict, and perhaps even collapse. Alternatively, we can decide to make America great again, just like the red hat says.

Here's a spoiler, though—I am going to tell you how no matter what we do, these last few miserable years will have changed us forever. America will be different than it was. But I am an optimist—betting against Americans is always a bad call—and I think we will get through this.

I will sketch out what went wrong. Then I will sketch out how things could get much, much worse. Will we undergo a national divorce? Perhaps a civil war? Might we fall prey to a foreign threat? Sometimes I will illustrate these scenarios with little fictional vignettes, because though you can talk endlessly of theory, sometimes the most powerful way to illustrate reality is to imagine how it all might play out in practice, as my novels about America coming apart demonstrate. So if my discussion shifts briefly into the story of a soldier, or a politician, or a regular mom trying to provide for her family, you know why.

After a parade of horribles, I will offer a parade of, at least, *less* horrible horribles, and then I will talk about how we might come out of this nightmare. Will we re-embrace the Constitution? Will we embrace a rightist strongman? After that, we will discuss the short term, such as what might happen in 2024 and what a conservative leader must do to save the country once he is sworn in in 2025. That agenda will make a lot of liberal blue checks apoplectic, but so be it. If they are busy dealing with apoplexy, they aren't trashing our country.

As Al Davis, famous sportsball person, said, "Just win, baby." We're in this for survival, folks, and we need to act like it. If you are busy clutching your pearls, the bad guys will eventually get around to strangling you with the strand.

Finally, I will tell you how I think all this is likely to end up, and what we must do as individuals to see that this crazy experiment begun on these shores far from civilization by a bunch of guys in powdered wigs continues. Civilizations fall. Someday, America will fall. But it need not be today or tomorrow. I think we patriots will win this existential struggle. America will not come out of this conflict unchanged, but I believe it will come out of it as still America all the same.

There you go. That's what I intend to tell you. So listen up, because now I am actually going to tell you.

CHAPTER ONE

THE PINNACLE

I was there at America's pinnacle, present temporally and physically, right at the very peak of American power.

But I did not know it then. In fact, it would not become clear to me until decades later. On February 24, 1991, I was a few miles west of Hafar al Batin in the Saudi Arabian desert along Tapline Road, at the main command post of the mighty VII Corps with my chemical decontamination platoon, awaiting the order to go forward. In November 1990, President George H. W. Bush announced we would be deploying from our home station in Germany to the desert to go recapture Kuwait. VII Corps, soon pumped up to one hundred thousand troops and tens of thousands of combat vehicles, was the steel wall that had awaited the Warsaw Pact invasion of western Europe for almost a half century. But by then, the Soviet Union was nearly dead, killed by American soft power. Now the full fury of America's hard power was about to fall on the bloated, inept officers and hapless goat-herding conscripts of Saddam Hussein's army.

We had expected to move our platoon up north at the beginning of the ground blitz and support the American 1st Infantry Division (Mechanized), the Big Red One, as it breached the Iraqi forward defenses. The breachers would get splashed—we assessed that Saddam Hussein had bottomless stockpiles of GS, GB, VX, and all sorts of other nasty chemical agents that would be used to hold off our attack. The job of 4th Platoon, 51st Chemical Company, of VII Corps's 2nd Corps Support Command (COSCOM), was to do what no one in his right mind would do and go where that stuff had been employed. Once there, we would clean off the contaminated vehicles and send them back into the fight. But it was not slated to end well. I saw the OPLAN, and there was no follow-on mission for the division. We were going to be rendered combat ineffective at the breach site.

So, we prepped to go. But we never did. The infantry punched through, and Saddam never used his WMD arsenal. The rumor was that word had somehow been passed to him through diplomatic channels that Baghdad would be added to the elite list that consisted of Hiroshima and Nagasaki should he use chemical weapons. I don't know if that's true. I just know all my troops came home.

I was micro-focused on the platoon's mission, so when the final victory was announced, I did not realize what was truly happening in the macro. I understood that I was an insignificant cog in a vast machine that had delivered our countrymen a remarkable triumph, but I would not fully appreciate the significance of the moment until thirty years later when, watching an unrecognizable U.S. military humiliated in the debacle at Kabul Airport, I saw America at its postwar nadir.

VII Corps Main was a huge patch of barren desert encircled by berms pushed up to about ten feet high by the engineers. Most of the inhabitants of the vast operating base were, like us, command and control units or combat support elements. The heart of it, though, was a gathering of woodland camo vehicles (we did not have time to repaint) and a volksfest beer tent brought over from Germany that housed the actual main command post. There, the huge battle staff planning, supporting, and overseeing the fight did its job. I walked through it often, and I heard radio calls going over the net that I later read about in books. I had been initially disappointed to be attached to VII Corps instead of being sent off to the cavalry regiment like some other platoons in the company. Years later, the historian in me appreciated the opportunity to have had a vantage point where I could see and hear history happening.

When President Bush declared the ground war over on February 27, 1991, after about one hundred hours, I did not understand what it meant except in terms of my approximately twenty-man unit. We knew we had won—the vaunted Republican Guard, with its Soviet gear, had been swept away by the unstoppable power of the VII Corps's American tanks and the attached Brit armored division. Not just swept away—annihilated, defeated utterly and completely, so decisively that our potential opponents around the world watched in stunned horror as it dawned on them what America could do.

It could do any damn thing it wanted.

But for those of us there, at the headquarters of the most powerful military formation in human history (the other corps, devastatingly potent though they were, were not pure armored/mechanized forces like VII Corps), the fog of war remained thick enough to obscure the reality. We were too busy performing the mundane chores of war to recognize the full implications of what had just happened. Under General "Stormin' Norman" Schwarzkopf, we had won a victory that would be spoken of along with such legendary battles as Cannae (which General Schwarzkopf studied and drew upon), if our ridiculous academic culture did not teach that history began in 1619 and then skipped ahead to the day Barack Obama was elected.

We changed the nature of the world through our display of irresistible might. Soon, Francis Fukuyama would write his book *The End of History and the Last Man*, assuring us that the new world order we had set in place was permanent. It was not, of course. The status quo is never static for long. This peak meant that the next thirty years would be one long decline.

But that day, America was unchallenged. It simply had no peer competitor. Weeks before, I had been heading east on Tapline Road to go somewhere to do something at one of the forward operating bases ringing Hafar al Batin. We descended into a miles-wide empty valley, a wadi that was full of nothing but dirt and the occasional uromastyx lizard for as far as our eyes could see. Then, a few days later, we dipped down into the valley again, and this time the landscape was carpeted with bases and gear and vehicles and men from horizon to horizon. This was Log Base Echo, the logistic hub that would support the invasion north into Iraq.

Deploying a bunch of tanks is power. But the ability to drop a city into the middle of the desert almost overnight is superpower.

Right then and there, at that dusty base just south of the Iraqi border, America took its place as the world's only superpower. The world beheld us in awe, and in fear.

But in the intervening decades from that high point, America has been in undeniable decline. Our ruling class has grown exhausted and corrupt, choosing expedience over the noblesse oblige that at least theoretically existed in the past. America's previous generation beat the Soviet Union; the one before that put a man on the moon. What has today's generation done but squander our blood and treasure? What are its achievements?

No, Facebook, Twitter, and Grindr do not count as "achievements." But they did promote change, in the sense that they fueled the polarization of the citizenry. America always denied class, and yet it always had a class structure. The thing that kept it from being pernicious in the way it exists elsewhere, as in England, is its permeability. You can change class easily, usually with money that bought you status. But in the early twenty-first century, the understanding of class as reflecting wealth changed. You could suddenly join the elite, or at least become an affiliate member, by the simple expedient of identifying with its values. And social media gave people the platform to do so.

Basically, class divisions became less about bank accounts (though the rich still dominated the heights of the elite) than about publicly harkening to the values of the elite. The left began to focus not on the dirty-fingernailed working man but on the college-indoctrinated white-collar gentry who never actually built anything. The gentry were not rich, nor were the young people who adopted the same mores even as they blended lattes at minimum wage and let their student loan payments for their gender studies degrees slide into default. But they mouthed the same platitudes as their betters and were now adjunct members—or, perhaps, graduate assistants—of the ruling class.

The kids began to rage for the machine as corporations fell under the sway of leaders who identified with the liberal establishment. And the liberal establishment was now America's establishment. The ideology of soft Marxism mixed with the racial hoodoo incubated in the most prestigious campuses of academia took over. The long march through the institutions ended with the marchers setting up camp in the offices of deans and studio heads, in boardrooms and C-suites, and even in places such as the Pentagon that had long resisted before falling to the enemy without a shot.

This elite ideology that rejected objective truth in favor of the unprincipled pursuit of power meant that even though its adherents had taken society's helm, no one was bothering to look where they

CHAPTER TWO

HOW CIVILIZATIONS FALL

America is going to fall.

That's inevitable. All good things come to an end. And so do all bad things. One day, Joe Biden will stop being president, assuming he ever actually started. One day, someone will buy CNN and make it a channel about people renovating their townhouses or doing something else that people in airports might enjoy passing the time watching. One day, Taylor Swift will enter a healthy relationship with a man and have nothing left to write crappy songs about.

Okay, that's maybe stretching it. Taylor Swift without drama is Taylor Swift without a reason to exist. But the point is that if you wait long enough, everything changes. Civilizations are no exception.

Our civilization, like all others, has a sell-by date. We don't know what it is, but it's there. At some point, there will be no U.S. of A., at least not as we know it today. And there will be no Western civilization as we know it either, but that's beyond the scope of this inquiry. The point is that the world as we know it will change—it has to change—and what replaces it will be something different from the world we all grew up in. With luck, what comes next will be something better. But history is not the story of luck. It's largely the story of everything going to hell.

Now, here we are not going to concern ourselves with random catastrophes and calamities. If a meteor hits us tomorrow and sets fire to the atmosphere, there's really not much to say. The same with a pandemic like COVID-19, except without the 99 percent+ survival rate. Ditto the dead walking the earth. Nor is climate change one of the threats we shall consider, mostly because it's a hoax. We're already past several deadlines established for our doom by credulous people high on their little taste of power who insist they love science. Instead, we are interested in human-caused collapse.

The soft shoulders of the trail of tears that is history are littered with the rotting husks of civilizations that came and went. Everyone knows about the Romans, and everyone knows that Rome fell—well, everyone but graduates of our prestigious universities, since dead Europeans are now officially unworthy of study. But the Roman example is particularly instructive because, while it was the Roman Empire that fell, Rome was not always an empire. It started out very differently and changed several times during in the 1,200 or so years of its Italian form; in its Byzantine incarnation, it kept going for nearly another millennium after the last western emperor was deposed in AD 476 by a German barbarian who was tired of pretending that there was still a Western Roman Empire at all. But Rome and Roman civilization did not vanish in a blink. "Falling," when it comes to civilizations, can mean fundamentally changing. It does not necessarily mean disappearing, though it can.

Now, plenty of civilizations have fallen and disappeared, some leaving a legacy behind but others blotted out except for ruins and legends. The Assyrians, for example, had a big-time empire in what we now know as the Middle East, off and on and in various forms, for a couple thousand years. They spearheaded advances in arts and sciences, built up famous cities like Nineveh, and were generally the big dogs in the pound that was the Levant, the area bordering the eastern Mediterranean from Greece to Egypt. These guys did not play—you crossed the Assyrians and they were likely to flay you and use your skin for drapes. Literally. They terrified their neighbors, including the Israelites (the Assyrians are referenced often in the Bible), and were generally considered invulnerable and unchallengeable. But then it suddenly all came crashing down in about 600 BC. The Medes moved in and took over. The Medes fell too, and then others came and went, each dominating that expanse of desert dirt, including the Romans for a while.

The Assyrians at least left some legacy. Other civilizations have fallen and left barely anything behind. Look at the Aztecs. Those monsters terrorized much of what is now Mexico until the conquistadors landed and Hernán Cortés marched on the Aztec capital. He would eventually conquer them with his small band of Spanish adventurers, but he had a lot of help from the locals. See, the Aztecs were jerks, and the whole human sacrifice thing did not win them any friends except among their unpronounceable gods. Hell, even their own bizarre gods didn't much seem to like the Aztecs. All that exhausting dragging people up the pyramid, heaving them onto the moist altar, prying out their hearts, and holding the beating organs up for their deities, and for what? What is the Aztec legacy today? The San Diego State football team is named after them. Mel Gibson made a movie about them with lots of scenes of people's hearts getting torn out. Beret-wearing Hispanic activists in Latinx studies classes at second-tier state colleges cite them when babbling about Aztlán. That's about it.

But if you really want the best example of a rising and falling civilization, you always have to go with the Romans. The Romans had their own founding myths involving abandoned kids and suckling off she-wolves and even some stuff about escapees from Troy, but for our purposes what happened was that a bunch of villages in a hilly area near the Tiber River came together and organized under a king. The king thing was the first phase, and it lasted for a while until the guys who were not the king—that is, everyone else—got sick of having sovereigns, booted the monarchs, and founded the republic. From then on, the idea of a king was so abhorrent to self-respecting Romans that the rumor that someone was aspiring to a crown could get him killed.

The Romans tried something new. They understood they were a bunch of ambitious schemers and *embraced* it. They enforced a system of checks and balances on power, so that no one man could dominate—and, not incidentally, so that any worthy citizen could aspire to greatness. You could attain power, just not such that it would deny your peers the chance to also have power.

The fall of the monarchy, the first big change in the nature of Rome, is important for our analysis because it was not the collapse of a civilization, but a foundational change that altered its trajectory yet left it still recognizably Roman. What we mean here by "fall" is not necessarily the total obliteration that the Aztecs suffered. Perhaps, in the context of America, the potential "fall" is best understood as a morphing of our society into something else. It might look like old America, but it would be fundamentally different.

That is the most likely type of "fall" scenario for America, as we will see later. But that does not mean that it will happen without conflict or upheaval, or without winners and losers. Just ask King Tarquin, who got his ass run out of Rome following a #MeToo issue and spent years trying to get back in. Regardless, this transition from monarchy to republic is one with massive echoes that we feel still today.

The republic was, at its core, about citizens having a role in their own government. That's "citizens," not subjects, and the distinction is important. The ridiculous idea of royalty and the notion of free citizens are irreconcilable, which is one reason the sight of Americans ga-ga-ing over the inbred mutants who make up the current generation of the British royal family is so unseemly and disgraceful. Citizens are not subjects. The Greek city-states, with their democratic experiments, would also influence the future, but the Greek moment of greatness was a flash in the pan compared to the lifespan of Rome. It was the Romans, and their republic based on the notion that a polity was to be governed by citizens within a procedural framework that protected individual rights, that most directly inspired the founders.

It goes without saying that not everyone in Rome was a citizen, and even among citizens there was no pretense of equality. There was a nobility of sorts; the patricians, and their snobbery over birth and ancestry, put the Victorian Brits to shame. The history of the early Roman Republic is one of the struggles by non-noble citizens, the plebs, to get a couch (the Romans dined reclining) at the table. They eventually did so, and the Roman Republic as we understand it took shape.

Rome saw itself as a nation of sturdy farmers, obsessed with honor, unbelievably stubborn and tough, creative but also willing to learn from others. The Roman Republic, led by twin consuls and advised by the Senate, conquered much of the known world. Rome took control of Italy, then came into conflict with Carthage, a major sea power just across the Mediterranean where Tunisia is today. Rome was not a sea power, but it learned, and it learned fast—there are parallels there to America's current crisis, which we will explore later on. Over the three Punic Wars, each of them worthy of a book unto itself, Rome eventually defeated Carthage—though not without taking a nonstop series of gut punches from guys like Hannibal.

Like that Chumbawamba song, they got knocked down, but they got up again, you are never gonna keep them down. Rome found itself both in charge of the western Mediterranean and rich beyond its imagining.

This prosperity changed Rome forever—the whole orgies-and-vomitorium phase of spectacular excess followed—and within a few decades the republican virtues that had sustained Rome's rise were being discarded with astonishing regularity. Strongmen emerged, military leaders whose soldiers' loyalty was to them, and not to the idea of SPQR—*Senātus Populusque Rōmānus*, or "The Senate and People of Rome." Sulla, Marius, and then the final dictator, Julius Caesar, each chipped away at the republic's foundations.

Their ambition for power led them to set aside the norms of the *mos maiorum*, Rome's unwritten constitution and generally accepted rules and rights. Expedience is the death of principle, and even these men seem to have told themselves that marching on Rome at the head of their legions, or assuming total authority within the city, or generally becoming in all but name the kings that the Roman Republic had been founded to replace, was a necessary and temporary evil. In fact, Sulla—after serving as dictator and killing everyone who looked at him cross-eyed (notably excepting Caesar, whom he grudgingly struck off his proscriptions list)—gave up his power. He retired to a life of wine and carousing with his theater folk pals at his villa near Puteoli until he died, perhaps by alcoholism or a burst ulcer, or, as the papyrus equivalent of the *National Enquirer* had it, by a plague of hideous worms.

We will never know if Julius Caesar would have ever given up the unlimited power he had won in his civil war against Pompey the Great, because he got ventilated by conspirators before that was ever close to happening. On the Ides of March in 44 BC, just before he was to lead sixteen legions on a campaign in the eastern Mediterranean to crush the Parthians, he was murdered by a bunch of *optimates*, "the best men" of Rome, who believed Caesar sought to be king. In current terms, think of them as a bunch of grads of Harvard, Yale, and Princeton rubbing out the competition, except many of the conspirators were soldiers who had proven their bravery in battle and not insufferable blue checks deploring the deplorables and jealous of people who can do push-ups.

Had Caesar overthrown the Parthians—incidentally, they then ruled much of the same desert as the ancient Assyrians had—who knows if he would have accepted a crown? He made a show of declining one not long before he got waxed. In any case, Caesar was not one to let norms or rules interfere in his quest for glory. And that quest for glory led to the next great Roman transformation, that of republic to empire. Immediately after Caesar's bloodstained carcass with twenty-three dagger holes (only one, which nicked Caesar's aorta, was believed to be fatal, proving the conspirators to be nearly as hapless as their present-day analogues) was picked up off the floor in front of a statue of his late rival Pompey, the fight to replace him began. The conspirators told themselves that they did it to restore the republic, but we will never know what they would have accomplished or screwed up, because they didn't count on Caesar's nephew Octavian.

Eighteen-year-old Octavian, who would soon become Augustus. That this precocious kid eventually took a name like "Augustus" did not augur well for the conspirators. Octavian was posthumously adopted by Caesar in his will, and the implacable youth went for some old-school payback. The conspirators died, badly, and then Octavian's pal in hunting down the conspirators, Marc Antony, died too. Octavian/Augustus was not into power-sharing. Nevertheless, he brought back the republic, but in name only. He was the First Citizen, the *princeps*, and he was totally in charge of everything informally and, when he deigned to assume an office, formally. A few dozen legions give you that kind of heat.

So, the republic was back, except it was not. The empire was born, and for another five hundred years or so, the emperors would—to varying degrees—pretend that the Senate was something more than a bunch of bitchy old men without legions and that the *mos maiorum* was still a thing. But it was most definitely not a thing. The republic was dead and gone, and Rome had undergone another massive transformation even though under the first few emperors there was always a faint hope that the republic would return.

But that did not happen. Rome had been remade into something new, something still recognizably Roman but very different.

The emperors, at least for a while, proceeded to expand the borders. At its maximum, under Trajan in the early second century AD, the Roman Empire ran from Britain through Gaul (France) to Spain and around North Africa through Egypt (which Augustus took as his personal property—move over Elon Musk) up through the Holy Land and northern Arabia and into what is now Iraq (and was once Assyria) and back through Turkey, Greece, Romania, the Balkans, the Alps, and some of Germany. In other words, the transition from republic to empire was not the end of Rome's arc of power—Roman power peaked a century and a half later.

Now, everything was not hunky-dory in the early empire. It had its troubles. It had its defeats. So did the republic. The Romans had a reputation as great warriors, but they lost a lot during both the republic and the empire. Under the aforementioned Hannibal, during the Second Punic War, a Carthaginian army snuck into northern Italy after coming from Spain by the expedient of crossing the Alps—with elephants, no less. Once on the other side, the unfrozen survivors of this legendary passage reorganized and crushed a responding Roman army at the Battle of the Trebia. Then the Romans tried again and got their behinds kicked at the Battle of Lake Trasimene.

One needs to understand the dynamic. The Roman armies of the time were citizen soldiers, largely small farmers led by patricians. Most of the senior officers were senators or men who were headed for the Senate. And Hannibal slaughtered them all. A huge swathe of the adult male population was wiped out, but the Romans did not quit. The Romans had several advantages that served them well early in Rome's history, such as a total unwillingness to admit defeat and amazing fecundity. Roman women pumped out endless numbers of Roman babies who would each grow up to wield a *pilla* and a *gladius* and carry a *scutom* into battle against the motherland's enemies. But this Hannibal guy was something different, and it was going so badly that the Romans picked a dictator, a single man with unlimited power for a short, proscribed period, to go deal with this crisis. Quintus Fabius Maximus Verrucosus settled on a most un-Roman strategy. Fabius was not going to take Hannibal on directly. Instead he shadowed the invader and made sure the countryside was purged of supplies.

The Romans did not like this, considering it cowardly. Fabius was nicknamed "the Delayer," and it was not a compliment, though it was objectively a sound strategy. Now, if the annals of the republic were within the Marvel Comic Universe, the Roman motto would have been "Hulk smash." The Roman way was to find the enemy and kill them all. And this was an effective strategy if the enemy cooperated by letting themselves be killed. But Hannibal had other ideas.

The Romans finally grew sick of the Fabian strategy. It grated on them, having this savage scion of a noble family from a city-state that sacrificed its babies to Baal the fire demon wandering around the Italian countryside generally acting like Antifa in Portland. And Hannibal messed with Fabius too, once escaping a Roman trap by tying torches to the antlers of cattle at night so the Romans would think a stampede was the Carthaginian army on the march, allowing his soldiers to slip out of the kill zone.

Fabius left the dictatorship, and the Romans put together another big army. The year's two consuls went to take out the African invader once and for all. The consuls that year were Gaius Terentius Varro and Lucius Aemilius Paulus. Consuls were elected annually in twos as part of the checks-and-balances initiative the Romans had pioneered. Of course, having two guys of equal rank and equal ambition—ambition being the mark of a Roman making his way along the *cursus honorum*—was a problem when they were together on a battlefield. A key military principle, which would still be taught in American military classrooms today if there was time to do so between blocks of instruction on white privilege and how diversity, as opposed to guns and bombs, is our strength. One mission, one commander. One mission, two commanders is a recipe for disaster, and what followed proved that.

Varro and Paulus decided to address the problem by assuming command on alternate days. Yes, this was a thing, but perhaps we should not sniff too hard at ridiculous Roman affectations when our own military thinks a valuable use of its time is conducting trans awareness training. Paulus, who usually gets portrayed as slightly less impetuous and dumb than his running buddy, declined to accept battle when the army approached Hannibal on the Apulian Plain. Varro, though, was down to fight. On August 2, 216 BC, on Varro's day, he engaged Hannibal's forces near a soon-to-be-famous village called Cannae.

He chose poorly.

The two armies lined up facing each other. Hannibal then suckered Varro's center inwards, folding around it like a crescent. Hannibal's excellent cavalry drove off the inferior Roman horsemen, and soon the massive Roman army was totally surrounded—double enveloped, as it were.

They all died, or at least almost all of them. Varro—like a drunk at a car wreck—walked away. Paulus, his face smashed by a sling stone, refused to retreat and died under a hail of spears. History rhymes here—an arguably competitively remarkable envelopment defeat was suffered by the Nazi 6th Army at Stalingrad in 1942. Its commander: Field Marshal Friedrich Wilhelm Ernst Paulus. Make a note—never give command to a guy named "Paulus."

It took years for the Romans to recover from having a huge chunk of Rome's ruling caste wiped out in an afternoon, and during those years Hannibal marched around Italy doing exactly as he pleased, though he could never muster the combat power to take Rome itself (his decision not to make the five-day march to the Eternal City in the wake of Cannae has sparked arguments among military historians for over two thousand years). But Rome did recover. It caught some breaks—Hannibal had his own problems with the idiot noblemen back home in Carthage. But the big advantage for Rome was that Rome's women got busy pumping out more babies. Soon, the legions swelled again, and new leaders who were not utterly incompetent rose to the top. They forced Carthage to terms and ended the Second Punic War.

Years passed, Carthage grew strong again, and Cato the Elder (a veteran of that conflict) began ending every Senate speech with the sentence *"Carthago delenda est"*—"Carthage must be destroyed." And it was, at the conclusion of the Third Punic War. Literally. The city was wiped off the map, and it was said the fields were sown with salt.

The Romans were nothing if not thorough.

During the empire, there were likewise victories and defeats. The most famous is a total wipeout in the Teutoberg Forest of Germany.

Under Augustus, three legions under Publius Quinctilius Varus marched into Germany to show the barbarians who was boss. At the Teutoburg Forest, German barbarians answered that question unequivocally. The barbarians were the boss. The Romans followed up with some punitive raids to exact their vengeance, but gave up on the idea of adding Deutschland to the empire. That's why there is no such thing as wiener schnitzel pizza.

It was said that Augustus wandered his palace back in Rome banging his head on the walls, wailing, "Varus, give me back my legions!" Make another note—never give command to a guy whose name's first syllable is "Var" either.

There were lots of other defeats. Later in the empire, Emperor Valerian was taken prisoner by the Parthians and literally used as a footstool by their king. But Rome survived them all, even if it was shocked to the core by the fact that it—the undisputed champion of the world—had lost, even momentarily. Similarly, America has suffered defeats—Vietnam, Afghanistan—and it has gone on. The point is that a civilization can handle dramatic, even calamitous, setbacks. That one nation is the strongest of the nations does not imply that it is invulnerable or unchallengeable. Defeats do not necessarily mean collapse, but they do weaken the foundations, and if you suffer enough of them you will collapse.

Rome did not fall to a crushing defeat in battle, but rather to slow decline over centuries. By the time the last western emperor, Romulus Augustulus (weirdly, the founder of Rome was likewise named "Romulus"), took the throne in Ravenna, Rome had been largely abandoned by the court, and the real power had moved east to Constantinople. The western empire was weak and exhausted, with huge swathes of territory taken by barbarians. There was no strength left in the people. Centuries before, the Roman citizens had outsourced their fighting, first to the urban poor, then to foreigners. Now there was no one left to heed the call to arms. Things fell apart. Chaos crept in. Roman culture was vanishing; the Dark Ages would soon come. Walk around one of our big blue cities at night and you pretty much get the vibe of the next thousand years. Filth, chaos, pestilence, and—in place of today's crack—mead.

Rome, at least in the West, did not fall as much as fade away. Even the traditional AD 476 date of the fall is less a hard end point than a convenient milestone, the time the barbarians stopped pretending that the West was governed by an emperor. Of course, in the East, the Roman Empire continued right up until the Muslim Ottoman army took Constantinople in 1453, a millennium later.

How does all this Roman history apply to America?

Well, not perfectly. Rome is not a template for America, but it is a useful example of the kind of challenges a superpower faces and the phases it goes through. America, too, rejected monarchy in favor of a republic. It then began to grow and prosper. Its people were tough and creative. Then it got rich and its people became softer and lazier. We are currently in the soft and lazy phase, and it comes at a time when our own *mos maiorum* is being undermined by people who bristle at the obstacles norms and due process create to their imposing their will. We are not Rome, but we are sort of like Rome, and if you study its fall you may come across some spoilers.

We know America will fall someday, but we have also seen that a "fall" need not be a complete obliteration à la the Aztecs. Instead, it can be a transformational change that need not be from a single crushing military defeat or even a few of them. It can be evolutionary. The old ways can simply stop meeting the needs of the present, and something different replaces them. Rome transformed fundamentally three times into something that was still recognizably Rome. The fourth time, not so much, for at that point there was really nowhere for it to go but into the abyss. Rome, by the end of the fifth century, had simply run out of a rationale for being.

So, what is in store for the United States?

Some kind of change, to be sure. That is the subject of this book, and with some luck it will be a change into something better than our mediocre present. Without luck, it will be much worse. But it will be something, and yet there is a taboo against talking about what it might be. Even alleged conservatives, especially the kind who write columns like "The Conservative Case for Accepting Leftist Premises and Surrendering to Them Like Gentlemen," whine that to think about the future is somehow to yearn for the fall of the present system. It's not. It's simply being realistic. After all, the idea that the United States will exist in its present form in perpetuity is ahistorical at best, but the idea that it will abide in some form is perfectly reasonable, at least through a few iterations. The question is what form the next phase will take.

The present form of the U.S.A. is just under 250 years old. The Roman Age of Kings lasted about a century, then the republic and the empire each lasted about five hundred years. So, it's not clear if we Americans are due for a change, at least chronologically. But are we due politically and culturally? That is a different question, and the answer seems to be in the affirmative.

It's impossible to coherently argue—as the left often does via its silly 1619 theory—that America is utterly unchanged from the Revolutionary Era. The culture is different. The population is different. The world is different, not least of all due to technology. It is impossible to reasonably dispute that we, as a people, have changed in important ways. But our system of government has not changed, at least not formally. Sure, we made some tweaks—senators are directly elected, you can tax income, women can vote, and Democrats can no longer have slaves—again, something the 1619 crowd glosses over. But the basic formal structure remains.

The informal structure, not so much. The administrative state has usurped both legislative and executive prerogatives, though it acts less independently than with a wink and a nod of support from the political branches that are happy to let faceless bureaucrats take the heat for the inevitable screw-ups of governing.

We have also changed our application of the Constitution, particularly in terms of the Bill of Rights. The founders might be stunned to hear that their First Amendment allows gay porn; they would be staggered to hear that the Constitution mandates gay marriage. But when you look at the form of our federal government, with three branches, checks and balances, and protection for civil rights (even if those civil rights are previously unknown), we have not changed that much at all.

Yet some people now want to change it—dramatically, structurally—mostly left-wing people for whom the whole idea of negative rights grates. Limiting government, the whole point of the Constitution, is anathema to them since they desire for themselves to wield power via the force of government. Of course they hate obstacles, that is, negative rights, also known as civil liberties, and of course they adore the idea of positive rights, which is known as giving free stuff to layabouts. If the Constitution promises to give people something, that means that those in power are able to control that giving, and they must also necessarily control the taking away. There is no free lunch no matter what modern monetary theorists tell you; if you are going to give favored people stuff, it has to be taken from someone, and that's certainly going to be from the disfavored people. Giving and taking was how emperors ruled, which seems to be the point.

If the leftists get their way, the transformation America will undergo will be from our own republic to, well, not quite a Roman

Empire analogue, since the new elite's search for power comes from crushing and looting internal dissenters rather than crushing and looting foreigners. It would be something else, a dictatorship to be sure, for socialism cannot be anything but. Social democrats are a contradiction in terms. Maybe the gulags would be more comfortable than some previous ones through history, but it would still be a dictatorship. And, of course, it would be sold as removing our liberty for our own good. If you want a picture of that future, imagine a condescending schoolmarm telling us to acknowledge our privilege and to use our inside voices—forever.

Yet that is only one way that America could fall. We shall look at several scenarios, bad and good—or at least, less bad. But we need to understand that America will fall, in the sense that at some point—and it may not be in our lifetimes—it will morph into something different. We can hope that what it becomes is still recognizable as America, just like the empire was still recognizable as Rome, but that is not the only option. It could become something very different, and something much, much worse. History is a not a drama; it's a horror movie. And we comfortable Americans have got it into our heads that there are no real monsters left out there in the 2020s. But we're wrong.

CHAPTER THREE

THE DECLINE

A merica has fallen from that pinnacle of power it occupied back in 1991. That was inevitable. High points are high points, after all. But three decades later, it appears to have landed flat on its face.

Remember that America's decline was a choice, one made by an exhausted, corrupt, and incompetent elite. Who makes up that elite? The cultural trust fund babies who inherited a great nation and have neither any appreciation for it nor a clue how to lead it. It includes unaccomplished rich people, credentialed mediocrities, and those allied with them transactionally (such as government employees) and by affinity (such as the Twitter blue checks and the social justice mobs). Together, this ruling elite is united by a dedication to its own power and status, and a contempt for everyone else not unlike that once felt for heretics. When Hillary Clinton called the people who were insufficiently in awe of her "deplorables," she meant it. It was a moral judgment; they were bad people because they failed to accept her caste's creed and secularly divine right to rule. You look at her hate-filled mug and you just know that if she could she would be tossing the torch on the kindling to burn the heretics.

And yet, people like Hillary run our institutions, and badly. Not only does the moral critique of their critics allow them to feel that they are pure, but focusing on everyone else's moral failings allows them to shift the discussion away from their failure to do their damn jobs competently. Here is a challenge—name a major institution today that works, that gets the job done. Let me save you some time. There is not one, not a single one, that performs better than merely adequately and few that perform that well.

Why would the elite choose to fail? Well, the elite did not fail. The elite succeeded, at least in meeting its own objectives. It got more powerful and richer. Normal people got to deal with the failure, whether it meant taking out loans to fill their SUVs' gas tanks or burying their kids killed in idiotic wars.

Maybe we are just going through a rough patch. That's possible. Now, to every thing there is a season, as the Bible says and also as folk-singing commie Pete Seeger cribbed for "Turn, Turn, Turn." Things get better and things get worse in a cycle. A pinnacle is called "a pinnacle" for a reason; as David Clayton-Thomas once wrote, what goes up, must come down. As a country, we've been going down, with a few jags upward, for over three decades now.

Ronald Reagan led us up to the peak, resurrecting the optimism and purpose that had made America great in the first place. The U.S.S.R. was supposed to be our perpetual nemesis, and he pushed it over without a shot. Stupid Saddam Hussein decided to be the guy we did the shooting at, and it turned out we were incredibly good at it.

But what is Batman without the Joker? Just a weirdo dressed like a flying mammal. Remember this was the pre-Ukraine bear which we thought was capable and scary. America without the Russians to confront was bereft of a purpose. After decades of defining ourselves in the context of our enemies, America had no serious enemies left. And the "New World Order" that George H. W. Bush babbled about was no substitute. "Come, let us work together to attain the vision articulated by a bunch of rich strange-os who meet up in Davos" was hardly an inspirational call to arms on par with JFK's challenge to put a man on the moon.

At home we ended Jim Crow. We had been to the moon. The Soviet Union was gone. We were rich. Why not party, since there was nothing else to do? So, of course, we elected the perfect party president in Bill Clinton.

If anyone on earth is the wrong guy to identify a higher purpose, it was the Man from Hope. He sort of tried. He sent Americans in to solve the problems in the Balkans, an action partly intended to distract from his intern/humidor issues and partly the result of the kind of transcendent hubris only a member of our worthless elite could aspire to. But separating squabbling lunatics fueled by a thousand years of grievances was not going to do it. He would also go into Haiti, pull out of Somalia, and refuse to intervene in Rwanda. Intermittently rescuing the rest of the world from its spasms of butchery and giving up when the going got hard was simply not going to work as America's new purpose—particularly when the doing was to be done by an all-volunteer military that was shunned by the same ruling class that sent it around the world to referee other peoples' fights.

Nor was there some other goal that we could work toward as Americans, like the Apollo program. Maybe we could go to Mars, but that cost too much, especially when the percentage of the federal budget dedicated to giving free money to deadbeats was expanding apace. No, there was really nothing to do except just to go on being a contented superpower. In a way, it was a return to normalcy. Between World War II and the Cold War, America had been facing off with foreign supervillains for a half century. Now, America had a chance to spend its peace dividend. And, of course, it spent it on the budgetary equivalent of hookers and blow.

What came out of the nineties besides sludgy grunge music? It was prosperous, sure, but America was hardly creating anything new economically or artistically. The exception was in computer science—the nineties saw the birth of the internet. Talk about a mixed blessing. The internet would eventually change how people bought, sold, and communicated, and it would also create the ability of people to live outside of the real world. Coming generations would see the world through their iPhones. The social consequences would be enormous, and mostly terrible. Look outside. Do you see kids playing outside like you did if you grew up in the seventies or eighties, or even the early nineties?

And things were not entirely swell at home. The civil rights movement had won, but there were plenty of people (and an entire political party) who leveraged racial hatred to their own advantage. The Los Angeles riots in 1992 were fueled by the likes of the noxious Representative Maxine Waters. The same people did all they could to make the subsequent O. J. Simpson trial a referendum on race hate, and the jurors voted in favor of it. The root cause of all of this, we were told, was the fact that normal Americans were still racist. And the objective fact that this was a lie did not matter to those with an interest in ethnic acrimony.

Things got uglier. Clinton's mutant attorney general Janet Reno presided over the incineration of several dozen men, women, and children at Waco for the crime of defying the feds. Later, some creeps blew up a federal building in Oklahoma City and killed 168 people. According to the left, Rush Limbaugh was responsible, apparently because he was an articulate and popular critic of the elite. In Colorado, two geeks walked into their school and murdered a bunch of their classmates. That was also, according to the elite, the fault of normal people for having guns. That this was nonsense did not matter. The Age of Narrative was beginning, and narrative always trumps mere truth.

Many of the seeds of our present divisions were planted back in the 1990s. And they were able to take root because there was relatively little ability by normal folks to prune them back. We were still in the era of the legacy media. Newspapers were even considered a prime investment opportunity, as the internet had yet to steal away their classified ads and, thereby, much of their revenue. People still watched the Big Three networks, and CNN had not yet lost its ever-loving mind. The mainstream media could set the agenda.

And the Republican opposition followed it. Sure, Newt Gingrich was a conservative, but there was only so much the GOP could do with the media establishment against it. Fox News only began operations in October 1996. Rush Limbaugh's radio show was really the only mass media outlet at the time fighting back. The conservative "Contract with America" got the Republicans the House back after decades in the wilderness, but there was a huge headwind for anyone wanting to fight over "cultural issues." Those were within the distasteful domain of the Jerry Falwells and the Pat Buchanans, and cultural warriors were the designated bad guys.

What we had was a Republican Party still propping up a bastardized version of Ronald Reagan's agenda from years before. It was all tax cuts, big business, and money for wars. You could throw in locking up criminals too, but that was the gist of it, and that was what Republicans did. Their agenda was corporation-friendly and cultural concern–unfriendly. This allowed the Republican establishment members to avoid truly uncomfortable encounters at the country club.

Sure, *National Review* would write occasional articles about the weird and ominous doings out in academia, but that was a sideshow. The pushback on the social issues was muted, but part of that was the fact that the Democrats were not yet in the grip of the woke madness that distinguishes them today. Bill Clinton's big achievement was "Don't ask, don't tell," which made it possible for gays to serve in the military but did not actually lift the ban—that would wait until 2011.

Yet many millions of regular Americans began to become unsettled. The bipartisan elite passed the North American Free Trade Act (NAFTA) and winked at "outsourcing," and pretty soon people were noticing that their jobs were packing up and shipping off to Mexico, China, and elsewhere. Immigration, legal and otherwise, was changing the demographics of the country, something no one had voted for. But the establishment just let it happen. Moreover, the corporations kept getting bigger, and they seemed awfully comfortable with the people in D.C.

Politics was becoming more ruthless, even in a decade when the stakes were arguably the lowest they had been in nearly seventy years. There was no Depression to contend with, no Hitler to beat, no Russian Bear to stare down, yet politics—which was never beanbag—was becoming truly intense. The Republicans tried to impeach Clinton over his fellatrix-related fibs, and the Democrats accused the Republicans of ideologically arming the OKC bombers. Yet, at the same time, the leadership of both parties remained firmly within the same ruling caste.

The 2000 election, including the Florida fiasco, was the culmination of those troubling trends. Al Gore was supposed to be elected—we were at peace, the economy was okay, and the bubbling cauldron of social issues was merely simmering. But George W. Bush won, via a Supreme Court decision, and the Democrats did not think all the hanging chad jokes were funny. They were outraged, and though they have sought steadfastly to hide it, they pioneered the "illegitimate election" claim. A substantial section of the Democratic Party simply refused to accept that W was the president. The entire

cultural apparatus swung into action against "compassionate conservative" George W. Bush. They called him a chimp and a moron,
and they writhed in delight fantasizing about his murder. And he
just stood there, taking it.

There was an interregnum in the W-hating when 9/11 reminded
us that there was a big, mean world out there. Bush decided to make
the response—and most Americans wanted a response—into a cru-
sade. The new enemy would be "terror," whatever that was. Of
course, Bush was establishment to his core—those fighting him were
members of competing factions of the ruling class. He could never
call the threat what it was—radical, jihadist Islam. His social set did
not speak such truths. Somehow it became uncouth to speak them,
most likely as a way to differentiate the elite from the great unwashed
who did not hesitate to.

So, the War on Terror began based on a lie. We were told that we
were fighting a tactic when we were actually fighting a specific set of
people who wanted, specifically, to convert or kill us all. There would
be many more lies to come.

Thus began the Afghanistan part of this patchwork of bungled
conflicts. The American people supported the idea of killing those
bastards, along with the bastards who helped them. They were all in
on that. There was a name for the kind of war they wanted to fight—a
punitive expedition. The Brits used to do that to uppity natives back
in the day. The Romans did it too, in their own inimitable style, like
during Operation *Paybackus Is a Bitchus* following the Teutoburg
Forest ambush. They would gather up a couple legions, march into
the territory of the malcontents, and kill every man they found.
Maybe, if they were feeling generous, they would merely enslave the
women and children. Tough but fair.

The American people would have been perfectly cool with our
superb troops going in, finding the bad guys, coordinating their

encounters with their seventy-two virgins, and then shaking the dust of their Third World hellhole homes off their combat boots.

But no.

No, Bush and the thought leaders of the establishment decided that we going to take it upon ourselves to *fix* Afghanistan. And it is hard to imagine a more broken place. Some of the advocates of nation-building would look at the ruin this scheme would come to and learn their lesson. Others would learn nothing from that failure, or from the failure of the *Weekly Standard* for that matter. They would form the core of the Never Trump mini-movement, a group of people dedicated to ignoring the plaintive whining of the Republican base in order not to be held accountable for their mistakes. What got them truly angry was not Trump's populism—remember that it was Bill Kristol who pushed populist Sarah Palin on John McCain—but the fact that Trump thought these guys were losers and did not hesitate to say so.

But "hacks" undersells the true extent of their incompetence, their unearned arrogance that heaped up piles of corpses and squandered piles of cash. The idea that a land that Alexander the Great could not subdue might be out of their grasp as well never occurred to the brain trust. The only failure greater than Bush's initial idea to crush the Taliban and then stick around was Joe Biden's disastrous decision to abruptly run away in 2021, complete with Afghans dropping off the landing gear of the fleeing C-17s. It was hard not to notice the hideous parallel to the bodies falling from the aircraft at the end of the misadventure and the bodies hurtling down from the World Trade Center at its beginning.

And then there was Iraq, the war that raises the question of whether the members of our elite are liars, or idiots, or both. The military truly believed that Saddam Hussein had chemical weapons in 1991, but by 2003 that had changed. There were no weapons of mass destruction; if our leaders were wrong, they were fools, and if they knew they were wrong and pressed on anyway, they were worse. Again, perhaps had they gone in, overthrown Saddam, and then got out of Dodge Iraq would not have gone down as one of the Top 5 Worst Foreign Policy Mistakes in American history. But they didn't. They went in without a plan to handle the aftermath of our predictable conventional victory. And nearly two decades later, with thousands of Americans dead and maimed, Iraq is a barely stable basket case that exists only because Iran allows it to.

Bravo, America's elite. Bravo.

It did not take long for the American people to realize that the Iraq and Afghanistan wars were going poorly, and to notice that the children of the elite were not the ones coming back dead or mutilated. The natural patriotism of normal Americans kept the discontent below the surface on that issue, but on other issues it was clear that the elite was still not listening. The ruling caste was excited about "comprehensive immigration reform," that is, amnesty, and it was unclear to millions of Americans, who themselves were expected to obey the law, why foreigners who did not were to be rewarded. Moreover, it was becoming obvious that the prosperity the corporations were experiencing was not shared by many of the people. These populist sentiments had no real voice; the then-leading conservative magazine *National Review* and others within Conservative Inc. much preferred to pine for the Gipper than adapt to the base's growing discontent. Worse, Bush—much like the chief justice he ended up appointing—seemed to go out of his way to avoid defending the interests of the people who had elected and then reelected him.

These issues began to come to a boil. And, with the deft and savvy touch for which the Republican Party is renowned, in 2008 the GOP establishment decided that what America needed was John McCain.

America did not need John McCain.

However, something did happen in 2008 that almost seemed a premonition of change, like the dove landing on Noah's arm with the olive twig in its beak. This was the nomination of the aforementioned Sarah Palin for veep. Here was someone about as far away as possible, both in terms of geography and in outlook, from the hated D.C. cabal. She was a Republican populist before the elite realized that there were Republican populists. At the same time, the Democrats nominated Barack Obama, who portrayed himself not only as center-left, but as a way for Americans to purge their alleged racial guilt. He was a black guy—a country can't be racist if it elects a black guy, right?

Well, the left did not keep that implicit bargain. Nope, America was *still* racist—in fact, more racist than ever before. Sure, they elected a black guy over a very white guy, but they were faking it.

Nor did Obama govern as promised as a center-left politician. He went hard left, pushing the faculty lounge pathologies that had been growing out of sight within academia upon normal Americans.

The Wall Street meltdown of late 2008 was a watershed. As a nation we were failing militarily (the surge in Iraq had beaten down, but not ended, the insurgency), and now we were failing economically. And this was not just another downswing in the business cycle. It was created by the gross incompetence and greed of a Wall Street that was totally tied-in with the federal government. And what was the federal government's response? It was to bail out—with *our* money (or, rather, money borrowed with our name on the IOUs)—those bad actors.

But there would be no bailouts for the peasants, of course.

The Tea Party erupted, a populist response by normal Americans to a government seen as totally out of touch regardless of party. The Tea Party had little choice but to caucus with the Republicans, as it was mostly made of the people excluded from the Democrat coalition. But if you listened to the Tea Partiers—which the establishment did not—then you would understand that while they detested the Democrats, they utterly despised the Republicans who were part of the same corrupt bipartisan establishment.

If any of the elite had bothered to look closely, they would have realized that something important was happening. But then, if our elite had that kind of self-awareness, it would not have provoked the reckoning.

The Obama administration made no move to return America to greatness. At heart, its members did not think America ever was great. The same attitude would explode later in the decade with the wokeness fad, but even then, there was an underlying conviction by the ruling caste that the peasants were not merely revolting (in both senses of the term) but were hopelessly morally flawed.

The Tea Party rebellion would establish several things. The first was the polarization of the Republican Party and the slow elimination of the squishes. Mitt Romney exemplified that sorry species—rich, immaculately coiffed, and utterly ignorant about what the people really wanted. His pandering on immigration and his claims to be "severely conservative" were typically ham-handed, consultant-driven attempts to play to what he thought the base wanted. But he did not know what the base wanted, and he did not care. He was not tone-deaf. He was just not listening at all. The least shocking development ever was Senator Mitt joining the communist-curious progs at a BLM protest march in 2020. If it was 1920, he would probably be marching for some similarly horrifying progressive nightmare, such as eugenics, chanting, "Three generations of imbeciles are enough" alongside Margaret Sanger.

Like W before him, he was of the ruling caste, and could never be expected to stand against it. His conservatism was more gussied-up Reagan-era sloganeering, but the problems that the people needed addressed by 2012 were much more than another cut to the corporate

rate might cure. The fact that Bush II would later publicly become close friends with the Clintons and the Obamas, who participated in crucifying him while he was too much of a gentleman to defend himself, simply confirmed to the people that there was little difference between the establishment figures of both parties.

Rehab counselors have a name for this behavior: codependency. The rest of us call them "backstabbers."

But boy did Bush II find his tongue with Donald Trump. W lambasted Trump and Trump's supporters, the same people who had defended Bush while he sat mute all through the aughts. Trump's crime was being *from* the ruling class—many of the elite figures had abased themselves begging for his largesse—but not *of* it. Trump sided with normal Americans (after all, he was from Queens, not Manhattan), and therefore could not be forgiven.

The myriad controversies of the (first, so far) Trump years have been recounted in great and stomach-turning detail elsewhere, but what they show is a deeply divided nation. Trump did not create the polarization of today, but he did highlight it. His election was a response to it, a cry for help by an abandoned base. The denial of his legitimacy from even before he was, improbably, elected over the ruling-caste mascot Hillary Clinton predated and dwarfed Trump's own complaints—some of them meritorious—about the 2020 election in terms of damaging the national order. Between 2000 and 2016, it became clear to tens of millions of Americans that their political victories will never be accepted, and that the elite of our society will never let them win.

The COVID-19 pandemic panic gave petty fascists their dream come true in terms of "emergency powers" for an emergency they never seemed to want to end. Teachers' unions refused to teach. Politicians spent trillions. Huge companies, mysteriously free of the restrictions imposed on smaller competitors, prospered while thousands of businesses closed their doors.

And in the midst of this, the arrests of various felons led to the Black Lives Matter riots, which liberal cities and states allowed to rage unchecked. After all, America was a white supremacist nation built on slavery; ironically, those running the institutions insisted that the people without power pay the price for this perfidy.

In 2020, every hound was unleashed to beat back the challenge that populism represented. The media tossed away any pretense of objectivity. It did not merely ignore the sensational stories of stripper-banging scion Hunter Biden's coke-fueled corruption in Ukraine and China, but worked with the tech overlords to actively suppress what would have been a story worthy of Woodward and Bernstein, if Woodward, Bernstein, and the rest of today's media were not eager regime lackeys. It was not until 2022 that the regime media conceded, "Yeah, about that laptop...maybe there was something to it." But no apology was forthcoming, largely because the liars were not sorry.

Nancy Pelosi stood up after a State of the Union address and ripped Trump's speech to shreds on camera. The new norm, it seemed, was no norms at all. There was one impeachment, then another. The Democrats cheated where they could, changed voting rules to their advantage where possible, and when Biden wandered into office, they unleashed the Department of Justice on Americans in an effort to intimidate and silence them. Even the establishment GOP, seeing a chance to regain the power stripped from them by the populist wave, joined in or, at best, sat silent. Exercising your democratic right to challenge your school board's perversion or race-hustling agenda was an attack on democracy, and terrorism too.

With Biden in power, the utterly predictable failures come at breakneck speed. COVID-19 was not suppressed, and after the death toll under America's Biggest *Matlock* Superfan passed that under Trump, nobody was talking about death tolls anymore. Afghanistan was a horror show, the incompetence and humiliation compounded by a suicide bomber who killed over a dozen Marines and a soldier, many of whom were toddlers when we first set foot in that benighted land. The economy remained sluggish, and Biden attempted to impose his will on America by leveraging Kamala Harris as the Senate tie-breaker to force through a nightmarish progressive wish list.

Red states led by aggressive governors fought back against the abdication of the deferral government in domains such as immigration and crime. Blue states doubled down on leftist failure. The chasm between the right and the left deepened. There looked to be no way out.

And today, things seem as though they can only get worse.

CHAPTER FOUR

ON THE EDGE OF CHAOS

To understand where we are now and where we could be going requires that you understand that, to the left—which is the dominant faction in America's establishment today—there is no bottom.

There is no status quo awful enough that the left realizes the errors of its ways and gives power back to normal people to fix what the pinkos broke. To imagine that there is a bottom is to fundamentally misunderstand the leftist threat to what we once knew as America. The leftist metric is not based upon prosperity or freedom for our citizens. Prosperity and freedom get in the way—if you are prosperous, the left cannot buy you, and if you are free, you will not choose subservience. Instead, the leftist metric is based upon the amount of power accumulated by the cadres. That is their alpha and omega. Their power, their control. Everything else is irrelevant.

So, it is cold comfort to observe that even as bad as things are, America has not quite yet hit bottom; the left is fully prepared to hit bottom and then keep digging. Centers of resistance to the leftist establishment still remain. There is a corps of feisty dissenting media, such as Fox and Salem. There are rebel social media outlets such as Gettr, Rumble, and Parler, designed as refuges for cancellation targets. There are churches and synagogues that have not yet submitted to assimilation by the cultural Borg.

Moreover, there are traditional families that have not been split asunder into bizarre parodies of actual families. Many of them are educating their own kids to be independent citizens, an exodus jump-started by the COVID-19 shutdowns forced by lazy union drones. And there are willful and disobedient deplorables out there who refuse to conform, who spread unapproved narratives and shamelessly defy their alleged betters. Sometimes they even dare do it to their betters' smug faces—remember the guy who told Joe Biden, "Let's go, Brandon"?

This is all an intolerable outrage to the left, for whom total domination is the goal—though once it totally dominates, it will necessarily create new bugaboos to focus its official hate upon.

We are not beaten yet, but damn, things look grim right now.

And while the left will never hit bottom and admit failure—because, as long as the left holds power, it has not failed in attaining its only objective—that does not mean that it will not have failure thrust upon it. As we will see, there are various scenarios where things go utterly to hell, but there are others where we come back and cast off the yoke of progressive tyranny. The indisputable fact is that this status quo cannot go on forever. The big question is what does America look like afterwards?

Remember that leftism is not a state to be achieved but a process to continue forever—it is the struggle, and through the struggle it accumulates and exercises power. Just as there is no bottom, there is no utopian end state that the progressive project will ever achieve. In fact, leftists do not even bother to sketch out what one might look like. The progressive agenda is just carrots for their allies *du jour* and sticks for their enemies. And the carroting and sticking will just go on forever. The fake oppressor–oppressed dynamic, which requires you to be poor and miserable in order to give rise to the envy the progressives leverage, cannot ever end. And when they cannot exploit real grievances, they manufacture them—perhaps the only manufacturing our establishment has not yet outsourced.

It's not even meant to end. Look at the civil rights movement. The Democrat-created and imposed Jim Crow laws were eliminated a half century ago and black Americans were fully integrated into society such that in three of the last four elections a black American was elected and elevated into the White House. And yet, the left—of necessity—perpetuates the lie that black Americans are not only subject to substantial oppression but that this oppression has been even worse under Democrat Barack Obama, former Democrat Donald Trump, and Democrat Joe Biden than under the segregationist Democrats a century ago.

It's objectively bullshit, but that fact is objectively irrelevant. Facts are not the point and never will be. This is about power, and the leftists' power comes from the clash of groups. The left picks the moral groups and the immoral ones, and the labels often change. Remember when the Democrats were the party of the workin' man? It's been a while, but that was a thing within living memory. Now those same truck drivers, hard hats, and assembly line workers are toxically cisgender, privileged racists dedicated to perpetuating white supremacy. This includes the ones who aren't white. Today, the self-appointed enemies of white supremacy are the overwhelmingly white people who run our institutions, the ones literally exercising supremacy. You have got to hand it to them. What the left lacks in consistency, it makes up in strategic flexibility.

Being unconstrained by reality does have its strategic and tactical advantages, but while the left is powerful, it is not all powerful. We sometimes imagine our progressive foes as Blofeldian geniuses stroking their kitties as they concoct unstoppable plans for world domination. But they are subject to the same flaws of human beings anywhere—they are greedy and dumb, envious and petty, impulsive and emotional. This is not an army of unbeatable, jut-jawed *Übermenschen* marching forward in some sort of socialist realist vanguard to a soaring chorus of "The Internationale." It's a bunch of unaccomplished scolds and nags with no upper-body strength and blue-checked Twitter accounts trying to pester us into submission. They have what authority they do because they occupy the heights of power in America today. That's undeniable. As we have observed, the left's long march through the institutions has ended up with it in charge of every major institution in American life.

Here is where we are now.

Leftists hold academia, where even the faculty in the formerly sensible STEM fields are now babbling about decolonizing calculus. The universities are an ideological incubator that grows and nourishes the political pathogens infecting our society. They did it out of the limelight, in the dark, for many years, a giant, taxpayer-funded laboratory creating such horrors as "critical race theory" and then sending out waves of ideological Typhoid Marys in the form of their graduates to spread their plague into society at large. It worked, too—the stupid things you would hear on campus from the weirdos with the drums and banners out on the quad that most people just ignored decades ago have been mainstreamed into boardrooms, newsrooms, and Washington, D.C.

They hold the media, of course, except for that cause of all of America's ills, Fox News. It is instructive how insane the mere presence of one fairly moderate dissenting organization makes the left. The left both requires an enemy and covets total control, so it inevitably freaks out over a single big network that dares to dissent.

Dissenting websites are likewise targets—Townhall, Breitbart, and the rest all live under the threat of total cancellation even as they nurture the conservative resistance. The potential for cancellation led to the creation of what the left calls the "right-wing echo chamber," as if the rag-tag collection of dissenting media outlets is some sort of organized collective working closely together instead of competing. The left, of course, visualizes its enemy in its own form, as a united force dedicated to ruthlessly promulgating its propaganda. The people have reacted to the media's lies by granting it a level of credibility somewhere between congressmen and magic beans salesmen.

They hold Big Business, even the big corporations that you might expect not to fall for the leftist lies. You would think that sports enterprises such as the NFL, the NBA, and even NASCAR, built on individual achievement and ruthless competition, might push back, but they were pushovers. When a garage pull got labeled a noose, the mandarins of the big circle-driving sport joined in the condemnation of their own audience's alleged racism.

The big corporations are happy to comply—they effectively buy themselves favored treatment from the left (often through government action) by going along and getting along. It was no surprise that our betters made it clear that it was imperative that the little stores in your neighborhood shut down during the COVID-19 pandemic, but also that the Costcos and Walmarts and Targets stayed wide open. And do not be fooled that it is merely greed that has the big companies cavorting with the left. Just as powerful, maybe even more so, is the social pressure to conform. When everyone around you at the charity ball or the club or in Davos is singing the praises of our senile president and deploring the deplorables, who wants to be the guy who drops the turd in the punch bowl by confessing that he voted for Trump, or that he likes normal Americans? Plus, the CEOs' second wives will never let them hear the end of it.

Elon Musk's Twitter provocation notwithstanding, they hold Big Tech, and they eagerly use their power to try to stifle the opposition. There was once a time when the tech titans were libertarian heroes fighting for a Wild West internet where freedom was the primary value. Then the guys who made a zillion bucks at twenty-six figured out that not only could they control, or at least try to control, the discourse, but that their powerful friends in the liberal elite would reward them for doing so in favor of the official narrative. Now, all that tech that was supposed to liberate us is devoted to maintaining and reinforcing the dominant paradigm. Social media was like being handed handcuffs and told, "These will set you free."

They hold Hollywood, and where it once was merely tiresome that popular entertainment was reflexively liberal it is now agonizing to be bombarded by Tinseltown's full-fledged, full-throated propaganda. Flip through Netflix and try to find a show that is not about some designated victim trying to survive the grim oppression inflicted upon him, her, them, xir, or whatever, by some designated villain. The designated villains used to be a hack cliché version of a businessman, a minister, or a general. Ironically, thanks to the fall of our institutions, these people now often are the real villains—the businessmen suck up to the Chi Coms and persecute patriots, the ministers worship the climate goddesses, and the generals are planning to go to war against people who voted for Trump and/or who don't want a vaccine that does not even work as advertised.

They hold even institutions formerly connected with conservatism, or at least with moderation, like big city law enforcement. George Soros, always a savvy investor, decided to pump tons of his questionably gotten gains into electing district attorneys who think that the big problem with crime is normal people complaining about it. As a result of their innovative prosecution program of not prosecuting people, crime is out of control. The fact that the consequences fall mainly on minority city-dwellers—who, we are informed, are especially morally worthy people—does not seem to matter. Criminals trump mere black and brown people in the hierarchy of victimhood. If your kid gets shot playing in the park, well, that's a small price to pay for letting scumbags wander the street unmolested by law enforcement. Dead children demonstrate the progressive commitment; it is a sacrifice that progressives willingly make to demonstrate that they are serious about their transgressive agenda.

Remember when we loved the FBI, always chasing bank robbers and commies? Russiagate and sending SWAT teams after protesters ended its love affair with the right. Edger J. Hoover himself would be horrified by everything about today's bureau, except its acceptance of cross-dressing.

The military used to be our most honored institution, one of the few that people had any substantial respect for even before the whole lurch woke-ward of the last decade. That's gone. According to the Reagan National Defense Survey, in 2021 just 45 percent of Americans had "a great deal of confidence" in our military. In 2018, the number was 70 percent. Perhaps getting your ass kicked by a bunch of mountain tribesmen and run out of town carrying the bloody bodies of your unavenged warriors tends to drive down your poll numbers. And perhaps fixating on "white rage" and the weather as America's greatest threats instead of, say, the Chinese, might tend to make you look ridiculous. In the 1990s, Americans tied yellow ribbons for the troops; in the 2020s, those same patriots are advising their kids not to join the wokeforce. Let the liberals send their own kids to die for their precious narrative.

So, we know that today the left controls the institutions in society, and we also know the left has done a terrible job running them. But this is not surprising. As we have seen, its goal is to aggregate power. It is not to perform adequately. In fact, adequate performance can be a liability—because adequate performance requires actions that go against the tenets of leftism, such as allowing free enterprise, locking up criminals, and killing America's enemies. Success actually repudiates leftism. Failure, on the other hand, supports the drive for more leftism. Look at how Obamacare screwed up the health care system, which was already a problem because of too much governmental meddling. Now it's even worse, so the left's answer is...surprise...to give more power and money to the left to fix health care. And that will be the answer when the left screws up again.

That is always the answer. No matter how bad leftists screw up—and just as there is not a single institution in American society that they do not have their claws into, there is not a single institution in American society that functions worth a damn—the answer the establishment offers to solve the problem is to further enrich and empower the same establishment that screwed up in the first place. In this way, failure enables still more failure, on and on, forever.

But this scam is not working anymore.

Nothing is working anymore, including a huge number of Americans.

Everything is worse. You can't go to the store and know the stuff you want will be on the shelves. If you find it, you need a wheelbarrow of cash to buy it. It takes forever to get an appointment with your doctor. You can't even rely on getting an Uber.

Our military is no longer unchallenged. Our border is wide open, though we thought we had outlawed illegal aliens. Crime has crept back into our lives after being exorcised in the nineties. Junkies and hobos wander our streets. Unaccountable authorities demand you wear a mask that they admit does nothing, and take vaccines to protect people who already took one—even though the vaccines do not even do that.

America was imperfect but it worked. And now it doesn't. Everything is falling apart, and it feels like such comprehensive failure across every institution cannot be organic. It almost seems like a plan, though the problem with explaining it with conspiracy theories is that our ruling caste is too demonstrably incompetent to pull it off.   .

Regardless, this is unsustainable.

The anger is building.

You can feel it.

To go out and speak to people is to feel their anger.

They are furious, unspeakably angry at the current state of affairs.

They see a country where the establishment has failed at everything.

The media lies.

Hollywood sucks.

Big Business is corrupt.

The government not only cannot solve problems but actively seems to want to encourage them. We have discussed crime and the refusal of Soros-owned prosecutors to prosecute. But on the federal level, we have an FBI that always seems to know about mass murderers before they mass murder, yet never seems to consider arresting them. Instead, the Most Wanted list includes dangerous desperados who dared put up their work boots on Mistress Pelosi's desk.

What happened with that shooting in Las Vegas anyway? Who knows—look, that insurance salesman took a selfie in the Rotunda! Let's roll!

In 2020, America watched the military arm of the Democratic Party loot and burn our cities. These "mostly peaceful protestors"—who mysteriously got a lot more peaceful when their rioting would make President Asterisk look bad instead of President Bad Orange Man—generally walked free. But the kid who capped a couple of convicts who were trying to kill him and disarmed, literally, a third, got prosecuted for murder. He walked, but the process is the punishment. When Americans got the real story—because the media lied about it so thoroughly that a shocking number of Americans believed Kyle Rittenhouse had shot black people—most of them thought that the verdict for terminating a guy who had been convicted of anally raping some kids should have been granting Kyle a Medal of Honor. The same with the McCloskeys in St. Louis, who defended their home from a mob of degenerate Marxists with their 5.56 mm freedom stick—another leftist prosecutor tried to jail them, and Missouri's governor had to pardon them to end their ordeal.

The wacky Viking guy who good-naturedly walked through Congress sat in jail without bail for nearly a year before pleading out and getting nearly four years. The BLM fan who mowed down a half-dozen Christmas marchers in Waukesha was out on bail of a grand total of a grand for trying to run over his pregnant gal pal. Hillary Clinton took and misused classified info and walked, while normal people who worked around classified material knew that if they did a tenth of what she did, they would be punching out license plates in Florence, Colorado, till Judgment Day.

We have two systems of justice, one for us and one for the elite. And everyone knows it.

Everything is upside down if you are a normal, law-abiding American. In 2021, millions of illegal aliens poured over the borders. In 2022, there will be more. The left blocked efforts to stop their coming in, and rejects efforts to kick them out. In fact, the left will seek to attract more of them, not only by throwing open the doors but by offering them free money to come on up north.

And with the tsunami of what we are no longer supposed to call "illegal aliens"—for some reason, we are instructed it is wrong to call them what they are—come the piles of fentanyl that killed 100,000 Americans in a year. That's 100,000 dead Americans, in case the number did not register. It does not register with our betters because those deaths often happen out in the hinterlands that just don't count, to people who just don't count. A dozen teens around Warren, Ohio, cash out on opioids and who cares? Some multi-intersectional box-checking TV star pretends some of the many, many MAGA men wandering the frigid streets of Chicago both recognized him and decided to lynch him during a 2:00 a.m. Subway run and not only do you have it wall-to-wall on the media but you have potentates like Biden and Harris tweeting their support. And when he's convicted of lying about it, they are silent—like they are about the OD victims killed by drugs they let flow into the country with the tide of what they hope are future Democratic voters.

All sorts of bad things happen out there in flyover country, and none of it counts. When their jobs get shifted to Ciudad Juarez or Szechuan, those rubes need to learn to code. When rich girls need their loans for their Princeton literature of gender fluidity degrees paid off, those rubes need to stop being so selfish and pay up. When another war in a place that you can barely locate on a globe comes along, the rubes need to enlist. Boy, those rubes sure need to do a lot of things, especially shut up and obey.

When they don't, their uppitiness must be punished. When a tornado destroyed their small town, too bad, they brought it on themselves with their infidelity. As some Hollywood hag named Nell Scovell—whose Twitter bio helpfully identified her pronouns as she/her, in case you feared she was being mis-pronouned—tweeted on December 11, 2021, apparently on purpose, "Sorry Kentucky. Maybe if your 2 senators hadn't spent decades blocking legislation to reduce climate change, you wouldn't be suffering from climate disasters. If it's any consolation, McConnell and Rand have f'ed over all of us, too." Leaving aside the fact that the phenomenon of tornados predates fossil fuels—objective reality being beside the point—just look at the contempt in that tweet. And she was proud to tweet it—proud because she knew that she would be high-fived and praised among her soulless

Hollywood clique for celebrating the dozens of deaths of those who refused to yield to their alleged betters.

They hate you. And the best they want for you is to obey. The worst? Elimination.

That's simply the only reasonable conclusion to be drawn from their words and deeds. Some will even tell you. Social media was awash in progressives hoping that COVID-19 would cull the prole herd.

And normal people are beginning to understand.

This creates a problem, for you cannot have a ruling class that utterly despises the ruled and expect it just to go on like that forever.

It's like the Beatles when Yoko showed up. It is unsustainable. Something has to give.

And it is giving. We are seeing the cracks in the façade. In fact, we saw them very clearly in 2016 when America elected Donald Trump. We were instructed by our betters that the choice was the greatest woman the establishment had ever produced, the smartest, most accomplished lady of all among our glorious elite.

America took a look at Hillary Clinton and promptly voted for the "grab them by the pussy" guy.

How desperate is a society that votes for Donald Trump? As good a president as he was, and to his credit, he did much that put off the reckoning for a while, this was still *Donald Trump*. We elected Donald Trump because he was the best alternative, and it was not even close. The short-fingered vulgarian, as *Spy* magazine used to describe him. The TV reality show blowhard. The mean tweeter. The guy who tapped Playboy Playmates. These are not characteristics you typically expect in a president, though one can imagine a Jack Kennedy or a Bill Clinton cavorting in a hot tub with Miss March and Miss June. How failed is your establishment in the eyes of the people when the people reject the proffered best and brightest for Donald J. Trump? If you suggested this in 1995, they would have chased you with a butterfly net and straitjacket.

Trump was a warning to the elite, but the elite refused to heed it. And *of course* they refused to heed it. There is no bottom when you don't care at all about hitting bottom. The goal of the elite is power, while the goal of normal Americans is to make their misery stop—or at least to ameliorate it. These respective goals are in conflict because, as we have seen, the left's success requires misery.

Now, Joe Biden, the basement-lurking zombie, was sold as a return to "normalcy." To regular folks, that meant before all this misery, back when America was at its peak, like in the eighties or nineties. Basically, normality would mean patriotism, prosperity, and peace. Those sound pretty good right now.

But to the progressives, normalcy meant the Obama years, when they were pushing hard to the left. When Biden was sort-of elected, the Democrats pushed as hard as they could to the left even though the voters had seen fit to literally provide them the barest imaginable legislative majority. They were not going to let a little thing like a lack of a mandate stop them from completing their socialist to-do list.

But when the checks and balances in the system temporarily checked and balanced, the progs were livid. No one should have been surprised about the liberal elite's subsequent calls to change the rules to permanently lock in leftist dominance through the Democratic Party. The Electoral College had to go because it provided non-progressives the opportunity to win presidential elections. That was racist. And the election laws had to be changed to allow Democrats to cheat—no voter ID, no cleaning the voter rolls, no oversight of any kind—since not letting Democrats cheat is also racist. And for good measure, the Supreme Court needed to be packed because to not pack the Supreme Court is racist too, and probably transphobic as well.

To do this, the filibuster needed to go. Yes, it is racist, of course, unless used to stop Republicans, in which case talking bad about the filibuster is racist. While these initiatives sputtered out, the damage to the foundations of our society remained in their wake. The effect of it was to delegitimize any tool or process that the non-elite use to make their wishes known and have their preferences enacted into law. But the idea that the majority of Americans will sign on to signing out of participating in their own governance seems like wishful thinking. Still, that is the demand. And there will never be normalcy, whatever that means, as long as that is the price.

Similarly, the elite's contention that we need to defer our liberties to the whims of a bunch of incompetent bureaucrats with M.D.s and a track record of lies seeks to write normal Americans out of their own sovereignty. The COVID-19 panic demonstrated to millions of Americans that they were being excluded from their own governance. Experts, especially ones who are as utterly inept as the Faucian hacks who change their advice both frequently and without explanation, were never meant to rule. But the elite sees value in disintermediating actual citizens from power by virtue of technocracy. If you don't want to be ruled by a narcissistic dwarf in a lab coat, you hate science.

The red and the blue states actively differentiated themselves. The blue states were eager to exploit the opportunity COVID and social justice nonsense provided to exercise power, while the red governors gained popularity by casting off power. In New York, the new governor—who took over when Democrat media darling Andrew Cuomo had to resign for behaving exactly how you would expect a Democrat media darling to behave with the local talent—heard about the Omicron variant and beat a path to the mic bank to announce she was banning elective surgery. In Florida, Ron DeSantis shrugged.

And people are choosing. In blue states, they are packing up and leaving. The price of a U-Haul to Los Angeles is a fraction of the cost of one heading to Houston. They are livid at the prices of gas and rib-eyes, at being called racist, at having their kids taught they are racist in schools that abandoned their kids completely during the pandemic. They are sick of criminals being set loose, as if the criminals are the real victims.

But there is more to this than just people voting with their Reeboks. There is talk of the possibility of violence. People are raising the idea of a national divorce.

Have they given up on America, or do they feel America has given up on them?

The institutions sure have. Academia, which they support with their tax and tuition money, drives off any professor who dares share the same general worldview as at least 50 percent of Americans. The corporations embrace woke nonsense, and their employers and schools force CRT-derived racist nonsense down their, and their kids', throats. Pinko DAs won't prosecute crimes; the FBI prosecutes the regime's enemies. The elite and their favored walk free, while under the judicial double standard folks like Kyle Rittenhouse, whose crime was not letting himself be murdered by criminal scum, stand trial against the threat of spending the rest of their lives in prison. And the things that normal folks enjoy in life, like BBQs or vacations or even their cars, are threatened by COVID lockdowns or scheduled to be sacrificed to appease the pagan weather gods. We have become a woke version of the Aztecs. Or at least our elites have. Can human sacrifice be far behind? And Hernán Cortés far behind that?

There's not even prosperity to ease the pain. We have seen the return of inflation, the demon that we thought was exorcised back in the early eighties by Ronald Reagan. Using COVID as an excuse, though they never really needed an excuse, the Democrats sought to squander trillions on tree equity, their donors' climate change scams, and assorted other nonsense. Inflation is a civilization's bane. The

Romans suffered from it too. They had long devalued the precious metals in their coinage, thereby devaluing their coinage at the same time as they failed to increase production. Diocletian, who probably read the Roman equivalent of the *New York Times*, looked at the situation where less valuable money was chasing the same number of goods and thought, *Gosh, it must be greedy businessmen who did this*. He instituted a detailed law setting and controlling prices for every commodity and trade his massive bureaucracy could catalog. And people reacted exactly as one would expect—they selfishly refused to work or sell for less than their labor or stuff was worth. And when people did not cooperate, Diocletian issued more orders, such as tying farmers to the land and forcing people to adopt their fathers' trades. You could see Elizabeth Warren pushing the same insanity, except instead of a toga she would be wearing buckskin.

Just wait until inflation really revs up here. Even before you have to fill your trunk with twenties to top off at the local Chevron, our Demented Diocletian is going to blame the looters and wreckers and try to command the free market into obedience. History tells us that it will not work, but then all the smart people with Ivy League degrees understand that history is racist and that they are much smarter than those old-timey people—and, lo and behold, they will do the same thing again, with similarly disastrous results.

Note that Diocletian resigned from being emperor and retired to his palace to grow cabbages. Apparently, cabbage horticulture was the watching *Murder, She Wrote* reruns of late-third-century Rome.

Diocletian's heirs fought a brutal civil war for supremacy. Rome fell just under two hundred years later. It staggered on after him, but its extended decline was agonizing. It feels like we are falling right now, though it might be that, in time, we look back on our current miseries with envy for how good we had it.

There is a sense in our country that we are too far gone, that we cannot go back to something like normal. The last two decades have been anything but normal, a nonstop barrage of terrorism, economic collapse, political battling, cultural warfare, and pandemic insanity. It was not one black swan but a flock of them. Biden was supposed to make things normal again, but he hasn't. He can't. And he doesn't want to. His handlers need us impoverished so *we* need *them*. They need us divided, so they can leverage Group A against Group B. They need a crisis—the flu, the weather, an insurrection!—so we cannot think and cannot debate and cannot stop them from solving the crisis by doing what they always wanted to do anyway. Our freedom shrinks. Our prosperity shrinks. Our anger grows.

Change must come, as this is unsustainable.

America is poised on the precipice. What cannot go on will not go on, and this will not go on. But the question remains—what next?

CHAPTER FIVE

A POWDER KEG

One must have a heart of stone not to shed a tear of joy watching the video of Ukrainian citizens lining up to collect their AKs to use to shoot Russian invaders. An armed people is a free people, and as of this writing the Ukrainians are still independent. There's a lesson there, one which our establishment does not want Americans to learn. But a whole bunch already have.

So, if you want to feel hopeful about America's future, just look at all the guns that Americans are buying. That Americans buy guns means they are not conceding defeat. They do not have to have a focused intent to start shooting; that is not the point. They are making a statement. Nothing says "I'm not throwing in the towel on freedom" like a proud citizen plunking down three grand for a brand-new Wilson Combat CQB 1911A1 pistol in glorious .45 caliber. Think of it as investment in freedom, because it is. And people are putting their money where their trigger fingers are.

Americans own more guns than there are Americans, and that is an unalloyed good thing. Citizens should own guns, and lots of them—the possession of cold steel that shoots hot lead distinguishes citizens from lower forms of life, like "subjects," "serfs," and "gulag residents." In a nation meant to be by and for the People, it is important that the People never cede to the State, which is their tool and not their master, a monopoly on violence. Having guns in the hands of citizens is the ultimate veto over tyranny.

And yet we Americans almost never use guns against tyrants.

Now, we do use them against criminals, and we do it a lot, though solid statistics are hard to come by for several reasons. If some cretin breaking into your Chevy Tahoe provokes you to pump a shell packed with double-aught into the chamber of your Remington 870 and he wisely skedaddles, you probably are not going to pick up the phone and inform the local constable, "Hey, I just basically threatened to blow a hole the size of a basketball in the thorax of some dude trying to nick my hubcaps." No, you go back inside your castle; crack a cool, frosty Dos Equis; and are grateful that you didn't have to hose off the sidewalk. Also, these days, ammo is really expensive.

The fact is that most instances of anti-criminal gun use—and make no mistake that a display of your gat is a "use" of a firearm to deter crime—are not reported, and the media and Gun Control Incorporated have no interest in their being reported. Every time a citizen triumphs over some delinquent thanks to the Second Amendment, it shoots another hole in their "guns = bad" narrative. Similarly, that's why you will never again hear about the aforementioned "Kalashnikov in every pot" assault rifle equity program.

What is clear is that Americans use firearms hundreds of thousands of times per year to ward off, or take out, criminals. Deterring and deceasing criminals are important tasks for citizens in a nation with widespread gun ownership, but they are not allowed in less civilized nations like the United Kingdom. There, one might terminate an intruder who breaks into an occupied residence and not be given a medal for his glorious act of social hygiene. In fact, as bizarre as it seems, the heroic defender of hearth and home is more likely to be persecuted than celebrated. It's mind-boggling, but true. Sad how far the sturdy and stubborn defenders of Rorke's Drift have fallen. Colour Sergeant Bourne would roll his eyes and smack you limeys upside your heads with his pace stick.

But thankfully, in the United States, outside of the blue, urban jurisdictions where George Soros has successfully invested his cash installing pinko prosecutors, our national consensus is pretty clear that if you threaten the life or limb of a law-abiding citizen and he ventilates you, well, too bad. Don't want none, don't start none with a suburban dad from Houston who has a SIG Sauer P229 loaded with +P hollow points stuffed in his fanny pack. Chances are the dad-bod commando spent time at the range while the punk got his tactical training playing Grand Theft Auto.

The gun gurus of the *Washington Post* might not be hip to the vibe, but the crooks get the picture. Polls of convicts in prison show that they fear armed citizens much more than armed police officers. This is how it should be. Crooks should be the ones who are afraid, not the citizens.

Of course, the same people who grind their teeth at the fact that you aren't helpless in the face of their criminal constituents willfully ignore the reality of effective armed self-defense. When the guy who was not allowed to own guns but got a gun anyway because the government failed to record that he was not allowed to have a gun brought a gun to a church in Sutherland Springs, it was an NRA instructor who ended the rampage and the rampager, permanently, with a gun. And our hero used a scary "assault rifle" to plug the murderer.

Perhaps in the collective hive mind of the *New York Times*, the Democratic Party, and liberal women married to insufferable liberal males who would cry if they heard the crack of a .38 round up close, we would all be better off leaving our personal safety up to the same law enforcement agencies that let the convict buy a small arsenal. But this seems unwise, and Americans decline to outsource their safety to a government that regularly fails at every task to which it turns its efforts. We would rather be our own pre–first responders, as the massive sales of firearms in recent years—forty million in 2020 alone—demonstrate.

The hyper-arming of Americans is *good*, and it bodes well for our future. A broken people does not buy guns. The fact that a huge bloc of Americans is unwilling to sit on its collective couch awaiting some government employee to wander by and save them when trouble brews is clear evidence that we are not ready simply to give up on our prerogatives. Buying a gun is a proactive act of citizenship; defending yourself and your community from criminals is not the act of a serf.

However, putting fear into the hearts of thugs, burglars, and ruffians, while both noble and necessary, is not the only, or even the most important, function of citizens packing heat. The primary reason we citizens should all own guns—putting aside the extremely compelling reason that is the fact that we damn well feel like owning guns—is to facilitate the deterrence and, if necessary, the defeat of tyranny.

Put another way, it's pretty hard to forcibly enslave a couple hundred million people who have guns. And the fact that they have guns makes it very unlikely that any aspiring tyrants will try, at least with brute force. And when they roll the dice, as Putin did, it ends up backfiring.

The idea of Americans having had enough, throwing down their iPads, getting up from their La-Z-Boy recliners, walking over to the mantle where they keep the ole AR-15 on a rack, affixing their tri-corner hats, and moving out to water the tree of liberty with the blood of tyrants seems far-fetched today, and it is. This is good—we don't want that kind of gardening. But it is essential that we maintain the potential to do it if it comes to that—think of it as an anti-tyranny vaxx—and the way to maintain that potential is to make sure We the People are fully capable of massive lead redistribution operations should the unlikely scenario arise where the answer to the problems before us is to shoot people.

We are far from that, for reasons we will discuss, so far that even to consider what such a circumstance might look like is to invite all sorts of hyperventilation and hyperbole from the left. They claim you are cheerleading violence, or you are working yourself into a Jeffrey Toobinesque frenzy imagining our streets awash with blood. This is nonsense, of course, the same kind of awkward gambit the establishment always employs to try to place off-limits a subject that it does not want discussed. The fact is that the subject requires consideration, most importantly as a remedy to both those eager to skip the hard work of political participation to solve our myriad problems and go right to direct action, and those who insist on pushing, poking, and provoking the American people with petty oppressions and galling outrages.

The reality is that political violence has happened before in our history. People have gone to the guns. It just hasn't happened very often in our history. That's good—our goal today is to fix the constitutional order, not fix bayonets.

Of course, when examining the role of an armed populace in our political paradigm, we need to start back at the Revolution. It was a bunch of armed subjects who decided that they preferred to be citizens, took their muskets off the racks over their mantles, and started busting caps in the direction of the redcoats.

And the redcoats—the British infantry (which included crack Hessian mercenaries)—were arguably the finest infantry in the world. The key takeaway is that a bunch of dudes with a mixed bag of rifles beat them. One might fast-forward to Vietnam and Afghanistan to get to the punch line, but that would miss some important details.

The first is that a call to arms in American history, on the rare occasions that it happens, is usually not a sudden thing. People don't go from zero to shooting at the government like a 427 Shelby Cobra off the line. Now people have the impression that the Revolution started when Paul Revere rode his horse and Johnny Tremaine and his deformed hand helped dump tea into Boston Harbor, but the indignities and oppressions that led up to Lexington and Concord did not just happen overnight.

It was a slow fuse. A frog boil, as it were, except the Frogs eventually helped us out. It took time to go from "Say, this isn't right" to "Hold your fire until you see the whites of their eyes."

The American Revolution was the culmination of a long process in which the colonists were slowly stripped of what they saw as rightfully theirs, that is, the rights of Englishmen. The Brits had a long tradition of individual rights. Yes, England was a monarchy, but the king had clear limits to his authority. There was representation of the people, imperfectly representative but jealously guarded (much like the Roman Senate and *comita*), through Parliament. And as Englishmen, which the colonists considered themselves until about July 3, 1776, the colonists knew their rights and demanded them. That included the representation they were denied in Parliament—to them, the quirk of geography that placed the Atlantic Ocean between them and London did not negate their birthright to be represented.

And there were other gripes as well, piled one on top of each other. The Declaration of Independence is one long litany of complaints about how the Crown had been screwing them over in contravention of their basic liberties. You can feel the anger in its text. The impression one gets reading the Declaration is one of outrage,

outrage that the norms and principles that they had grown up believing in were being disregarded.

Does this seem familiar?

The fact is that if the Crown had acknowledged the colonists' grievances and addressed them—that is, treated the colonists as other Englishmen were treated—today we too might well be chewing terrible food with bad teeth and watching *Doctor Who* on the telly.

So it is understandable that the colonists did not just run to shoulder their muskets the first time the British government started messing with them. It took years, many years and many ever increasing oppressions and humiliations, to get to trigger time. But when they finally reached their breaking point, when they finally decided that it was time for the colonies to channel the breakup of Lindsey Buckingham and Stevie Nicks and go their own way—we're probably Stevie in that analogy—then it got ugly.

The American rebels—the insurrectionists, if you will—acted both individually and collectively. The colonists individually had their own rifles, useful for hunting and defending against attacks by the alleged ancestors of Elizabeth Warren. But collectively, they had local militias, not a bunch of weirdos in tacticool web gear drag but all the males of military age who got together on the town common and tried to train themselves into a semblance of some sort of military formation. A fair number of the men had fought before, whether skirmishing with the local tribes or off on the frontier in the French and Warren War. George Washington himself had been a colonel in that conflict, with mixed results (he had been captured at one point). So, it was a mix of experienced men and inexperienced ones. And they had to fight the British Army, which hopelessly outclassed them—on paper.

There was no way, at least at the outset, that the colonists were going to prevail in a stand-up fight against the Brits. But the colonists had other attributes the redcoats did not. They were fighting for their homes and their liberty, not on some distant shore for a paycheck and the prerogatives of a king they had never seen. And though the senior officers were always focused on getting the colonial forces trained up so they could stand up to the British infantry in a stand-up fight, the guerrilla tactics of frontier combat frustrated and infuriated the English commanders and soldiers.

The example of a handful of farmers ambushing a supply column of powder and rum, then fading back into the foliage, is asymmetrical warfare, the application of a weaker force's strength to the stronger party's weakness. The Americans had a lack of firepower and lack of close-order discipline as their weaknesses, but terrain knowledge, local support, and mobility as their strengths. The Brits had firepower and discipline, particularly manifesting in a terrifying bayonet charge that would follow devastating volleys of musket fire, as their strengths. They also had a huge industrial advantage, but that was an ocean away. Their need to ship things across the pond, and their reliance on logistical trains on land, as well as the relatively slow movement of their heavy infantry, were their weaknesses. So, the colonial tactic would be to avoid a situation where they could shoot you to bits and run you through. Instead, a wily rebel would look to hit swiftly at lightly defended supply columns and the like, then vanish. Concentrate your forces as a rebel too early, and you will probably lose.

Now, that would soon change as the troops improved their conventional warfare skills. After all, in an insurgency, the rebels don't typically win by guerilla warfare. They win after guerilla warfare creates the space for the rebels to generate conventional warfare capability. It was not the Viet Cong that took Saigon. In fact, the Viet Cong arguably never fully recovered after they prematurely dropped their guerilla campaign and came out in the open to take on U.S. forces directly during the Tet Offensive in early 1968. They got crushed, despite Walter Cronkite's hysterical simpering on network TV to the contrary. It was a bad idea to fight the U.S. Army and Marine Corps toe-to-toe in any case, and worse to expose themselves to the full fury of their artillery and air support. No, it was the North Vietnamese Army, a conventional force driving tanks like the T-54, that broke into the presidential palace on April 30, 1975, and finally won the war.

Sure, the Democrats' betrayal of our South Vietnamese ally played a part, but you get the point.

And there are exceptions, arguably such as the Taliban's victory following Joe Biden's second disgraceful abandonment of an ally—that ancient freak voted as a congressman to cut off the South Vietnamese almost a half century before. But generally, by the time the insurgents win, they are something like an actual army.

During the Revolution, Washington and the other commanders kept trying to fight the kind of set-piece battles that they had been trained to fight during their time waging war for the Crown. And sometimes, it worked, sort of. At Bunker Hill, they shot the British attackers to ribbons from dug-in positions on Breed's Hill, only being driven off with losses at the point of redcoat bayonets after running low on ammo. Later, French officers, such as the legendary Marie-Joseph Paul Yves Roch Gilbert du Motier, Marquis de La Fayette, and the eccentric Prussian Friedrich Wilhelm August Heinrich Ferdinand von Steuben, would train the Continental Army in the ways of war back on the European continent. It was a traditional siege at Yorktown where the British finally gave up in 1781, allegedly to the sound of the redcoat band playing "World Turned Upside Down," the eighteenth-century equivalent of cranking "You Won't Get Fooled Again" at a Trump rally.

But the world would never have turned upside down if those colonists had rushed out to the Lexington and Concord greens years before with only pitchforks and sticks instead of their privately owned fire-arms. And this is one key reason why the establishment so hates the idea of an armed citizenry. It leaves the revolution option on the table. In the Australian and Chinese COVID oppression, we saw what happens when you take it off. If you start killing Americans' dogs and cats like the Chi Coms did during the Shanghai lockdown in 2022, you best get your affairs in order because your ass will be a bullet magnet.

Since the Revolution, in nearly 250 years, there has never been any similar uprising—at least in scope. There have been incidents, though, where privately owned weapons changed the dynamic. Before the Civil War, there was the border war between Missouri and Kansas. It was less an uprising against the government than a battle between political factions. Here, armed citizens facilitated the fight and made it possible. Pro-slavery bands and abolitionist militias ranged the territory murdering and looting. Dozens were killed over several years in a run-up to the Civil War.

John Brown cut his crazy teeth out there in the bush. He would later come back east, gather his acolytes, and try to steal federal weapons out of the Harper's Ferry arsenal in order to fuel a slave revolt. Robert E. Lee led a unit of Marines to suppress his raid, and Brown's band decided to fight it out with those conventional forces—a big tactical mistake for guerillas, similar to the one the Viet Cong made in Hue when it got wiped out by the Marines a bit more than a century later. Brown got hanged for his trouble and a-mouldered his way into song and legend.

Of course, Brown's execution was arguably a strategic victory for the abolitionists, in that his death provoked outrage that would eventually, at least partially, fuel the Civil War. His haunting last statement was, "I, John Brown, am now quite certain that the crimes of this guilty land will never be purged away but with blood. I had, as I now think, vainly flattered myself that without very much bloodshed it might be done." It was a chilling warning that proved horrifically correct. It is also important to remember that information operations, like the one Brown conducted, sometimes have a greater strategic effect than kinetic ones.

The Civil War would leave hundreds of thousands of Americans dead in a nation with a fraction of today's population. It featured some use of privately owned weapons, mostly on the frontiers and likely among the rebels early in the war. But having an armed citizenry did not facilitate that war the same way it did among the colonists. The Civil War was largely a conventional war—the South grabbed federal depots and arsenals dotted throughout its territory to arm its men. It further established the American way of war—the Union leveraged its size and mighty industrial base to pump out the endless battalions of well-equipped men and countless trainloads of supplies and equipment that crushed the more rural South. Future enemies from Hitler to Hussein would feel their pain.

The Civil War was *sui generis*. The other examples of internal warfare in American history were of much, much smaller scale. One well-known example of an armed uprising against the government that utilized privately owned weapons, like the Revolution, also leveraged the training and experience of returned veterans. In 1946, a group of citizens, many just back from fighting in World War II, fought against the corrupt Democratic machine government of Athens, Tennessee. After the local sheriff and his thugs seized ballot boxes following an election and took refuge in the jail, the veterans—having armed themselves—surrounded the place.

The corrupt sheriff would not give up the ballot boxes, and the shooting started. It escalated into dynamite being thrown, along with Molotov cocktails. In the end, the deputies surrendered after their intrepid leader ditched them. Nobody was killed, though several people were hurt.

Tellingly, the battle led to only temporary relief from corruption. Not all the GIs were upstanding citizens themselves. The veteran government fell into bickering, and soon politics returned to business as usual in Tennessee. The legacy of the Battle of Athens, often cited by those who see violence as the solution to what ails America, was distinctly mixed. In the end, it solved nothing.

But this example is not an argument for disarmament. It is one for understanding human nature. Guns can be a force to freedom and a force for tyranny. Communists use guns. Nazis use guns. American troops use guns. And so do American civilians. It is the ideology and motivation behind the gun that matters, not the tool. The moms who demand action cannot seem to make that distinction, but that does not mean there is no distinction to be made.

Guns are essential to freedom because they allow people to resist a tyrannical status quo with force, but as we have seen, at least in America, that is much more the exception than the rule. Moreover, the few results when it has happened since the Revolution are, at best, mixed. So why maintain the option?

Well, because of that first time when it did not go wrong. We always need that Second Revolution option lurking out there, just in case.

And stripping us of that capability is precisely why the establishment is so dead set on pulling an Australia on us. In the mid-nineties, after some creep went on a shooting spree in Tasmania, Australians disarmed. Now, despite some superficial similarities with America—they are a frontier people, like us—Australians are very different from us. They started off as a penal colony, and the mindset seems to have stuck. When COVID hit, they went into extreme lockdown mode, and moreover, their cops went into full Stasi mode. Besides monitoring social media and spying on people, they literally beat the hell out of people failing to obey the regime's draconian lockdown edicts. The footage of burly kangaroo kops pummeling people found insufficiently masked made quite an impression on Americans. Many Americans, observing this unrestrained savagery, determined that Australian policemen were entirely too certain they weren't going to go too far and get shot. Mostly because there was no way to stop the government from going too far.

That is the key point—American citizens know that they have that ultimate power and cherish it. They understand that the decision to allow or disallow any act by the government ultimately resides with themselves. Oh, as we have seen, they almost never use that power, but the fact that they could, that they could lock and load and force a confrontation (maybe, assuming that sufficient numbers of the regime cat's-paws would actually fight other Americans for the benefit of the San Francisco/Manhattan axis if it really came down to that) is critical.

It is not just a practical consideration but a psychological one. To have a pistol is to have power. After all, Chairman Mao—whom our ruling caste envies, consciously or not—said it best: "Political power grows out of the barrel of a gun." Of course, there's more. In a 1938 speech to the party, he actually said, "Every Communist must grasp the truth, 'Political power grows out of the barrel of a gun.'"

And every Communist does—that's why they are so intent on making sure we have no guns, and therefore no barrels, and ultimately, no power.

To strip us of our guns is to strip us of our power. It is to make us accept a lower status than citizen. And, almost as important as it is for us to be disarmed for the practical reason that we can't fight back, it is likewise vital to our would-be oppressors that we *realize* we have been disarmed and therefore stripped of our power. To disarm us is to confront us with our second-class status. It is the key to our accepting ruling-class subjugation.

And Australia is the example of that. It is a noble and strong people submitting to humiliation and oppression not merely because they have no practical means of resistance but because they have psychologically abandoned the idea that they could resist. That is the establishment dream here, of power unrestrained by the knowledge that a bunch of Americans packing heat could simply say "No" and put a stop to the liberal scheme *du jour*. But more than that, it is the goal of having a population that cannot even conceive that resistance is possible.

But how bad would things have to get before that happened?

CHAPTER SIX

LIGHTING THE FUSE

American history teaches us that the answer to the question of when patriotic Americans should start spewing lead is pretty much always "Never." We have never seen, since the founding, a scenario where that drastic action could be justified, and we should pray we never do. Civil wars are bad—they are highly uncivil, and our own War between the States 1.0's kill count, in absolute and per capita numbers, dwarfs the butcher's bill from any of our other conflicts. Political violence is a bad thing, a thing to be avoided, and even to discuss the possibility of its happening here is to risk spasms of sputtering outrage from the people who would be least prepared for such a scenario yet most likely to provoke it.

But none of that should obscure the truth, and the truth is that such a scenario *could* arise. It's not likely, but unlikely things happen all the time—you recently spent a couple years walking around with a thong draped across your piehole and, beyond a hypothetical contingency, none of us saw that coming.

Here is the truth. The United States could reach a point in which an armed revolt is not only justified but a moral imperative. And this does not mean some goofy mini-riot in a public building led by horn-hatted weirdos and manned by elderly vets wandering through the Capitol Rotunda in red caps. That was an "insurrection" the same way Joe Biden is a genius. A real insurrection would be a disaster of unfathomable proportions and, therefore, it should never be contemplated lightly.

So let's contemplate it with the appropriate heft. When might it be okay to pull the trigger?

In over two centuries, we have never reached the point where the people have decided, in significant numbers, to engage in armed struggle. Oh, we have had some folks at the margins do it. Indians, for instance, kept up armed resistance for decades, though it is debatable whether it is reasonable to call them "insurgents" when the point of their resistance to the federal government was that they declined to accept their obligations under a social contract they never signed.

America also experienced some other very low-grade insurgencies, inevitably led by bad people. The Democrat-founded Ku Klux Klan probably does not qualify, since it was effectively the paramilitary wing of Southern Democrat governments dedicated not to fighting the feds but to terrorizing the black population in order to keep them enslaved in reality, if not in name. In that sense, it represented less an insurgency than a quasi-governmental reign of terror.

Blacks, of course, were disarmed by law as a way to ensure they would not resist. Seems familiar.

At the other end of the spectrum were those insurgents who wanted no government at all. In the 1800s, anarchists attacked various government and other targets, eventually even assassinating President William McKinley. But their campaign of terror ultimately went nowhere—being anarchists, it's not like they were a disciplined force laser-focused on a single objective. The anarchists were relegated to the fringes of American society, as most Americans thought them nuts, manifesting again in the twenty-first century in different forms. Some were less anarchists than outright leftists; they practiced low-level mass street fighting with few real casualties and a wink and a nod from the traditional left. Hipster anarchists—such as Michael Malice (who was once the subject of a Harvey Pekar comic book)—found space on the right, but did not practice organized violence.

The twentieth century brought some violent mini-insurrections that came to naught. Leftist guerillas seeking Puerto Rican independence tried to smoke President Harry S. Truman while he was living at Blair House in 1950 and shot up the House of Representatives in 1954. Terror attacks would sporadically continue in the United States (primarily in New York) until the seventies. Democrat Jimmy Carter pardoned the surviving convicts from the fifties attacks, while Democrat Bill Clinton pardoned a dozen subsequent Puerto Rican terrorists and Democrat Barack Obama commuted the sentence of another. This was more winking and nodding to the violent extremes by the Democrats, and if this country were ever to go up in flames, that tolerance for violence might be part of the witches' brew that led to it.

Interestingly, in 1950, several towns in Puerto Rico—but for the filibuster, still not a state but a mere commonwealth—rose up for independence and were attacked by Puerto Rican National Guard forces in what was called the Jayuya Uprising. This iron-fist response included mortars, artillery, and airstrikes by P-47 Thunderbolt fighters. The rebellion was quickly suppressed, and a few people died. This foiled insurgency demonstrated a strategic error we will see again, that of an insurgent force prematurely attempting to hold territory against a conventional force. If it had created an underground guerilla movement it might not have been wiped out in a matter of days.

The sixties bred a variety of terrorist groups that conducted a surprisingly widespread series of attacks, mainly bombings, well into the seventies. The Weather Underground, Symbionese Liberation Army, and other groups, all some species of Marxist, robbed, shot cops, and blew stuff up. This included themselves—one of the most effective Weather Underground operations was detonating a bomb in its own townhouse in New York. The pampered red-diaper babies who made up that motley band of over-educated communist sociopaths were utterly ineffective as fighters, but their indulgence by the liberal establishment—many of those convicted were pardoned—allowed them to take key positions in American society. The loathsome Bill Ayers, who in any serious nation would have been swinging from a gibbet instead of granted tenure, was allegedly one of those most responsible for the rise of Barack Obama in the Chicago district he infested after coming in from the cold.

So, the leftists' answer to the question of when you start shooting is, "When you don't get your way." The Weathermen—which, in an early form of the linguistic gyrations for which the left has become renowned, renamed itself the "Weather Underground" so the chicks would feel empowered—came out of the sixties movements that failed to bring change fast enough to suit its radical members. The hackneyed Bob Dylan lyric "You don't have to be a weatherman to know which way the wind blows" gave them their name, and as befitting any group both pretentious and frivolous enough to cop a moniker from "Subterranean Homesick Blues," their terrorist vanity project left a bunch of people dead and maimed. It accomplished little else except to set its surviving members on a pathway to influence among the Democrats for the next half century. The son of a couple of them, Chesa Boudin, eventually became the pro-crime Soros DA in San Francisco.

Why they chose terrorism and violence is a direct result of who they were—spoiled brats, often raised by affluent and indulgent parents who sent them off to universities where their poisonous politics suppurated in safety. They were Marxists who rejected the working class—in a preview of today, the sweaty hard hats were their enemies and the enlightened cadres, like themselves, were to be the primary beneficiaries, with a token tip of their Red Guard caps to oppressed minorities. They were also elitists who rejected the hard work of democracy. Our American democracy (which we all know is really a republic, but the inapt use of the term "democracy" to describe our system is so ingrained as to make constantly correcting the error a gigantic time suck) was the problem, after all.

The people, the stupid people the cadres told themselves they were fighting for, wanted nothing to do with the college kids' bizarre pseudo-socialist utopia. In 1968, when the fawning media was telling the masses that the kids were leading the world to revolution, the actual voters of the United States elected Dick Nixon on a law-and-order platform. In 1972, the very left-wing George McGovern—remarkably, from today's perspective, a senator from South Dakota—was utterly crushed by Nixon in a total repudiation of everything the Weathermen sought. Those who didn't cut their hair, bathe, and go get jobs doubled down and kept up a few more years of low-intensity conflict.

Obviously, democracy did not work, since it did not give them their desired outcome, so violence it was. In a way, the terrorist left (and those who more or less supported it) were all in on Carl von Clausewitz. For them, war (even their tepid, performance-art version of it) was simply politics continued by other means. Can't get the proles to vote for you and your schemes? Fine. Shoot some cops and stick a bomb in the Capitol.

So there was no real dividing line for them between political combat and combat-combat, but then their total alienation from the idea of the United States as an entity erased the possibility of there being one. Why not go instantly from zero to killing, since their ultimate goal was to destroy and remake the country in their Marxist image anyway? The Weathermen allegedly stated that fixing America would require the deaths of several tens of millions of uppity Americans, but it was a sacrifice they were willing to make *others* make. When you are talking death on an industrial scale, you have decisively abandoned the mainstream paradigm. But shattering norms was not an issue—since the whole point was shattering norms.

This is in complete contrast to the question of abandoning the traditional political process in favor of violence when it faces normal, patriotic Americans. As we have seen, American citizens rightly treasure their ability to take up arms and change their government should it turn tyrannical. The emphasis is on the "should it turn tyrannical" part. The premise is that America is not naturally and intrinsically tyrannical, which the bloody left would argue it is. For normal people, before violence becomes morally appropriate, a tyranny would have to replace our democracy. In other words, unlike the way our nation appears in the eyes of the Marxists, who hate the whole idea of the United States of America and wish to tear it out root and stem, we normal citizens assume that the natural state of the United States is non-tyrannical and worthy of patriotic devotion.

Consequently, in order to convince Americans that they must take up arms against their government, they must so totally lose control of their government that it ceases to be by and for the People. In other words, things have to change so radically that the constitutional framework by which we have lived for going on two-and-a-half centuries has effectively collapsed. And, as we have seen, nothing like that has happened here since the Revolution. But that is not to say the hard-left Democrats would not give it a try.

What does it mean to say that the government of the United States has turned tyrannical? When does bad government step over the line into irredeemably oppressive? At the outset, there is the question of degree. Every endeavor that people engage in is going to involve people failing to meet the standards set for them. Greed, lust, envy, hate, and other character flaws endemic to humanity will manifest in governance, all governance, even where the framework we set up seeks to mitigate them.

And our Constitution does that. One of the most remarkable things about the ancient document is how astutely the framers took into account human nature when trying to set up "a more perfect union." Take, for instance, the concept of checks and balances. Why would one need checks and balances if people were not so fallible? The Romans during the republic certainly understood that. They elected two consuls per year to wield executive power, not just one (though in rare cases they would select a single dictator for a short, set period). They expected the ambition of each hiker along the *cursus honorum* to counter the ambition of his fellow travelers; hopefully, that equilibrium would lead to good governance, or at least not atrocious governance. Of course, the tens of thousands of Romans dead in part due to bickering consuls at Cannae might dispute that, but the principle was sound even if it was spotty in practice.

Regardless, checks and balances exist as an imperfect means to check and balance the sordid side of human nature as it manifests in the exercise of power. And government is power, in our case power expressly delegated by the people to the government in order to perform certain functions collectively, the most important being to protect the rights of the individual.

Not all of the checks and balances are those within the governmental structure itself, such as the presidential veto or the Congress's power of the purse. Certainly, those are important, but they really pale in comparison to the other checks and balances. Voting is one of the two ultimate checks and balances since it allows us citizens to select—at least it is supposed to—those who exercise the powers granted to the government by the Constitution.

The other ultimate check and balance is tens of millions of citizens with an AR-15 at home. If things truly go to hell, the citizens go to their gun safes. But when could this ultimate check and balance come into play?

If the primary purpose of the Constitution is to provide for the protection of the rights of the individual, then the failure of the Constitution must mean, at a minimum, the failure of the government it establishes to protect those rights. But, again, it cannot simply be some individual failures or even relatively widespread ones. Injustice is hardwired into human experience. Rights are necessarily going to be violated all the time—that is simply reality. So, a single, discrete incident where rights are violated could not ever serve to terminate the essential legitimacy of the United States government. In fact, the Constitution assumes the rights of citizens will be violated, which is evident because it creates processes to remedy such violations, such as establishing a judiciary.

Nor would even widespread and long-lasting violations of key rights justify essentially declaring the Constitution DOA and going to the mattresses. Again, the Constitution anticipates such wrongs and provides processes that address them. Take the Democratic construct of Jim Crow. For nearly a century, black Americans were subjected to hideous discrimination and oppression written into the law. And, worse, institutions created by the Constitution even served to (temporarily) sustain them. The case of *Plessy v. Ferguson*, (1896)

163 U.S. 537, upheld the manifestly unconstitutional notion that the state could enforce separate but (allegedly) equal accommodations based on race. In *Korematsu v. United States*, (1944) 323 U.S. 214, the Supreme Court upheld the detention of Japanese Americans based on their race. These were grotesque violations of basic civil rights, and yet they were allowed to persist—for a time—under the Constitution. But they were also undone within the context of the Constitution. That's key—within a tyranny, citizens do not have the ability to undo injustice.

Would black Americans or Japanese Americans have been justified in going to war against the United States? In fact, both groups went to war *for* the United States even as they endured these wrongs, and distinguished themselves in combat against actual dictatorships. As painful as these wrongs were, even large-scale rights violations like these did not justify armed insurrection against the government of the United States. The reason is that these violations of basic human rights could still be, and eventually were, addressed by the processes within the Constitution.

You don't fight when you can fix it some other way. In these cases, you had Congress. You had courts. You had elections. And even if the courts and legislatures and the voters came to the wrong decisions initially, there was still a functioning process to create change to conform reality to the vision of the framers. The system worked, even if it took a long time.

That is the difference between the left's view and the view of patriotic citizens when it comes to the role of violence in the system. The left is concerned with its own power, and nothing else. If it can exploit the Constitution to get power, then it will do so. And it will happily negate those processes to ensure that the power it gained cannot be undone. Alternatively, if the left cannot use constitutional processes to get what it wants, it will choose insurrection. The left has no investment in the Constitution, no loyalty to it. It would last, under the left, only for as long as it was useful to the accumulation and preservation of leftist power. That's why it was so easy for the Weathermen to abandon politics for urban warfare in a mere heartbeat—these Marxist creeps were in no way attached to a Constitution they sought to destroy eventually anyway.

Normal citizens think about the issue of political violence differently, to the limited extent that they consider it as a practical possibility at all. For the left, violence is on the spectrum of options. They move to it seamlessly. Just look at how quickly they began coming up with excuses about how the Black Lives Matter/Antifa riots of 2020 were perfectly legitimate responses to their not getting their way. But for normal citizens, to embrace violence requires them to opt out of the system on the grounds that the system no longer functions.

Our system is a mess. It sometimes seems to be in free fall. But the Constitution still prevails today despite myriad and manifest injustices. Yet a black-swan scenario where normal citizens might embrace violence could arise, and in the current crisis people are thinking about the unthinkable. Could America descend into some sort of civil conflict? Of course it could. The chances are that it will not, thanks to the Constitution's remarkable strength and flexibility. But what would it look like if America actually became a tyranny?

Unfortunately, it would look like a lot of the present trends had continued unbated and the present wrongs that American citizens are suffering had gotten immeasurably worse. But we have already seen that, for our Constitution to function, significant numbers of Americans may need to endure even massive violations of their rights for extended periods. You cannot just get mad—even if eminently justified—and take your political ball and go home. For the Constitution to work, people must rely on the Constitution and its processes to correct injustices.

What this means is that for America to reach a state of tyranny, there must not only be massive and systemic violations of rights but, simultaneously, the elimination of any meaningful ability to address those wrongs, either under the Constitution or otherwise. That is, for the Constitution to fail, it must actually cease to function. The checks and balances must be eliminated, including the voting check and the gun check retained by the American people.

And, alarmingly, the elimination of checks and balances is the precise goal of the American left. They do not see them as important components of a dynamic and resilient system that allows for self-correction within itself rather than necessitating going outside it. They see checks and balances as obstacles to the real purpose of government, which is to provide a vehicle for their own exercise of power.

For example, they seek to eliminate the filibuster, which we will discuss more later. This requirement that the vast majority of legislation is subject to a sixty-vote threshold for consideration by the Senate essentially forces compromise and consensus. It ensures that massive changes cannot be implemented by a bare majority. Now, the filibuster is not a constitutional requirement but is, instead, part of a tradition that takes into account the Senate's constitutional role as the legislative brake. The House represents population, the People; the Senate was supposed to represent the states, though 1913's Seventeenth Amendment requiring the direct election of senators disrupted that somewhat. The tradition of progressives imagining that they are smarter than the founders is over a century old.

Still, the Senate's role is to check the passions of the People. And that feature is a bug to Democrats who followed the 2020 elections with the intention of fundamentally transforming the nation via a House majority of a half-dozen and a Senate they controlled only through Kamala Harris's vice-presidential tie-breaking. By the barest of margins, they essentially sought unlimited power. And that was scary. No one sane wants to have his freedom reliant on the whims of Kyrsten Sinema or Joe Manchin. But that's where we were in 2021 and early 2022.

So too was the concurrent push to pack the Supreme Court. In Washington, it is always amusing to observe the establishment Republicans opining about "judicial restraint" and "applying the law as written" and so forth as the keys to good judging. Those of us who practice in actual courtrooms draw a federal judge assignment and immediately go online to find out which president appointed the jurist. Democrats are much like lawyers, in that they are result-oriented. A liberal judge will not always be liberal in regular cases. In one Ninth Circuit argument on an esoteric business law issue, your author found an appointee of Barack Obama who had been whispered about as a future SCOTUS justice to be the smartest and most engaged one on the three-judge panel. In a similar argument, your author engaged in a polite but vigorous disagreement—okay, a shouting match—with another flaming liberal, and also with a theoretical conservative who was later whisked off the bench for alleged #MeToo issues. Still, a liberal judge is usually liberal.

But in political cases, a liberal judge will always, every single time, no exceptions, side with the left. Most conservatives will side with the right, but occasionally you get a Justice Gorsuch who decides to be a maverick and read a 1960s discrimination law as totally, completely, of course applying to transexuals.

Control of the Supreme Court means control of the Constitution, and we know that for liberals, "control" means control with an iron fist. It allows them the freedom to morph the law into whatever they wish it to be. For example, the leftist justices and leftist lower court judges have repeatedly found that "the right of the people to keep and bear Arms, shall not be infringed" actually means "the right of the people to keep and bear Arms can totally be infringed." If you imagine that they won't discover a hidden asterisk in the Bill of Rights leading to a footnote to the First Amendment's right of free speech that reads, "except for what Democrats and their lackeys call hate speech," you are fooling yourself.

Now, combine that with the informal power exercised by the corporations, particularly by the mainstream media, social media, and internet companies that provide the forum for debate and discussion in our democracy. Unlike in Athenian democracy, which was a real democracy, a citizen can't just cruise down to the *agora* and watch the big debates of the day and perhaps even be heard himself. If the corporations decide to deplatform, say, everyone to the right of AOC, then the central premise of representative government—that citizens can meaningfully participate in their own governance—vanishes with the flip of a circuit.

But luckily, no corporation would ever intervene to silence opposition to the establishment narrative.

Oh, right.

So, with Congress locked up, the courts in lockstep, and no ability for dissenters to participate in politics, our elections would be merely a high-five to the status quo. In other words, that could very well look a lot like the situation where the Constitution's self-correction function has been, quite deliberately, negated.

And what option does that leave normal citizens except submission?

And that's a problem.

CHAPTER SEVEN

THE UNRAVELING

We dodged a bullet in 2021. Sure, we got hit with plenty of others, but not the .50 caliber round. We dodged it in large part thanks to a couple of Democratic senators, one who knew that he would have to run for reelection in a Trump +37 state, and a flighty one who was essentially a Saguaro Scarlett O'Hara fiddle-dee-deeing her way to maverick status as only Arizona pols can.

But what if there had been a couple more Democrats in the Senate, and the pressure to push their most measly of margins to the max?

The thing about transformation is that it is transformative, and sensible people do not undertake transformation without massive electoral support demonstrating a societal commitment to a fundamental change. But the progressive left is not made up of sensible people. Sense has nothing to do with it—only obtaining and keeping power does. So, their temptation is to make huge changes not via consensus among the citizenry of the kind resounding mandates demonstrate, but solely via power. If they can squeak it though, fine. Even if they can't—during the "Build Back Better" and "voting rights" fiasco, we learned that when fifty-two senators defy the forty-eight who support the Democrats' prerogatives, it means the death of "Our Democracy."

But just because you can does not mean that you necessarily should. Not if you care about a healthy body politic.

When FDR pushed through his New Deal, he had a massive majority in Congress. Republicans would have had to dramatically improve their standing just to have qualified as an afterthought. You can argue that the program was unwise, and it *was* hugely unwise, but you cannot argue it was powered through without the consent of the governed. With those numbers, it was the insistence of the governed. The people elected Franklin Roosevelt knowing what he wanted to do, then reelected him three more times and thereby granted him an indisputable mandate for his policies. We've been paying the price for their mistake ever since, but there is no reasonable debate over the fact that they made it.

That would not be the case in today's polarized America. Instead of building a consensus among the electorate, then getting a mandate in an election, and then getting the policies passed through the old-fashioned "I'm Just a Bill" process the Gen Xers learned about on *Schoolhouse Rock*, today's play is to get the major changes passed regardless of little things like buy-in by the people as expressed through an electoral wave. And it's not really the policies that are the issue. The climate-hoax payoffs to favored constituencies, universal preschool up to age thirty-five, government-subsidized abortions for pregnant people of all genders—these are the kind of relatively routine pork barrel payoffs to favored constituencies we have always seen. They are money dumps that have the sheen of wokeness on them. Everyone knows that the only thing that paying billions to hire a zillion "diversity consultants" is going to do is employ a zillion Democrat-voting diversity consultants.

No, what is different are the initiatives that, but for the filibuster, the Democrats would shove down our collective throats in order to ensure their perpetual power. The filibuster requires sixty votes to allow argument to conclude on a piece of legislation in the Senate. There is no equivalent rule in the House, which operates on a straight-up majority basis. The idea is to slow things down, to build consensus, and to encourage compromise. You remember that "the Senate is the cooling saucer" analogy from civics, if you grew up when they taught civics. If you were several generations older, you might know what a "cooling saucer" is. Regardless, the filibuster effectively creates a sixty-vote supermajority requirement for most legislation. So really controversial stuff—like much of the pinko punch list—tends to die on the floor.

Progressives hate that, at least when they are in a sub-sixty majority. It provides a nearly insurmountable obstacle to their exercise of power. It provided an obstacle to the loathsome Harry Reid's power when he was Senate majority leader. The Republicans refused to let some circuit court nominations proceed, so he invoked the nuclear option—that is, by a mere majority, the Democrats eliminated the filibuster rule, but only for circuit court judicial appointments. Harry Reid got his circuit court judges, and when the cunning Mitch McConnell got the chance to jam through three Supreme Court judges by nuking the filibuster as to SCOTUS justices, he did—much to Democrats' chagrin. They don't call the tortoise-looking parliamentary genius the "Murder Turtle" for nothing.

But with just a couple more seats, the Democrats could kill the filibuster for everything and bring us to the brink.

First, they would change the Senate by making the District of Columbia a state. Now, there are constitutional issues with this innovative move, but a pliable Supreme Court—oh, we shall get to that—would allow them to bypass irrelevancies like the text of the Constitution that bars D.C. statehood. The capital was something like 92 percent for Biden in 2020. Statehood means two more Democratic senators forever. And the cradle of Marion Barry would, no doubt, provide inspiring ones.

For good measure, they would make Puerto Rico a state too. That's two more perpetual Democrats. There are no other arguments in favor of making a state out of this commonwealth, but if you bring up the arguments against it you are literally David Duke. Heck, why not integrate a poverty-stricken island with a very different culture than the rest of the country into the United States as the fifty-second state? And don't worry, its history of insurrections in favor of independence that led to assassination attempts, mass bombing, and open warfare could never, ever become a giant problem of epic proportions.

So, there's a permanent four-seat cushion for the left in the Senate. But that's fine. After all, the Senate is a racist bastion built somehow on racism because low-population red states like Wyoming and Alaska get equal representation with big blue states like California and New York. Now, low-population blue states like Vermont and Rhode Island also get that same representation, but that is not an issue. In fact, that's a good thing because it helps Democrats. Not giving Vermont, the Miracle Whip of states, two senators is totally racist.

See how this works?

But packing the Senate is only the beginning—you don't want to take chances. That's why you have to let the feds take over the election system. This is super convenient, since the Democrats are currently the feds—it's their bureaucracy, their Congress, and, as part of the scam, their presidency. And, if they take over our election system, they will *always* be the feds.

Is it insurrection to suspect that a federally controlled election system might be used to turn elections in the direction of the party controlling the federal government? Yes, obviously.

As part of election reform, they inform us we need gerrymandering reform. Clearly, Republicans are getting too much of a say in redistricting and Democrats not enough. Merrick Garland, whose diss may be McConnell's greatest legacy, sued Texas for gerrymandering as Biden's AG in 2021. Yet he somehow overlooked the Jackson Pollock nightmare that was the Illinois map.

We also need to ban voter ID. It is super popular, with 81 percent support in 2021. You can't get 81 percent of Americans to agree on anything except maybe that the Lincoln Project should not babysit your tweens. But the Democrats insist that banning voter ID is imperative. It's too hard for black people to get an ID, according to white people who are experts in such things. Note that this inability to get an ID does not apply to something labeled a "vaccine passport"—apparently the same daunting challenges that regular IDs present to the constituents whom Democrats infantilize do not apply to jab-related documents.

Ballots must also be mailed to everyone, but voting rolls must never be cleared. Ballots can be gathered up and brought to the counting locations by anybody—how could vote harvesting go wrong? Now, a cynic might wonder if the Democrats actually want to make it easier to cheat, and that cynic—as is so often the case these days—would be absolutely right. It's all a transparent attempt to facilitate cheating by Democrats within a process entirely controlled by Democrats.

But there's more. There's amnesty, for everyone, and no border at all. Actually, the "no border" part is already in effect. As the Biden administration's actions, or conscious inaction, demonstrated, just because there's a law doesn't mean that the regime has to enforce it. For tens of millions of people streaming north, it would be a quick transition from Third World peasant to American voter. And they probably aren't going to vote Republican.

It's safe to say this will benefit Democrats, as in it will further ensure that Democrats never lose a majority in either house or the presidency ever.

But what about the courts? Surely our robed solons will dispense justice in the face of such manifest wrongdoing!

No, and that is the part that takes the danger to a whole new level. Even with electoral shenanigans and adding seats, there exists a possibility of the GOP's retaking power. This is more than a theoretical one, considering the ineptitude of Democratic administrations. Just look at Joe Biden, nearly halfway into his alleged term of office, polling on par with head lice, bowel obstructions, and Nickelback. Even with Democratic "voting reform," Republicans could, with difficulty, squeeze out the occasional congressional victory (the presidency would probably be gone, though). After all, we had an overwhelming, outside-the-margins-of-fraud wave in 2010, and 2022, as of this writing, is looking very promising in terms of crushing liberal dreams. But if the Democrats conquer the courts, the electoral remedy is gone. The courts will decide the elections, and they will always decide it in favor of Democrats.

How might they take the courts? By doing what even FDR could not convince his legislative minions to do. Pack them. Sure, they could do it at the Supreme Court level—add five seats and SCOTUS is theirs forever. But they can also expand the lower courts and fill those new seats with pinko commies who make AOC look downright Trumpy.

Leftist courts would effectively deprive disgruntled, patriotic citizens of any remedy. They won't be able to elect non-regime candidates, and they won't be able to avail themselves of the courts to redress their grievances. Unconstrained by the sixty-vote threshold, the Democrat id would be in full effect. The Democrats would make it rain dollars, supercharging inflation from merely awful to Weimarian levels. They would attempt to force workers into unions, and generally drive the economy into a freeway piling. The social proclamations would be even more gruesome, with gun bans, car bans, pronoun mandates, and misgendering felonies—whatever they dreamed of would be made real. All America would be Berkeley, which itself is basically COVID-era Australia with fewer kangaroos and more seminars on decolonializing chemistry.

And the oppression would not only be governmental but corporate—the corporations, particularly the social media companies, would be partners with the regime. If silencing you informally through corporate deplatforming was not enough, the government could do it. And a leftist Supreme Court would rubber-stamp it.

At the end of the day, without the people behind it, the Bill of Rights is only as strong as the parchment it was scrawled upon. You either defend those rights with due process or with a rifle.

How does this play out? What would America falling apart actually look like to the Americans caught up in it? How might it happen?

As Hemingway observed about bankruptcy, it happens slowly, then all at once.

Our story begins in a grocery store in blue California. Jane walks down the aisles, barely taking notice of how the few various products that remain in stock are lined up right at the front, with empty space behind, to give the impression of plenty. But there isn't plenty.

It's the peanut butter that does it, or the lack of it. No Jif. The kids only eat Jif. They won't touch Skippy or that Ralph's house brand stuff. And there's no Jif—again.

She complained about it to her friends on Facebook, or Meta, whatever they call it now. She wrote, "I can't believe I can't find Jif anymore! I voted for Joe and then Kamala to get back to normal and I can't even find peanut butter!" But Facebook refused to post it, telling her, "Fact-checkers and experts agree that reports of product shortages are false and constitute harmful misinformation."

Jane has had it. She tears off her mask—Dr. Fauci, still doing daily media despite breaking his hip the previous winter after slipping on ice in Aspen, had issued dire warnings about COVID-24 and the need for an eighth booster—and shouts, "This is bullshit!"

Everyone in the store stares at her from behind their masks. A woman with a pinched face and a cart full of Chardonnay and dinners-for-one screeches, "Shut up, insurrectionist!" But a man down the aisle rips off his mask and says, "Hell yeah, lady!" Then he adds an old favorite—"Let's go, Brandon!" The bitter crone pulls out her Android and dials 911.

Jane's husband Dave is at home. On Zillow, his three-bedroom house is worth $2 million, though it has no backyard and the balcony leaks. But no one is buying—and when they looked online at properties in Idaho, they were comparably priced.

It's not like his job was keeping him in the Golden State. Truthfully, he felt a little like a sap for working at all. His neighbor didn't work, and he lived on benefits almost as well as Dave and Jane. Of course, his neighbor had rented that house from the owner and just stopped paying rent a couple years ago, which certainly helped make ends meet.

Dave got only a fair performance review at work last year. He was a decent manager, he was told, but his race indicated that he had a number of inherently bad characteristics. Dave considered complaining of reverse racism, but he understood from one of the innumerable HR briefings there was no such thing.

Now he sat on the couch waiting for Jane to come home. The big screen was blank. With all the streaming services, he had a thousand choices, but there was nothing on.

Dave used to watch Fox News when Jane went out on an errand, but he was not watching it now. It was off the air. It had pushed misinformation, the government said. He was not really that into politics, but he had heard that the Supreme Court upheld the right of the government to stop insurrectionist speech.

A mail-in ballot sat on the counter. What did it matter? The election was over; the same guys had won. He would not have even bothered to send his in except that they kept track of people who refused to—*not participating in the election was a form of protest which itself was tantamount to supporting insurrection.*

He walked by his kid doing homework in the dining room—a privilege worksheet where the children analyzed how their race affected their power in society. The kid was smart; Dave had told him to go along and get along, and the boy—Dave made sure to periodically confirm his son's gender, just in case it changed—was now on the middle school Diversity, Inclusion, and Equity Council. The students were busy policing the rest of the student body for racism, transphobia, and fatphobia, which Dave simply accepted as being a thing when he first heard the term. Dave did not remember the last time he saw his kid with a math book.

He made sure to watch what he said around his currently male-identifying child, just in case.

Dave needed some air. He stepped out onto his cramped patio where the Weber sat unused. He might as well get rid of it, he thought. Meat was ridiculously expensive, with sirloin at eighteen dollars a pound. Regardless, grilling contributed to global warming. So did gas-powered leaf blowers and lawn mowers; his yard looked like a jungle.

On the sidewalk out front, a couple of young men in hoodies carrying tire irons looked inside the window of his Camry. Dave knew enough not to leave anything out inside the car where it could be seen, and the two passed it by satisfied there was nothing worth taking. One caught sight of Dave staring and pivoted.

"What the hell you looking at, bitch?" the thug shouted.

Dave turned and went back in the house. He used to have a shotgun, but Jane didn't like it and made him turn it in during the mandatory buybacks. After all, this wasn't Texas.

"That's right, bitch, walk away." His co-conspirator laughed as they strolled to the next car.

Dave did not bother calling the cops. He had learned that this was not going to get him anywhere, that the 911 dispatcher would *tell him there was nothing that could be done about a couple of gentlemen simply out for a walk.*

His son looked up at him, having heard the encounter, and then looked back toward his work. Dave felt his throat tighten. He was furious, angrier than he had ever been, raging at his total impotence in the face of oppression from all sides. And there was nothing he could do.

In Texas, they could do something. When the president signed the law outlawing the private possession of firearms—the Safe Childhoods Act, which was upheld by the expanded Supreme Court 10–5—the governor of the Lone Star State and the governors of several others jointly announced this law would not be enforced in their states.

"No," they said.

President Harris was, of course, both livid and incoherent, with her instructions and orders confusing her cabinet and her generals. They understood her enough to know that there needed to be an example made. Such brazen defiance in support of the racist notion of gun ownership—experts and fact-checkers, Twitter reported, had determined that racism was the genesis of red America's love for guns—had to be crushed. Certainly, the official media was all over it, bewailing the outrage that was these governors defying the federal decree. But the rebels were clear—there would be no enforcement of the gun confiscation statute in Texas or any of the other states that had signed onto the Second Amendment Compact.

"Come and take them," the governor said. He had considered saying "Molon labe" instead, but that was a bit esoteric for the masses and clearly over President Harris's head.

When she looked at the generals, they fiddled with their collars. "Ma'am," the chairman said. "We have a problem with AWOLs."

She did not know what that meant.

"Absent without leave," the general explained. "Basically, about a third of our troops deserted when the rumor spread that they would be ordered into the insurrectionist states to reestablish authority."

"You still have the other two-thirds," she replied.

"Ma'am, a unit that loses that many of its troops quickly is generally considered combat ineffective."

President Harris just stared blankly.

Pete threw a garbage can through the front glass windows of Tiffany's on Fifth Avenue, but he knew he would not be looting the place. All the diamonds and jewelry had been evacuated weeks ago as the mobs had spread through the city. The storied New York Police Department was at about 60 percent manning, which the politicians had played off as intentional, part of "reimagining community order" in the Big Apple.

The truth was that both ends of the personnel pipeline were hemorrhaging. There were few recruits coming in, both because generous benefits made sitting on one's couch playing Grand Theft Auto *a viable career path, and because the kind of recruits that used to join up— legacies, vets, and traditionally inclined individuals—were no longer showing up to pin on a badge. Why would they? Morale was rock-bottom, and anyone interested in the gig was told by anyone who had actually been on the job that he would be crazy to join up. On the other end of the pipeline, just about everyone who could retire did so as soon as his pension vested. Among those without the years, an astonishing 50 percent of serving officers had a disability claim pending. "Stress" and "PTSD" were favored grounds. Others took the bonuses that departments in Florida and Texas were offering and moved south.*

The cops still on the beat kept inside their cars when they could and made no effort to look for trouble. They had seen what happened when the cameras came out during an arrest—you could rarely get the DA to prosecute a case involving an actual criminal, but a cop caught getting physical on tape? Charging him was never a problem.

Pete admired his handiwork. He wore no mask—why conceal his identity when no one was being arrested? Plus it was well-known that COVID did not infect mostly peaceful protestors like himself. This was the first time they had pushed as far as Fifth Avenue, but the lack of opposition inspired him and his comrades. It also inspired many of the people who usually worked near there—mostly to flee Manhattan forever for the red states.

He was not angry about his college debts anymore—they had been wiped away by Congress, making his sociology degree free—but he was angry in a more general sense. At twenty-five, he had never had a real job, only a few gigs. He got enough money from the government to stay alive, but he felt utterly without purpose. Religion? No one he knew believed in that nonsense—he had literally never met a regular churchgoer. But he burned with faith nonetheless, an undefined amalgam of socialism, critical race theory, and received wisdom delivered by Twitter blue checks to the endless timeline he read on his iPhone 15.

It made sense to smash things because nothing else made sense, and tossing a trash can through a glass window was his way of confronting the evil all around him. He hated the corporations but defended them against the hated racist, fascist Republicans. He hated the government, but he defended it against the hated racist, fascist Republicans too.

The rest of his friends were rushing down the sidewalk, breaking more windows. The street was deserted except for the mob. He followed. What else was there for him to do, except keep hating?

Jorgenson emptied off a mag from his M4 into the house, breaking out some of the few remaining shards of glass his fellow Bureau of

Alcohol, Tobacco, Firearms, and Explosives (ATF) agents had not already shot out. His black tactical helmet weighed down on his head and made it hard to look through his optic. No movement. He found himself hoping his burst had not hit one of the kids he knew was inside there. It was supposed to be just another routine gun grab—the New Jersey records had identified the homeowner as possessing weapons but not having turned them in. A social media deep dive—actually, they had not had to dive very deep at all—had revealed that their subject was a proud Second Amendment advocate who promised never to give up his guns. They would make an example of this guy and send a message.

The squad would go in heavy, in full tactical gear, and not give the target a chance to grab one of his weapons. His wife and kids were in there too—they might be a little traumatized when a dozen black-clad SWAT members rushed in with assault rifles, but they would get over it. A camera crew from federally subsidized CNN, tipped off in advance, would catch it all—it was important to publicize what happened to insurrectionists, the all-purpose term for anyone not willing to get onboard with how things were now.

Jorgensen himself thought that confiscation was bullshit, but he had five years and then he could retire to Tampa. The law was the law, right? Hadn't the Supreme Court said that there was no right to keep and bear arms? As law enforcement, he could keep his.

The team moved forward to the porch fast, and that was when something went off. Two guys down with two shots, probably a high-powered rifle firing big rounds instead of the light 5.56 mm rounds their M4s fired. The subject was waiting for them. It was a damn ambush. The rest of the team retreated and took cover, opening up on the house. Aimed fire was the response. Well-aimed. Another ATF officer went down with a round through his goggles.

We should have known, Jorgenson told himself, reloading a mag. This was the first shoot-out their office had walked into, but out in those other states, it was different. A dozen ATF officers had been shot in the last month attempting to confiscate weapons. In one case out in Idaho, the local sheriffs had helped the shooter escape.

But this was blue New Jersey.

He looked at the windows. No movement.

How did the gun nut know we were coming, Jorgenson wondered. A leak? Possible—a lot of the agents pinned down right now had been pretty vocal about what they thought of their new mission before the agent in charge made it clear that that kind of insurrectionist talk would get them fired. The most outraged agents had walked out on their jobs and their pensions. There were not many of those, though.

Or maybe the subject had an accomplice, someone else who had seen the black SUVs coming and warned his buddy. That guy could be anywhere.

Two hundred meters behind the line of ATF vehicles, a man with a Winchester 700 was set up just back from the brush, the way he had learned in the Marines. He carefully placed the crosshairs of his Leupold VX-6 HD scope on the back of Agent Jorgenson's neck, between the helmet and his body armor, and squeezed the trigger.

These anecdotes barely scratch the surface of where we are headed if we don't change course. Our society is angry, and there is a palpable sense of betrayal that the America we were promised is not the America that was delivered. Everything seems like it is falling apart. So, the question is, "What happens next?"

job, and their divine right. We conservatives all love the framers, but the framers all generally agreed with each other on the basics—it helped that many shared a classical education while few, if any, majored in gender studies—and that common grounding is absent between the red and blue today. You can't just offer up revitalized federalism as the solution to people who didn't recognize or embrace the concept of federalism back before it was vitalized.

A national divorce would mean a clean break, a formal end of the United States as we know it and the creation of (at least) two separate political entities on the North American property currently jointly occupied by Ms. Blue America and Mr. Red America.

So, how would the subject of a formal severance ever even come up outside of hypotheticals raised by provocateurs of varying levels of seriousness on opposite sides of the aisles? Five years ago, if you had mentioned it, they would fit you with a straitjacket. Your author knows—he started writing conservative action novels with this notion as the background and people called him a nut. Half a decade later, they call his novels visionary. You're welcome.

If it really were to happen, it would probably have to start at the grass roots and bubble up into the ruling caste's consciousness, essentially taking it by surprise like the Tea Party did in 2009 or the anti-CRT school rebellions that elected Glenn Youngkin in blue Virginia did in 2021. To mix up a handful of metaphors, the only way it could put down roots would be to remain under the radar, lest the idea be strangled in its crib.

A consensus for a national divorce is not going to be astroturfed and imposed from on high because the people on high don't want it. The moment the establishment realizes that it is a serious idea, the bulk of the establishment will come down hard. The idea will be insurrectionist and treasonous and Putin's probably behind it and it's definitely racist. The establishment has to stop it by making it radioactive since a national divorce represents a decisive change to the status quo, and if there is any kind of status our ruling class likes, it is the quo kind.

Some striver may see it as his lane to prominence, but he will be harnessing an energy that is already growing. For it ever to be a possibility, the people are going to need to embrace the idea in the face of universal scorn, much like the America First populism that Donald Trump embraced and surfed into the Oval Office. Trump did not invent the brand of populism he represented. He had long advocated something like it, even as far back as when that high-pitched billionaire elf Ross Perot was pushing a version of it in the early nineties. In the mid-2010s, the conservative populist ideology was just waiting for someone to exploit it, and The Donald had the vision to do it. Sixteen Republicans ran for the nomination against Trump in 2016. No one noticed that there was this M1A3 tank idling there, with the keys in the ignition, just waiting to drive over the gooey likes of Jeb! Bush right into the White House.

The idea of a national divorce is not exactly like that, as a split is less about an ideology than a reaction based on frustration—the other side won't listen and the love is gone, and now we're going to pile its clothes on the front lawn. The establishment would likely have no idea of the intensity of support for it until it was getting real traction, and that traction would likely come from its adoption by a wily pol who figured that he could do really well as a big fish in a pond approximately half the size of the present one.

Besides a grassroots movement and a leader, it would also likely take some sort of transitional event to jump-start serious divorce momentum. It is not going to take off simply because someone or several high-profile people start pushing it. To make it happen requires a "this changes everything" moment. Such a moment could come from one of the future scenarios we will discuss—a potential armed civil conflict or some outside event having to do with, say, China. But until you get the combination of the people wanting it *and* one or more leaders carrying the flag *and* something epochal to make it the solution to an even worse problem, you are not getting a national divorce.

Yet, if anything, the last couple decades have taught us that the worst-case scenario *can* happen. Therefore, let's examine what it might look like if all these things came to pass and America decided that its next destination was Splitsville.

The basic notion is that the red people would take their part of the community property and the blues their portion and they would go and live in separate parts of the U.S.A. Fortunately, as we all know, divvying up the pot in a divorce is never, ever, ever a giant hassle that becomes an endless, massive battle and ends unsatisfactorily for everyone except the lawyers.

Dividing polities is hard, and there are not too many examples from recent history to look to in order to see how to do it with minimal hassle. You do want to look to the Balkans, but as a cautionary example. Yugoslavia's breakup devolved into a massive civil war. That mess was still sucking in U.S. forces during the Trump administration when Ric Grenell finally negotiated something like a peace between Kosovo and Serbia. If we wished to divorce, we should carefully review how they broke up Josip Tito's territory and then do the opposite.

The Soviet Union, the Humpty-Dumpty of international communism, had a great fall. Now, of course, all the ex-KGB men are trying to put it back together again. Well, how's that whole Ukraine thing working out for you, Vlad?

More successful was the 1993 division of Czechoslovakia into the Czech Republic and Slovakia. They just divided up all the goodies by population and there they were, not that anyone else knew or cared.

There were Czechs and there were Slovaks, and they were different in ways that only matter to Czechs and Slovaks. The commies had pasted them together; with the U.S.S.R. gone, they could go their separate ways and did so without much trouble. They apparently still have some beefs, but they aren't killing each other. That's a low bar, but thank goodness they got over it.

So, it can be done, though the division of a country that is pretty much a footnote hardly compares to the monumental job of divvying up a superpower.

The first task would be splitting the real property. For simplicity's sake, you would probably try to stick with existing state lines to start. Let's begin with the easy ones. Blue gets Hawaii, red gets Alaska. Next, it's pretty clear that Texas and Florida are going to be in the red—in fact, it's pretty clear the red part will be primarily the south and middle of the country. New England, including New York, is definitely blue. But California has to be blue too, along with Oregon and Washington, and it seems hard to see how the coasts could be directly connected. Basically, you are really looking at the Northeast Coast and the West Coast as the blue with red in between.

But nothing is that simple. How about the Midwest? Ohio is super red, and Illinois is pinko-blue, or at least Chicago is. Indiana is pretty red, as are Iowa and Missouri, so now we have a checkerboard thing happening. What would you call Wisconsin, Minnesota, and Michigan? Are they blue? Minnesota, okay, but the other two? Are they red or blue or color non-binary? What are their political pronouns?

Red certainly takes West Virginia, and blue probably gets generic Virginia even after it rejected Terry McAuliffe. But Pennsylvania? Who knows? It's politically promiscuous. And you have Colorado being liberal right there in a sea of red. New Mexico too, and who knows what color the maverick-generating hotbox that is Arizona would want to ally with. It seems red, but would probably flirt with blue just to be contrary and piss everyone off in the tradition of John McCain, Jeff Flake, and Kyrsten Sinema.

Of course, a state is a big entity, and while a state like Massachusetts is pretty much all blue through and through, others are divided. California is blue on the coasts and red in the interior. You get outside of Chicago and you are deep into making-America-great-again territory. Ditto Pennsylvania—it's famously Pittsburgh, Philadelphia, and Kentucky in between. Same with New York—head upstate and pretty soon you start encountering common sense.

But the red states have the opposite problem: suppurating abscesses of leftism in otherwise healthy political ecosystems. Texas has Austin, as well as blue tumors called "Houston," "Dallas," and "San Antonio." The Rio Grande Valley used to be reliably blue too, until Joe Biden decided to yell "Olly olly Oaxacan free" to every Third World peasant south of the border. Ohio has Cleveland, Louisiana has New Orleans, and Missouri has St. Louis, and all of them are various shades of blue.

In other words, a clear division where you carve out all of your political opponents is simply not in the cards. No matter how you draw the lines, some of your opponents are going to remain on your side of the fence.

If the purpose is purity, to be rid of the troubling presence of the opposition, then a straight-up split, state by state, is just not going to get it done. There is no way you can gerrymander Austin into the blue. Nor can you parse out the vast stretches of rural cow country dominated by the big blue cities in the big blue states.

What's the answer? You could let nature take its course and let people move out to the part of the country they are most comfortable in. Maybe a bunch of people in Austin will decide that living under the tyranny of red freedom and prosperity is simply too much to bear and move to flats in Baltimore where they will definitely enjoy the winters and hip local music scene.

That would certainly happen to some extent—there would be a great sorting, but there would not be a *complete* sorting. You would have patches of red in the blue, and blotches of blue in the red, and doesn't that sort of defeat the point of the exercise?

Now, there could be sterner measures. The new countries could act to eject the interlopers who, until the divorce, were mere lopers. They did that in the Balkans post–Josip Tito, and there it was called "ethnic cleansing." This would not necessarily be ethnic cleansing—though considering the identification with red and blue with various ethnicities, the label "political cleansing" might be a distinction with less of a difference than anyone would be comfortable with.

Leaving aside the question of how a new nation might decide whom to boot out—do they go through the voter rolls in Red America and wave goodbye to anyone registered "D"?—there is the other question of how you might enforce such a decree. Not a lot of Americans, at least we could hope, would be too thrilled about going door to door evicting friends and neighbors based on voting histories. Maybe you could get former agents from the old United States' FBI to do it—they'll famously do whatever scummy thing they are told to do. Still, people probably don't have the appetite for that, though if we get pushed to the point of splitting up, they might work one up.

In all likelihood, a national divorce simply is not going to happen, unless the violence threshold has already been crossed, in which case all bets are off.

A more realistic approach is simply to crush the other ideology politically and allow the dissenters to stay, understanding that they will be powerless in their new country. Think California under the Democrats right now. Upon splitting up, each side would retire to its respective new capital—that America would have the opportunity to ditch the dismal swamp that is D.C. is one of the few solid arguments in favor of a divorce—and write a new and improved constitution. And in those new and improved constitutions, they would install towering guardrails designed to ensure that their respective political minorities could never, ever undo what the divorcers did.

Red America would likely track the present Constitution, being conservative and all. But there would be alterations. The revised version would do things like modify the Second Amendment to add "No, we're not kidding—everyone gets to pack heat, and that includes assault rifles." Maybe they would undo the Seventeenth Amendment and end direct election of senators. Expect that the word "abortion" would finally get into the Constitution, except it would be in the context of banning it starting at the time of the first date.

The Blue America constitution would be a different kind of abortion. The left, which is smarter and wiser and more moral than the dead white slave owners who were the framers—just ask them—would toss out the U.S. Constitution in favor of something written by a bunch of college professors gone wild. Say goodbye to those irritating negative rights that prevent the government from doing stuff to its citizens. Say hi to positive rights about all the things government is going to do for its subjects.

And you will see all the rights the old one had, except to keep and bear arms, of course. You'll have freedom of speech and of the press and of religion. They will just add a whole bunch of asterisks. If you watch the left today, you understand that its focus is never on the right itself but on how whatever situation is at hand demands an exception. "I believe in free speech, but with rights come responsibilities and _____ speech is irresponsible. Free speech does not mean speech without consequences."

Of course, the point of rights is not to have "responsibilities" or "consequences," and leftists know that. But the right of free speech is an obstacle to the left, so free speech must give way. Just fill in that blank with whatever you want—"racist," "insurrectionist," "climate denial," whatever. And you can be sure the diverse, inclusive, and equitable justices on the blue Supreme Court—you know quotas will be in their constitution too—will rubber-stamp whatever exceptions are needed to gag the dissenters.

So, you have a red constitution that is a tightened-up version of today's model, and you have a blue constitution drafted by AOC and Bernie Sanders that channels the U.S.S.R.'s fake one. How will that work out?

Certainly well for the extremes in the blue. The powerful will be protected and their sinecures secured. Understand that the cadres will take care of the cadres. The ultra-poor will do fine, with "fine" meaning their daily spoonful of scraps will be assured. They won't do well in an objective sense, but they will do well enough not to starve or have to work. But for the people in the middle, it will suck. Who thinks that all those billionaires who are keeping the brighter tomorrow at bay by refusing to pay their fair share will stay put in the blue if they can't avoid being taxed into oblivion? They either cut a deal with the establishment to avoid getting soaked—you know, like they do today in undivorced America—or they will head to Dallas.

No, in Blue America it will be the working saps who get to pick up the tab, only now they will not just be supporting the welfare bums. They will be paying for the cradle-to-grave coddling of the Julias. "The Life of Julia" was a horrifying Obama-era slideshow that presented how the expanded government the left dreamed of was going to take the place of the men who should be in a woman's life as she ages from toddler to geriatric. In a Blue America, the government would be daddy and hubby and everything else with a figurative penis that she will ever need. At one point in the slideshow, she decides to have a child and—since no dude is present—it's unclear if Uncle Sam pays for the test tube and turkey baster session, or if some bureaucrat gets *prima nocta*. In any case, multiply that horror show exponentially and you have an idea of the vision of life under the blue.

Red America's new government, on the other hand, would likely cater to the vast middle, with low taxes and lower services. These differences would turbocharge the migration trends. Some slothful layabout in Baton Rouge might hear about the hefty handouts to be had north of the border and go blue, while industrious citizens not interested in toiling to fund Doritos and cell phone plans for bums would head red. The blue increases its number of outstretched hands while decreasing its number of hands pushing the plows. The red loses its losers and wins the competition for winners. Give it a few months before the blue states are crying about how the red states are making true socialism unattainable, as it always is, by not being dreary basket cases too.

Certainly, red Americans would likely have to suffer the nightmare of mean tweets—count on Blue America's regulating social media into abject, craven submission—but people might be willing to do that in exchange for not being impoverished and oppressed by a government run by the kind of petty fascist bureaucrats who have made academia the nightmare it is today.

We need to consider the relationship between the two Americas sharing CONUS, the military's name for the continental United States. We can assume they would cooperate, or at least promise to cooperate, in things like military security. But do you think the blue would pull its weight Army-wise? It would inherit half the forces and promptly let the gear rust. The red would be forced to pick up the slack, draining its resources. It would likely take the nukes, since most of the missile fields are in the middle of the former country, but what about the subs? Our boomer submarine bases are mostly in the blue—the blue would have the entire Pacific coast. The Chinese would be unable to believe their luck.

This would be a challenge for Red America, as it would have little choice but to make up the difference out of self-preservation. While the scenario in the author's novels of no citizenship without service might be extreme, it seems likely some form of compulsory service would be necessary. At least Red America would have the weapons to do it. Notably, much of America's arms industry has already migrated south, and that would certainly accelerate in a national divorce. In 2021, Smith & Wesson moved from gun-hating Massachusetts to gun-friendly Tennessee. It is one of many companies to do so. And it is doubtful that the remaining aerospace companies in California would stick around in a country that has no interest spending billions of dollars that could be handed out to shiftless freeloaders buying Lockheed's wares.

What about foreign affairs? Red America would love Israel. Blue America would suck up to anyone who hated Red America. What about treaty obligations? Would both new countries stay in NATO? Would NATO even want the red knuckle-draggers? The EU would feel very comfortable with the globalists running Blue America, but they would need to trade with Red America. On the upside, Red American president Ron DeSantis might finally get around to invading Cuba and hanging all the communists from light posts like that over-hyped satyr JFK should have done.

Another issue is energy—the blues are against it. States like California have succeeded in largely outsourcing the dirty work of energy to the red states in order to appease their angry weather gods. It's unlikely that, upon the divorce becoming final, they would announce, "Remember global warming? Just kidding!" and start exploiting their fossil fuel resources again. No, the blue would become dependent on the red for power, and the red would be thrilled to build a bunch of smoke-belching coal plants and nukes on its scarlet turf to meet its new neighbor's needs. Of course, that will create useful leverage for when the blues get too big for their gender-neutral britches.

Don't forget food. California grows a ton of America's produce, but it's been letting land lie fallow because it won't build the water infrastructure needed to support it. Gotta keep those snail darters darting. Keep in mind that the Colorado River waters much of California's agriculture, and it originates in Red America. This is not an issue for the red. The red would be thrilled to pick up the slack and feed its neighbors...for a price.

Of course, the blues would rail against the ecocide committed by the awful red people. In fact, all of blue's problems would be attributed to the red. Just look at how the left operates now. It's always the red guy's fault. Crime. Poverty. The weather. Everything that goes wrong under the control of the institutions the left absolutely controls is the fault of the red people failing to give enough power and money to the people who are already in charge.

There's no reason to believe they would ever rewrite the playbook after a national divorce. The over-under on a blue demand for reparations from the red is about five years.

Dividing up the banking system, figuring out how to pay the obligations of the present U.S. government, plus dealing with a zillion other issues would be a huge undertaking. The United States' legacy of mismanagement would not just vanish. The national debt is over $30 trillion thanks to both Republicans and Democrats, though mostly to Democrats. How does that get paid off? And would the reds get sucked into a fight over the gold standard? Who gets the gold in Fort Knox? And how does everything else get divided up?

Blue America would have many (but not all) prestigious universities, though it is unclear how many people even today still buy the Ivy

League scam that these institutions are anything but endowment-fueled hedge funds that provide their customers networking opportunities even as the faculty indoctrinates them in the regime narrative. Blue America would also have the Pacific ports that provide the gateway to allow in cheap Chinese goods. But Red America might wake up and stick a tariff on foreign junk to simultaneously turbocharge American manufacturing and kneecap Beijing.

Of course, red and blue might end up tariffing each other. At best, you would have a tense relationship between red and blue, complicated by the blue's need for a scapegoat for the inevitable failures of socialism. Now, since the blue will be massively reliant on the red for food and energy, and because it is unlikely to invest in a capable military, its options vis-à-vis Red America would be rather limited. It could cut off trade, depriving Red America of its exports. These would include Hollywood dreck, assuming the studios did not move to places like Georgia to join the massive entertainment establishments already there today.

Presumably, the border would remain initially open and citizens of the two nations would be able to travel freely between them, but we have already seen how this could be a source of tension as quality people leave the blue only to be replaced by the dregs of the red. Moreover, the illegal alien issue would be a problem as well. The red states would stop that nonsense cold, but California still has a long border that the blues are ideologically incapable of sealing—assuming anyone would want to come north into California anymore. But if illegals used the open California border as a route into Red America, that would be a problem.

The trouble is that these problems would not get better over time. They would get worse, compounding over the years and being driven in large part by the entirely predictable false narrative by the leaders of Blue America that the problem with blue governance is

A National Divorce   113

that those red people over there are red. The blue is going to get poorer, and its bizarre cultural fetishes are going to get stupider and more insane—within a few years people will look back wistfully on the good old days where the worst thing they had to deal with was some doofus insisting xe is a nonbinary two-spirit and that you need to use xe's bespoke pronouns. There will be violence there because the blue system ensures that the establishment maintains a tight grip on all expression and power. With no procedural outlet to let off steam—denied both a public forum and access to governance—marginalized groups within the blue will see no alternative but violence to create the possibility of change. They will have been told to turn in their scary guns, but most will plant them in a hole and wait.

This could mean red rebellions, but also rebellions from the even harder left. The latter seems more likely—the Antifa and BLM types who rioted in 2020 will not stay under control forever unless they get what they want. The blue establishment today wants them as an unofficial military wing to be deployed as needed; it does not want to share the table with them. But how long will the street radicals be satisfied with that?

Blue America could fall into chaos, since it would have its own version of the Stasi but not a larger structure capable of dealing with large-scale insurrection—a *real* insurrection, not a bunch of eccentric geriatrics in MAGA hats marveling at Pelosi's powder room. The kind of people who make up effective military organizations will go to the country with effective military organizations while Blue America's rump military might well end up run by Field Marshal Alexander Vindman. At least their chow halls would be top-notch.

In contrast, Red America is likely to build up security forces capable of suppressing chaos spread to it by the failing blue. The question would be whether it would feel the need to go on the offensive.

The prospective border between divorced Red and Blue Americas would be endless and nearly indefensible; it is not outside the realm of possibility that Red America would determine that a collapsing Blue America would need to be stabilized with force. And so you would see the war a divorce was designed to avoid.

Two Americas would not mean two strong Americas. At best, it would mean one, and that one would be hampered by the need to undertake the security for both. The logistical and practical requirements of splitting the country in two would create endless problems and weaken both nations. They would be focused not on growth but on dealing with the challenges of the breakup. Yes, Red America would likely prosper more based on its embrace of a freer market and basic freedoms, but it would not be a superpower except in the sense that it has a whole bunch of H-bombs on Minuteman missiles in North Dakota. And a real conflict with Blue America would be almost inevitable.

Do we want that?

A national divorce is a cute idea, born of frustration. But it is impractical and counterproductive. However, it does have one thing going for it, one thing that is very, very significant.

At least in the short term, it's not a civil war.

CHAPTER NINE

THE SECOND CIVIL WAR: BLUE REBELLION

The last time America had a civil war, it was caused primarily by rich Democrats trying to keep control over a subservient population for their own selfish benefit. And that last time, America suffered about six hundred thousand dead. The next civil war, if it comes, will be caused by mostly rich Democrats trying to keep control of a subservient population for their own benefit. And if America were to suffer only about six hundred thousand dead in round two, it would have gotten off comparatively lucky.

Civil wars are the most uncivil of wars, fueled by emotion and superheated feelings of hatred and betrayal. Regular war is no picnic, and atrocities are the norm rather than the exception throughout human history. But in civil wars, you have a smoldering anger that is often more intense than that against relative strangers. We fought the Nazis until they surrendered, and except for stretching the necks of a small number of the worst psychopaths—arguably too small a number—we got to work building Germany into a BMW- and strudel-making powerhouse. The same with Japan, where ethnic hatred and Imperial atrocities combined to make the Pacific War a merciless slaughter. By mutual agreement, though with different motivations, we did not take a lot of Japanese prisoners. After a pair of our newly developed hot rocks crisped a couple of Japanese cities, our righteous fury over Pearl Harbor was satiated. Within a few years, occupied Japan was shipping America transistor radios, economy cars, and Godzilla movies.

But the hard feelings during and after a Civil War 2.0 might not subside quite so quickly. After all, our fights against foreigners were way over there, across the sea. This would be a war here at home, a battle you could literally drive to. In fact, it might even happen in your own neighborhood.

Reconstruction after Civil War 1.0 was no picnic, though it could have been much crueler. Some argued then that it should have been. But in that conflict, there was always a recognition that this was sometimes literally brother against brother. The generals, blue and gray, had often gone through West Point together and fought side by side in Mexico and along the frontier. Lincoln, while steadfast in his determination to defeat the rebels and reunify the country even if that meant wading through a river of blood, always focused on the fact that reconciliation would eventually have to happen if the Union was to be a union in fact and not merely in name. His second inaugural address makes that clear:

> With malice toward none; with charity for all; with firmness in the right, as God gives us to see the right, let us strive on to finish the work we are in; to bind up the nation's wounds; to care for him who shall have borne the battle, and for his widow, and his orphan—to do all which may achieve and cherish a just, and a lasting peace, among ourselves, and with all nations.

As usual, our Creator dealt America a winning hand in terms of leaders when we needed them. We've actually got quite the winning streak going. Without Washington, we would probably be caring about soccer, drinking warm beer, and calling a car's trunk "the boot." FDR caused a bunch of problems with his ridiculous New Deal, but he kept us out of socialist revolution during the Great Depression and helped defeat the National Socialists. Ronald Reagan was the right man to get those communist bastards to tear down the Wall. And Lincoln was the right man to preserve the Union both in the short term, with bloody bayonets, and in the long term, with a commitment to reconciliation.

What are the chances we draw another Lincoln should we decide to rerun the War between the States? They are not good, not at all.

The first Civil War was not truly ideological. The South was pretty much on board with the principles of the Constitution, except for the idea of black people getting to be any part of it. The Confederates thought of themselves as "Georgians" or "Virginians," not Marxists. But today, our intra-American conflict is explicitly ideological. One side is (often covertly but increasingly overtly) Marxist, with all that that entails, and the other side embraces the principles of liberal democracy, with all that that entails. If it comes to blows, someone has to win, and then what? You cannot hope to easily push back together people who long ago broke apart.

A victorious Red America would still have to purge the poison of neo-Marxism from the body politic, and that would not be pretty. It would be near insanity to allow it to keep festering, an abscess un-lanced and suppurating, waiting to infect the country again. It would be ugly.

But think of what might happen if the left won a second civil war? You don't have to guess—history offers plenty of examples of the consequences for the people who blaspheme His Holiness Karl Marx. Gulags for the lucky ones, a bullet in the back of the neck for the rest.

Harsh? Even crazy? Americans butchering Americans? Well, here's a quick quiz—what is the leftist victory that did not end up with bodies stacked like cordwood?

Trick question. There isn't one. It's always a bloodbath.

So, with the consequences dire, the struggle itself would grow ever more pitiless as the stakes of defeat became more and more clear. There were atrocities in the Civil War but, with the exception of the Confederates' hellish Andersonville prison camp, not systematic ones. Don't count on that this time. Remember that the Weathermen's Bill Ayers—Obama's mentor—once observed that purifying the U.S. of A. would require liquidating twenty-five million Americans. And if you are reading this book unironically, you are certainly one of them.

What would a second American civil war look like, specifically one in which the blue side rebelled against a red government? That is difficult to say because the facts on the ground make any kind of scenario possible, from low-intensity skirmishing to conventional fighting. Moreover, the scenarios in which it might happen are very different. However, we can make some educated guesses about how the scenario might play out. Almost certainly, the scenario would be some sort of insurgency in which a coalition of leftist forces (formal and informal) fights an ideologically hostile, conservative federal government, assuming the right is ever allowed access to power again.

The level of conflict could range from bad to cataclysmic. There are different levels of insurgency. We have already discussed some very low-grade ones from the recent past, like the sixties radicals and the hapless Puerto Rican rebels. At the other extreme, we have the example of the Civil War, in which eleven states came together to fight the Union. A second civil war could start with low-grade warfare and eventually escalate into the mass-mobilization type of rebellion seen in the 1860s, where two relatively effective central governments faced off and conventional armies fought conventional battles. At that level, you might also see foreign intervention. Who would be the France in this next revolution, and which side would it assist?

Let's dive deeper into the least likely and probably least cataclysmic scenario, a blue rebellion against a red-led U.S. government, that is, a federal government wholly or largely controlled by conservative Republicans. Maybe Donald Trump wins the election in 2024 because Biden gets weirder or because Kamala Harris takes over and simply remains as bad as she is now, and the Democrats lose what is left of their minds. An election starring The Donald as Grover Cleveland could make that happen. Imagine the meltdown as inane Twitter blue checks announce that the democratic election of the once and future president is the ultimate attack on democracy.

It's important not to underestimate the stupidity and cynicism of these leftists; many are stupid enough to believe the hype and others are cynical enough to stoke the flames. It's all fun and games for a while, but there are real consequences to the Totalitarian Trump narrative. After all, at some point, if you repeat enough that the guy you hate is literally Hitler, you might just start treating him like a literal Hitler, and the installation of a literal Hitler would justify busting caps. This kind of scenario, the utterly plausible one where the Democrats and the media perpetrate this Big Lie, is how the violence might start.

Putting aside that Donald Trump is not, and will never be, literally Hitler, or Hitlerish, or even remotely Hitleresque, what would be the correlation of forces? The first question in planning a battle is to look at the situation, and the most important part of the situation is the enemy forces. In fact, Paragraph 1.A of a formal military five-paragraph order—assuming our military still does military stuff between its regularly scheduled regimen of anti-patriarchy briefings and losing wars—is "Situation: Enemy Forces." So, what do the leftists have?

And yes, the neo-Marxists of the American left are the bad guys, in case that was unclear.

The most likely leftist insurrection scenario—and by "insurrection," we do not mean some oddballs bum-rushing the Capitol—comes in the immediate aftermath of Republicans taking power following the massive repudiation of Biden or Harris, should they put the senile old pervert out to pasture. It might be Trump as president again or Ron DeSantis, or anyone in the GOP—it doesn't matter, as they will all be equally Hitler in the eyes of the left. He or she puts a hand on the Bible in front of a crowd that contains no Democrats because doubting elections is going to be okay again and the election is naturally rigged since the Democrats lost, and the clamor from the mainstream media that started the moment local Democrats found it impossible to cheat enough to snatch this red victory away will rise to a thunderous crescendo.

Democracy having failed, as evidenced by voters rejecting the Democrats, will lead to Plan B. Plan B is "By Any Means Necessary."

The most likely initial step is some sort of lower-grade left-wing insurgency, probably with Antifa types and similar degenerates adopting organized deadly violence as an escalation of their current property crimes and street-thug bullyboy schtick. There were only a few dozen Weathermen, but there are thousands of Antifa-type criminals, and the term "criminal" is used with intent. The majority of the people out doing the semi-organized street violence in Portland and elsewhere in 2020 and onward are actual petty criminals dressing up their sociopathology with a patina of politics. When Kyle Rittenhouse conducted his act of societal hygiene by capping three scumbags with an AR-15, two of them terminally, they all had criminal records, including one gem who did a stretch for sodomizing young boys. When you pick three dudes at random and 100 percent are criminals with 33.33 percent of them potential CNN producers, that tells you all you need to know about the composition of the military wing of the Democratic Party.

Right now, the mobs' violence is well-organized and well-funded, apparently in large part by leftist dark-money donors. There is nothing to stop them from escalating to mass murder if the puppet masters need it to escalate. Such violence would be pure terrorism—it's not like they could kill all their enemies. Instead, they would seek to cow them. Dissenters would be beaten or killed. Cops would be targets too—not to wipe the police out but to demonstrate to them their own hopelessness in the face of the onslaught. Particularly effective might be show trials of thought criminals or law enforcement. Stalin saw the value of that. You publicly break them, then you murder them. The lesson is clear.

The blue metropolises are the perfect environment for this type of scenario for a number of reasons. For one thing, cities have resonance with the public. They matter. They are symbols. Control a city and that means something, even if holding it is tactically irrelevant. This kind of insurgency would be less of a kinetic fight to obtain victory by causing physical damage and holding territory like a traditional army than an information operation. A kinetic operation achieves its battlefield effects by killing people and breaking things. An information operation achieves its effects by working on the minds of the intended audience. The information operation component of a low-grade leftist insurgency like this would be to demonstrate the powerlessness of the red federal government and cause the public to feel insecure, weakening the Republican administration, by taking control of the cities and showing that President Trump can't do a thing about it.

If this seems familiar, it is.

And the left could do so in the large cities without substantial pushback, at least from the local authorities. We have seen municipal police, controlled by sympathetic local politicians, refuse to intervene to restore order, and there is nothing that would necessarily force them to get off the bench and do their jobs if the Antifa types escalate to lethal violence. We saw cops abandon their own police precincts in the face of mobs instead of introducing them to the proverbial whiff of grapeshot that Napoleon used to subdue uppity Frogs early in his career. In the Los Angeles riots in 1992, Reginald Denny got dragged from the cab of his truck and nearly beaten to death on TV without an LAPD cop in sight because the gendarmes were told to pull back. Do not imagine that the local fuzz is going to establish order, because the people who run the local fuzz in the big cities will not want them to establish order.

Nor can you defend yourself as a citizen of a big blue city. The establishment does not want you armed citizens being an obstacle to their scheme either. We have also seen, in the cases of Patricia and Mark Thomas McCloskey in St. Louis and the aforementioned bane-of-pedophiles Kyle Rittenhouse, how corrupt leftist district attorneys will criminalize self-defense by normal people in order to prevent anyone from stopping the Democrat cat's-paws. Yeah, they walked, but not until they fought off the attempts of a corrupt leftist system to punish them for what a sane society would award them medals for doing.

Combined with a friendly media that would be eager to characterize a slaughter perpetrated by these semi-humans as part of a "mostly peaceful protest," and with leftists in the ruling caste who would provide political cover, it is easy to see that eliminating such a sheltered insurgency could be difficult. The federal government has limited law enforcement forces, and it is logistically difficult for the feds to conduct operations without local support. A second Trump administration's response would be hamstrung by the lack of local cooperation, as well as by disloyal deep-staters, in rooting out these barbarians. How excited is an FBI that was super-psyched to raid Roger Stone going to be when turned on left-wing urban guerillas? Among other things, those leftist bad guys might shoot back, unlike elderly gadflies.

Don't necessarily count on the military either. Remember how in 2020 General Mark Milley resisted deploying federal troops into the cities? He actually praised the disgraceful combat soldiers who kneeled with the BLM thugs instead of clearing the streets of them with the butts of their rifles. Instead, ridiculous brass asks them for a woke reading list, the better to prepare for total submission. While we will later discuss the need to clear house—actually, bulldoze house—at the Pentagon and elsewhere, remember that the vulnerable point for the new red administration is at the beginning of the term, before it fully consolidates power.

While such a mob insurgency could arise in blue cities across the country and challenge public order, the key question would be about the effectiveness of such a strategy. Remember, it is primarily an information operation, and that means the people will have to take the right message from what they are seeing played out. So, the key is the audience and whether the citizens accept the offered message—essentially, "The red president is powerless and you need to turn to the Democrats to keep yourself safe." That worked in 2020.

But what if the message the people take the next time in response to a ramped-up insurgency is, "Gee, we've been too soft on these mutants and it's time to start stacking bodies?"

The kinetic options are limited for this kind of insurgency. The degenerates could operate within blue cities under the cover of their allies, but what is the advantage? Once they leave the protection of a woke justice system and go into the suburbs where the same rules do not apply, the calculus changes. A reign of terror in the cities would not only risk alienating the loyal voters in the cities, but would galvanize all but the wokest wine moms in the suburbs. After the local sheriff's deputies terminate with extreme prejudice a dozen dirtbags coming to pillage in the suburbs, a lot of Democrats living in those suburbs would shrug.

Basically, the Antifa insurrection model is self-defeating if the information operation fails to work as hoped. The role of the mobs is not actually to do damage or hold ground but to sow fear and provide a scary example to which Democratic politicians can point and stage-whisper, "If you elect me, they go away." And after the riots of 2020, of course, they did go away the moment Joe Biden was allegedly elected. So it's not a crazy strategy; it has a track record of success, though with the 2020 riots they could push a false narrative that they were fighting for some amorphous concept of racial justice (that was a lie, but lies are what the liberal establishment does). Here, they would try the racial justice angle again, along with "We're defending democracy somehow." But without video of some cop purportedly smothering a drug-addled convict with a lengthy rap sheet, that's much less compelling.

So, what would this kind of low-grade insurgency look like?

A pair of the 864th Engineer Battalion's bulldozers smashed through the barricade of burning cars and trucks blocking SW Market Street, and as they pushed the occasional pings of bullets bouncing off the enclosed driver's compartments echoed across the streets. The shooters were not defending at the line of vehicles but further back—the S2's intel brief before the operation to secure central Portland had noted that there were a few veterans with the Antifa guys, and those traitors had probably ensured that the leftist street thugs understood that an obstacle without covering fire was not an obstacle at all. The shooting was relatively light, but it made the operation more difficult. Many of the soldiers had been under fire before, but it was somehow different when it happened at home.

The infantry units behind the engineers, crack troopers from the 25th Infantry Division deploying down I-5 from Joint Base Lewis-McChord south of Seattle, moved up. They were not operating as they would in conventional combat. They had no combat air support and could not call in artillery—an infantry unit's primary killing system. They had been ordered to leave their machine guns at home, which caused considerable heartburn—how do you do MOUT (military operations on urban terrain) without machine guns?

But there were designated snipers pulling overwatch from surrounding high-rises. None fired. The rules of engagement (ROE) provided by the judge advocate general (JAG) officers were highly restrictive. The bad guys had to be positively identified, and have a weapon, and be pointing the weapon, and had to have already fired on the troops in order to justify using deadly force, plus under no circumstances could the forces engage if there was any danger at all of civilian casualties. What was really disturbing was that the ROE given the troops seemed to directly conflict with the president's public statement, "Our troops will be authorized to shoot to kill to defend their lives and the lives of citizens in these cities taken over by criminal mobs." The enemy—though there were strict orders not to refer to the enemy that way—therefore had all the initiative. Unarmed "civilians" would regularly surround Antifa shooters, rendering them untouchable.

The troops and their officers, at least the unwoke ones who did not openly sympathize with the Antifa thugs who had declared all of downtown Portland a "liberated area" (and there were several unit officers who did), grumbled. Three soldiers had been shot so far, one critically, and they had all had to be choppered back to Madigan Army Medical

Center at Lewis-McChord for treatment because the local government refused to allow any local hospital to treat the Army "invaders."

The soldiers had earlier encountered two Antifa guys, one with an AR-15 and the other with an AK-47, in Shemanski Park. The guy with the AK yelled a mother-referencing obscenity and pointed his gat toward the squad, and both of them died very fast and very thoroughly. All members of the squad were now back at Lewis-McChord restricted to quarters as the investigation was underway. The New York Times had headlined its report "2 Activists Killed by Soldiers; Mayor Decries Reckless Use of Deadly Force." The Pentagon put out a press release announcing that it was "fully investigating these troubling allegations" and reaffirming the military's commitment to diversity, inclusion, and equity. Neither mentioned the criminal records of both men, which included battery, theft, multiple drug offenses, and indecent exposure on a Zoom call. Ironically, Jeffrey Toobin, on CNN's coverage of "Trump's Brutal Crackdown," lent his strong support to these gentlemen.

The battalion commander had his infantrymen move forward through the breach made by the dozers. Alpha Company was to go first to secure the immediate area and eliminate any opposition. Federal marshals in camo with long rifles would accompany them because, even though the president had invoked the Insurrection Act, the JAGs were still asserting—incorrectly—that Posse Comitatus prevented active military personnel from conducting law enforcement operations in that situation. The U.S. Marshals would handle the arrests and the transportation of prisoners to the federal holding camps erected outside towns, as the local police and sheriffs would not allow the feds to use their jails. There was no local law enforcement in sight, as the cops had been ordered to stand down. But it was unclear if they could stand up even if allowed to. Rumor had it that half of the Portland police force had quit within twenty-four hours of the insurrection because the chief had refused to authorize the rescue of two officers who were surrounded and ordered by their bosses to surrender to the mob. Then the pair had been tried and hanged by the insurgents as an example of "People's Justice." The governor called it "regrettable" and blamed the president. The mainstream media simply ignored the atrocity in its nonstop, slobberingly solicitous coverage of the rebels.

The troops were making the breach when a JAG lieutenant ran to the battalion commander, who was on the radio coordinating with the helicopters overhead.

"Sir, you have to stop," he panted.

"What the hell are you talking about, lieutenant?"

"You have to stop the assault," the breathless lawyer said. "They went into court. There's an injunction."

"A what?"

"The lawyers for the rebels got an injunction against the military's assaulting the insurgents," the JAG replied, handing over a legal paper.

The light colonel looked over the sheet of paper.

"District Court of Hawaii?" he said. "We're in Oregon."

"It's a national injunction against the president's taking military action of any kind. It's unconstitutional. Taking action, I mean."

"I'm not a damn ambulance chaser, but I remember that the Constitution says the president can suppress insurrections," the colonel said.

"Not anymore," the JAG officer replied.

"Damn it," said the commander, taking up his mic. "Alpha six, this is Trident six actual, pull back. I say again, pull back, over."

The Dales, Mark and Renee (her last name was actually Sommers-Dale) and their kids Jordan, Ainsley, and Olive, were out of kale. In fact, they were out of nearly everything. The Uprising, as Rachel Maddow's chyron called it, had begun a week after the inauguration of that fascist whose name the family would not speak following what Stacy Abrams had assured them was massive election fraud on November 5, 2024. "It is our duty to defend democracy by questioning this election, by refusing to accept it," she had said, her ample frame sweating a bit from the exertion, and the Dales had nodded along. When the Uprising began, they cheered.

But now, ten days since they had last been able to shop—their local bespoke grocery store had been looted and had not reopened— the Dales were unsure of what to do next. Going outside was…problematic. Mark worked at home anyway, so only Renee was impacted by the People's Liberation Committee's order for businesses to shut down as part of the national "General Strike against Fascism." How her work in the HR department at the university buoyed fascism was unclear, but they told each other they had to do their part for the struggle. One of their neighbors, who had put up a sign promoting the T-word before the election, resolved to go into work at his auto dealership. A patrol caught him and beat him to a pulp with sticks in the street. The Dales told each other that this was unfortunate, but he had brought it on himself. They counted on the sign in their front yard listing all the different lives that mattered as a totem to ward off evil.

Jordan and Olive were happy to eat oat cereal for dinner again, but that meal used the last of the almond milk. Ainsley, who was allergic to oats, as well as peanuts, corn, and lettuce, had to make do with dried mango chips. Mark and Renee discussed trying to drive to another store, but they did not know for sure if there was even one open in liberated St. Louis. They did know that they could not leave the zone, that the People's Committee had decreed that trying to depart was white supremacy. The Dales were already very aware of, and sorry for, their pallor.

"How are we going to feed them?" Renee asked.

"Questions like that are exactly what the fascists want you asking," Mark replied in a disappointed tone, and for a moment Renee wondered whether he really meant that, or whether he was merely covering for his own impotence.

That night, like every night, the patrols rode through the neighborhood, armed people (mostly with bats and clubs, but also with guns) riding in pick-up trucks with spray-painted red anarchy symbols on their doors. The Dales watched them pass by through thin slits in the closed blinds, sighing with relief that the riders kept going, and then turned back to MSNBC. Their favorite network told them that the cities were in revolt against fascism, and the Bulwark staff writer who represented true conservatism joined the other six panelists in agreeing wholeheartedly. Renee briefly considered, but then suppressed, the stray thought that if the red government was truly fascist then MSNBC would not be allowed to cheerlead an insurrection.

MSNBC was their only real source of news. Their Facebook group for fellow progressives inside liberated St. Louis had been shut down. It had been a great source of information about what was open and what was not, but too many people could not keep themselves from complaining and criticizing the People's Committee despite Facebook's warning that misinformation about the liberation movement violated its terms of service.

"What else could Facebook do? Let them keep spreading misinformation?" Mark asked when Renee told him. Now they had no real local news; the local broadcast stations, taken over by the People's Committee, ran endless struggle sessions where various

people confessed their racism, sexism, ageism, fatism, transphobia, and other secular sins.

At about 11:33 p.m., one of the People's Committee patrol pick-ups stopped on the street and a half-dozen people piled out with their clubs and guns.

"Turn out the light!" Mark hissed, peering through the blinds, but Renee did so too late. The riders saw, and they approached up the walkway.

"Open the door!" they yelled, pounding on it with their clubs. Olive walked down the hall, rubbing her eyes.

"Mommy, what's happening?"

More pounding. Renee had grown up in a small town in Colorado. She had been proud to escape that legacy, proud to have rejected everything those people stood for. Her dad and their brothers were hunters, and it occurred to her in that moment that if a group of armed men came to pound on any of her relatives' doors, the intruders had best have their affairs in order. Several years before, Renee had told several of her family members that she would never speak to them as long as they still owned their "AR-15 military grade murder tools."

Mark had supported her decision. "You can't enable people like them. You have to take a courageous stand."

Now Mark was standing before the door as they kicked it open, defenseless, tears running down his face, begging them not to hurt them.

They laughed as they came inside, intent on doing just that.

The Milam County sheriff's Ford Explorer came up State Route 79 fast into Rockdale. It was the way the mob from Austin had come—the mob had secured the city, but then chose to push out to the suburbs. The campaign to push the insurrection out into Texas did not go the way the mob had hoped.

The deputy driving the cruiser was the only one without an AR-15 or Remington 870 in his hands—the other three deputies were ready for action. The driver's rifle was right there beside him, and his vest held five full mags. It had been six, but a quartet of losers from Austin had stormed an H-E-B and encountered the deputies coming out. That accounted for the empty sixth mag.

A string of pick-ups blocked the road, and two dozen locals milled about. Everyone was strapped, most with long guns and holstered pistols. The deputy recognized many of them. Jimmy Hanson had gone into the Army after high school, Tommy Sauer into the Marines. They wore their rigs and carried their AR-15s like they had done it before, because they had.

Tommy waved the sheriff's cruiser through the roadblock and pointed to the silver Camry with shattered windows and bullet holes in the unibody. The deputy pulled up and idled. Three shapes, red and twisted, lay in a row on the asphalt. Their weapons leaned against the car.

"What happened?" the deputy asked.

"Well," Tommy replied. "We were in fear of our lives."

"Yeah," Jimmy added. "A lot of fear."

"I see," the deputy said, assessing the situation. "My investigation concludes it was justifiable. You guys going to take care of the mess?"

Tommy nodded.

"No paperwork?" Jimmy asked.

"No time," the deputy replied. "We're going into Austin in a few hours. Local LEOs, Texas Rangers, the Guard. We're going to clean it out for good."

*"I thought the TV reported that some court said you can't go
into the cities," Tommy replied.*

"The Fifth Circuit says different."

"You need some help?" Jimmy asked.

*"Sure. We're swearing in temporary deputies. Come on down to
the airport. That's the assembly area. Bring your gear."*

*"Don't need to swear in," Tommy said. "My oath never expired.
We'll clean this up here and get over there."*

*"See you then," the deputy said. "Because this bullshit ends
tonight."*

*The cruiser accelerated away, and Tommy looked at Jimmy and
the rest of the citizen paramilitaries.*

"Okay, let's find us some shovels. Who's got some lime?"

Militarizing the Antifa types to use lethal force in a massive way
forces a choice for the citizenry, especially when they threaten to leave
their urban enclaves. Killing is a bridge too far for many liberals, and
killing in their own neighborhoods is a bridge on the next continent.
Turning mobs into insurgent forces alienates normal people and forces
them to choose a side, since the silent payoff option—vote Democrat
and they behave—goes off the table. Normal people would likely
choose order no matter how hard the mainstream media shilled for
the butchers. And plenty of them would be ready to intervene
themselves.

A low-grade, limited leftist insurgency is one scenario, but what
about a more massive leftist offensive against conservative Americans?
Is that possible? Yes, but is it practical? Perhaps. The left has states
under its control, lots of them, and some are rich. As we discussed
regarding the national divorce, a coalition of liberal states would likely
include the West Coast, New England, Illinois, and some other out-
liers. But those states are not contiguous. They are divided up by vast

swathes of patriotic red, and that matters both militarily and logistically. Remember that logistics is what the pros look at first; guns are important, but starving guys don't fight well. Supplies—food, fuel, ammo, power—matter. If you can't support your fight, you have already lost it. Just ask Putin.

Blue America's problem is that, to a large extent, its population consists of those needing to be fed rather than those doing the feeding. New England has Big Finance, the Ivy League, and preppies, but with huge, ravenous cities such as New York and Boston, it is a net importer of food and a net importer of energy, especially after the inexplicable decision to decommission its nuclear power plants. The West Coast is better off, though much of California's breadbasket is fallow because of mismanaged water policies. The Colorado River, which provides agricultural California a huge portion of its water, flows in from Red America. This is all critically important because the difference between a large American city and Mogadishu is about a week without food, water, and electricity.

There is also the questions of arms. As we have discussed, the blue states have already purged themselves of those wicked gun- and bullet-making people. This presents a significant problem for the blues. If you are them, you gotta fight with what you start with, ammo-wise, at least until you can rearm from friendly foreigners.

Another distinguishing feature of a multistate blue rebellion is that the red federal government would have the majority of the U.S. military under its control. Further, the red civilians are well-armed, and many are vets. This means the red feds are likely to have capable, large, and probably aggressive paramilitary forces at their disposal too. So, in this scenario, the red government begins with that big advantage—one that would not be mitigated (as in a blue-government-versus-red-rebellion scenario, which we discuss next) by large numbers of the predominantly conservative military deserting.

The blue states in revolt would not be powerless, just not nearly as powerful in terms of raw combat power. In terms of military forces, the blue states all have their own National Guard forces (Air Force and Army) of various strengths that answer to their governors in peacetime, as well as some U.S. forces stationed on blue soil. The thing is, the bulk of the national military forces are stationed in the red states, particularly the South. California has half the Marines with Camp Pendleton and Twenty-Nine Palms, but here's some more sand in the gears. How many of the troops, who are primarily, though not entirely, from conservative areas and backgrounds, would fall into formation as part of some sort of blue military force? You get a general out in front of a division and he announces that the famed 10th Mountain Division out of upstate New York is joining the rebellion against the GOP literal Hitler in the White House, and how many of the troops stick around to see how that story ends?

Probably not as many enlisted soldiers as the generals might hope. Nor is the officer corps necessarily all-in. Today's senior leaders who issue the commands are overwhelmingly deep-blue, and the mid-level and junior leaders who carry out the commands at least *appear* to be blue, but how deep beneath the surface does the blue go before you hit red? Right now, the stakes are relatively low. If you are a field-grade officer who does not buy the woke agenda, you can keep your head down, mouth the platitudes, tell yourself you are doing it for the country, and hold on until you hit your twenty. But if the guns come out, these folks will have to make a choice about where they stand, and not all of them will simply go along with the blue flow. There is a non-zero chance that the next morning one of that 10th Mountain general's patriotic staff officers takes his SIG and blows the traitor general's head all over his pancakes and his copy of the *New York Times* with the headline reading "Insurrections Are Good, Say Experts and Fact-Checkers."

With logistics challenges and a lack of conventional military forces, it would be unlikely to see a blue rebellion as a purely military phenomenon. It would be largely political, with information operations the main effort and military efforts supporting. They could mobilize the military forces under blue control, but that mobilization would likely be defensive. Unlike their Democratic forefathers from 1861, the blue states would not necessarily march into the red states to knock the Union out of the war and force a negotiated peace.

But a Fort Sumter situation is not impossible to imagine. Fort Sumter was a Union fort on an island in Charleston's harbor. The South Carolinians bombarded the installation, which the Union evacuated. It was the first shooting in what would be four years of shooting. The blue states could easily seek to take over defended federal installations on rebel territory in a Civil War rerun—in fact, that seems the most likely source of initial conflict in a macro-level conflict like the one we are discussing. It might also be a law enforcement facility, as opposed to a military one, though the thought that many denizens of any federal agency within the corrupt Justice Department would not eagerly flock to the treasonous banner of leftist revolt is probably wishful thinking. In any case, an initial Fort Sumter incident would not be primarily a kinetic operation but an information op—the message would be, "We blues are serious—back off."

A military conflict is a loser for blue rebels going up against a red federal government. They win by convincing the red government not to leverage its power—essentially, the same strategy they have successfully used to tweet-shame Republican sissies into not pushing back against leftist cultural offensives. They don't want to make this steel versus steel. The military forces that the left might have in such a civil war scenario are a poor fit for offensive warfare, but they would be useful in a defensive scenario. And a defensive scenario—one that raises the costs of suppressing a blue revolt—supports the strategy of getting the reds to just give up and acquiesce to the rebels.

If pushed to the wall, if the left did not fold, that would mean cleaning out cities. Urban warfare is the bloodiest kind of warfare, and even a few leftists willing to fight can create carnage if they embed themselves among civilians. Think of Stalingrad, Grozny, Aleppo, and Mariupol. And think of the hate that has already been ginned up in the last few years. When the killing starts, it will not stay selective and precise for long.

War is war. A civil war that lasts any length of time would almost certainly degenerate into a bloodbath. It might start somewhat polite, but after you bury the bits and pieces of your kid, that will change. No one will be safe. "Terrorism" by one side will justify terrorism by the other. The blues will target "insurrectionists" while the reds will hunt down "collaborators." And the bodies will pile up.

It would be a battle of wills. A blue rebel kinetic victory is not in the cards. They have to get the red federal forces to choose to stop. But an even more important factor for the counterinsurgents than the size of the blue fighting forces is the size of the blue territory. It's huge, and the U.S. military is not designed, equipped, or manned to recapture and dominate that kind of land mass. There are not enough boots on the ground to occupy America in any scenario—we will see that this would be an even bigger problem in a leftist counterinsurgency against patriots. This means a red federal government counterinsurgency would be focused not on capturing territory but on defeating enemy forces. In other words, beating on them until they surrender.

The red fed strategy for reconquering Blue America would probably not be Sherman's March to the Sea II. That's what the blue rebels would want—lots of media pictures of wreckage and crying kids designed to melt the hearts and bend the spines of the red populace, leading to a clamor in favor of negotiations that would inevitably lead to the blues getting whatever they want. Instead, the red government's strategy would be to starve them out. A ruthless red president would take advantage of the extended lines of communications among the blue enclaves and squeeze. After all, those Brooklyn community gardens can only grow so much kale.

Oh, and there might be the need to channel Lincoln and muzzle the leftist press to keep it from being the propaganda fifth column it inevitably would try to be.

A siege is the obvious aggressive play, since storming a city is like Peter Dinklage trying to wrestle a greased-up Andre the Giant. You need a lot of soldiers to take even a small city; you don't need anywhere near as many to defend it, assuming the population is friendly or at least docile. If the blue states fought to hold the cities against a determined attack, it would be a bloodbath for red patriots, blue rebels, and especially for the normal citizens caught in the middle.

What would it be like for normal citizens? Hell on earth right here in America. Obviously the logistics chain that brings them food and water would be broken. Medical care would be primitive. Think about life without power in the northern states in winter. All the stuff we take for granted goes to the fighters. Civilians? They survive as best they can. And that does not even account for the collateral damage from bombings and shelling. Remember how Representative Swalwell (D-Fang Fang) observed that all those AR-15s the knuckle-draggers own mean nothing because the government has nukes? What he was really saying, in his own flatulent way, was that there are no rules. Bombing the rebels? Launching missiles at them? Mass attacks? That's all on the menu.

And there would be atrocities. Social media exists to stoke anger. It does it well. Millions of Americans now hate millions of other Americans and wish them dead. In a civil war, they can make that a reality. You look at the collective giggling on the left over the killing of Ashli Babbitt and you have to ask what the limit is. How many of us would they kill to prevail? One? A hundred? A thousand? A hundred thousand? And vice versa?

Military forces and law enforcement are two key components of the order of battle, but both are dwarfed by the tens of millions of regular citizens with guns—paramilitaries. Military hierarchies exist in large part to control young men and channel their killing in an acceptable direction. But these paramilitaries would have no firm organization, no professional officer and noncommissioned officer corps to control the bloodlust. That is true of the Antifa types, and that would be true of patriots. We saw paramilitaries at work in the Kansas–Missouri border war. One side massacred a town, then the other paid its enemy back in kind.

When you talk about a civil war, understand what you are talking about. Slaughter. So do not do it lightly.

William Tecumseh Sherman got it right talking about another civil war: "War is hell. You cannot qualify war in harsher terms than I will. War is cruelty, and you cannot refine it. Those who brought war into our country deserve all the curses and maledictions a people can pour out."

Will the heavy weapons be used? Yes, because no side will forgo them if it gives the other an advantage. Will they starve cities? Yes. After all, what paratrooper from Des Moines is going to want to kill or die liberating New York City from the control of the same people the knuckleheads in New York City elected to rule them? Plus the resulting news footage—you can be sure the media would not hand-wave away the carnage as "a mostly peaceful invasion"—would be disconcerting to even the most ardent unionist.

While it would take divisions upon divisions—which the American military does not have, though a massive mobilization of paramilitaries would provide more combat power—to seize a city by force, it's really easy to cut transport corridors. Block the freeways, stop the trains, and halt water traffic, give it a couple weeks and your local urban area will be full-on Lord of the Flies. You could be even more aggressive and cut power—our power grid is right there in the open. Now it's dark, people are hungry, and they are not going to be kept warm or satiated on speeches about wokeness from the likes of Mayor Lori Lightfoot.

What's the flex for the blue states? They will certainly start rationing, because that sort of exercise of power makes them turgid. They will crack down on any dissenters who have not yet fled, because defund the police was never intended to defund the secret police. And maybe they make a plea for help from foreigners. Can you see, say, New England, cut off from power, the interstates blocked by Marines, begging its fellow travelers running the EU for help? Or even China? Of course, any help has to get here. The EU is unwilling to defend its own land, so it's hard to see how it might whip up an expeditionary force of sufficient size from folks in Dusseldorf, Naples, and Marseilles to cross the Atlantic to help out their gallant globalist allies in resisting the evil, red-dominated U.S. government.

Then, of course, they would have to get here first. America still has a Navy, of a sort, and perhaps faced with the reality of a second civil war a red U.S. government might choose seriousness over frivolity and direct that the Navy stop indoctrinating its sailors on the threat of white rage and start training them to sink enemy ships again.

The real challenge for the red U.S. government, when faced with suppressing a massive blue revolt, would be beating back the calls for easing off the offensive. Lincoln faced that kind of criticism too, but he held firm to victory. It would be tough. You would see chaos in the blue cities, and hunger there too. Of course, there would be no hunger in the Hamptons—the same people who won't give up the private jets they use to wing their way to climate change conclaves in Davos are never going to miss a meal during the conflict they start. Soft Republicans will howl that refusing to feed the insurrectionists is a terrible crime; you can identify who these sissies will be by searching the web to see who most vigorously demanded that hellfire and damnation be rained upon the unarmed, elderly selfie-snappers of January 6, 2021.

The red president would have to keep the pressure on, heedless of the wailing and gnashing of teeth, until the blue comes crawling back to surrender unconditionally. Surrender, unconditional and total, can be the only outcome unless you want to go through all of it again. And unconditional surrender would lead to transformative changes—at least it had better. The leaders must be punished—assuming the January 6 political prisoners have already been pardoned, the dank dungeons they were consigned to for trespassing and otherwise embarrassing the congressional establishment would be perfect for the ringleaders of the blue revolt. They must go away, and hard.

And then the leftist infestation, including all the gangrenous wokeness embedded in our society, must be ripped up from the country, root and stem. Of course, that necessary campaign might actually be one of the things that sparks a blue revolt in the first place.

It's one thing to sketch out the general characteristics of a multistate blue rebellion in the macro, but to understand what it would really be like requires taking a look at it from a micro perspective. And it would not be pretty.

The video screen in front of Governor de Blasio—like a cockroach, he survived his legendary failures as Gotham's mayor to become "President de Blasio of the Progressive States of North America" after outmaneuvering his main competitors Kamala Harris and Pete Buttigieg with a full-on embrace of socialism—was filled with static. This made it hard to see ex–California governor Newsom—now "Vice President Newsom of the Progressive States of North America"—and his perfect hair. The president was at Gracie Mansion in the PSNA's capital, New York City, which he had requisitioned from the mayor for his own. The vice president was in the West Coast capital of Sacramento, and the damn reds were scrambling the hook-up to the Chinese satellite that was facilitating the teleconference. All the landlines which ran through the red territory were, of course, cut.

"Damn it," de Blasio swore. "This is important!"

"I know," Newsom responded, his voice crackling with static. "I agree that the fact that both the presidency and vice-presidency being held by white cis-het males is literal actual violence to BIPOC and trans citizens of the Progressive States, but—"

The link went dead. De Blasio's aide looked at his notepad—there were a dozen action items that the leaders had needed to address, not least of them how to defeat the U.S. government blockade that was starving the blue cities and how they might obtain the recognition of the PSNA by the Chinese government. The Chi Coms had been pretty adamant that they would under no circumstances recognize a breakaway province—they seemed really touchy about that issue for some reason—even one that would promise whatever Beijing asked in exchange for support in the rebellion.

De Blasio calmed himself with another bong hit; the aide thought of suggesting that perhaps the objections to the heritage of the two chief executives should not have been the first action item addressed in this emergency teleconference. He grabbed a muffin off the plate on the table and took a bite as the president exhaled a cloud of baked kush. The aide always made sure to eat while on duty because food was getting impossible to find outside in the city. In fact, over the last few days, the aide had not even left the presidential compound at

Gracie Mansion to go home. He told himself it was because of the massive work required to run the revolution, but he was also terrified to go out on the streets. The police were gone; the only law enforcement operations were against the traitors, looters, and wreckers who were disloyal to the revolution.

The revolution was not going well—the aide would never say that out loud, but it was true. Generators kept the lights on here, but out in the city it was pitch-black. Chicago had surrendered the other day. That blue patch of rebel territory in the center of the map, detached from the coasts, it had been the first city subjected to a siege. The media had worked hard to portray the suffering of the people cut off from fuel, food, and power by the red federal troops under the dictator President DeSantis, but as always, he showed no sign of caring.

"Chicago will surrender unconditionally," DeSantis told a joint session of the abbreviated Congress a week after the alliance of blue states had announced the revolution and declared themselves an independent nation. "And when it does, we will move on to the other insurrectionist areas and subdue them as well. Victory is the only possible outcome—a restored union, indivisible, with liberty and justice for all." Though this promise a month ago was greeted with a standing ovation, many in Congress had expressed grave doubts about the ruthlessness of DeSantis's approach. Senator Mitt Romney had said, to a wall of cameras eager to publicize Republican dissenters, "We must understand that we are not enemies, and the idea of using food and heat as a weapon against fellow Americans is abhorrent."

Asked about this critique, President DeSantis had replied, "No one gives a damn what Mitt Romney thinks. Unlike him, I won election as the president of the United States, and I will restore our union, no matter what."

Dawn stepped gingerly over the shattered glass of the front window of the Whole Foods and into the grocery store. It smelled like singed arugula lettuce and scorched goat cheese, even though the store itself had not been torched like most of the other buildings on the street had been. But it had been looted, and thoroughly. There were a few other folks inside, like Dawn walking down the aisles looking for anything left after the shelves had been picked clean. Nothing, not even a can of mung beans.

She felt the panic rising inside her—what were her kids going to eat? It had been weeks since this all started. The mayor had gone on TV, looking like a bizarre alien as usual, and announced that Chicago would follow the example of the East and West Coasts and "consciously uncouple ourselves from the racist, sexist, and transphobic reactionary government in Washington." She promised there would be no violence if the federal government did not start any, and that a new day of progressive government had come.

Dawn was initially happy about it—she hated the Republicans, having never once voted for one, and it seemed that this might be the only thing to do under the circumstances. After all, DeSantis had come to power in what was clearly a rigged election—Maddow had reported how the GOP was not only suppressing voters of color but was actively rewiring voting machines—and he immediately began firing loyal public servants like the FBI director, many generals, and Dr. Fauci. The Republicans were even going to pass a law banning teaching critical race theory, which was vitally important to teach, though it was not actually taught in schools.

Was mandatory evangelical Christianity next? Maddow thought so, and she was never wrong, according to Maddow.

But the worst thing was his pardon of all the insurrectionists of January 6. DeSantis was literally guilty of treason, and it was only right that the progressive states rebelled against the deplorable and primitive red ones.

The protests had started after DeSantis targeted Chicago for a blockade. The streets were packed with marchers marching against the man in Washington, D.C. "We are all in this struggle together!" the mayor had promised, and kept promising as food supplies dwindled. The mayor never looked any thinner, but Dawn did every time she glanced in the mirror in her townhouse.

The protests against DeSantis continued every day, and there was soon looting and burning. "It's merely property damage, and that's not really violence," Dawn told herself, but she never went outside or let her kids out either. During the state of emergency, school was by distance learning until the power went out. Then there was nothing—no internet, no news, nothing. The kids were scared, especially when they smelled smoke. But Dawn, even as she reassured herself that she remained in solidarity with the protestors, bolted her door. The heat was off, and they all slept together in her bed wearing sweaters to keep warm.

Dawn caught a glint from between the slats of the shelves and knelt, careful to avoid the gooey liquids pooled on the linoleum. She peered under the lowest shelf and saw it, a can with the reddish label coming off it, lying on its side about eighteen inches back from the aisle. She stretched her arm and just managed to grab the loose label. Carefully, she pulled it out and looked closer. Chef Boyardee Beef Ravioli, 15 ounces. Dawn smiled and stood up.

"Gimme that, bitch," the man behind her said, his voice low and menacing. He grabbed the can and ripped it from her grasp.

"Please," she begged. "My kids are hungry." She had never before been confronted with a situation where physical strength and force was a factor, and it disoriented her. She had a sense that someone in authority should appear and resolve this injustice for her. But no one did.

The man just laughed and turned away, jauntily tossing his can in the air and catching it, and Dawn fell to her knees crying.

The two black SUVs were waved through the United States Army checkpoints on FDR Drive. Lieutenant Colonel Reaboi glanced right at Roosevelt Island across the water and then back at Manhattan. The city was still, beaten, broken, and, as of a half-hour ago, surrendered.

The drive was off-limits to civilians, though there was no gas left in the city after the month-long blockade to fuel any privately owned vehicles. Most of the traffic was commercial big rigs contracted by the United States government to bring in food. Every convoy was heavily guarded by fully combat-ready troops manning M240 machine guns in the turrets of their vehicles. The city was under martial law, and the food riots seen under the rebel administration were not going to be met with winks, nods, and excuses while the U.S. government was in control.

The day before, about a hundred people had charged a food distribution point inside Central Park. When the smoke cleared, half of them were dead and the other half were maimed. Far from down-playing the incident, the local media, now under federal control, made sure that it was made crystal clear what would happen if the occupying forces were attacked. There were no more such assaults.

Reaboi, like his men, was in plainclothes, but they all wore web gear and carried tricked-out M4 carbines. There was no need for the SUVs to be marked—all the troops manning the checkpoints knew these were special operations guys, and no one got in their way.

A line of a dozen blue and white NYPD cruisers passed them heading south, lights and sirens going. The call had gone out to all New York City police officers on every TV and radio station imme-diately after the surrender and the occupation of the main media studios (Colonel Reaboi's guys had been tasked to seize CNN's New York facility—one of the sergeants had observed that Brian Stelter really did look like a potato) to return to duty, including those fired for "racism, sexism, and/or bias against justice-involved individuals." About half the force was back on the job, and that was crucial. There were not enough soldiers in the whole damn Army to conduct an effective long-term military occupation of Manhattan, much less all five boroughs. They needed to rebuild civilian control.

"We're nearly there," his driver said from behind dark glasses. Reaboi checked the seat of the thirty-round Magpul magazine in his weapon out of habit. He didn't expect a fight, but he was ready for one. There had not been a lot of shooting during the two-month Second Civil War, but there had been some. It was always possible some of these leftists would be die-hards and things would get messy like they did in Portland. Those Antifa guys learned the hard way that there was a world of difference between local cops with instructions to play nice and pissed-off U.S. Army infantrymen with loose rules of engagement.

They got off the drive and Reaboi got on the radio.

"Let's do this fast and clean," he said. The other guys checked their weapons.

Ahead was what looked a bit like a plantation big house dropped into Manhattan from Gone with the Wind. *Gracie Mansion, yellow and baroque, had a patio along its front face. Several individuals, salty-looking chaps, lolled on the wood planks watching the team approach. The SUVs rolled to a stop on the grass out front and the operators poured out, weapons up, shouting.*

"Get down, get down!"

Reaboi's team swarmed up the front steps; the other split into two teams and charged around back.

The men on the patio stood with hands up, wisely unmoving, as the operators took them to the floor, relieving them of their handguns and expertly zip-tying them—years of experience securing randos at target locations in Kandahar and Baghdad paid off.

"Where?" Reaboi said, pulling the one who seemed to be in charge up off the wood. "Where is he?"

"Inside."

"How many guns?"

The man laughed. "No guns. Just us."

Reaboi dropped the guard face-first back to the wood and reformed with an entry team of three. The first pulled the front door open and then Reaboi and a sergeant were inside, rifles seeking targets, shouting at the civilians inside—there were several, all terrified—to get down.

Reaboi's eyes settled on the HVP—the high-value target. President de Blasio sat on a couch, his eyes wide and his arms up and spread, his red-glass bong in front of him.

Reaboi nodded, and the sergeant secured the ex-president's hands with a black zip tie as Reaboi covered the other civilians.

"Take him out," Reaboi ordered, and the sergeant did so in a distinctly ungentle manner. The other civilians sat frozen. They would be secured until the intel exploitation team a few minutes behind the assault element arrived to interrogate them and go through Gracie Mansion in exquisite detail.

"Hey," the former president of the rebel nation said, pausing. "Can I take my bong?"

"Get him out of here," spat Reaboi, as he prepared to call into headquarters and report the end of the Second Civil War.

A blue revolt against a red government is essentially a non-starter unless the blue forces can win the information battle and convince the red government to let the blue areas go off and form their own Marxist human centipede. To do so relies on the exploitation of the innate decency of normal Americans, and the hope that their compassion can be leveraged into allowing the left to achieve its ends by convincing the right to take its most effective strategy off the table. Look at the intense pressure by the left and its media upon Republicans to forgo "culture war" issues. It's not because the left does not think cultural issues are important, but because the American people do think they are important. When Glenn Youngkin ran for governor in Virginia in 2021, he refused to give up what turned out to be his most effective strategy to please the outraged left, and he won. In an actual revolt, you would see the left push to keep the right from using its strongest strategy, too.

But the left would not choose to focus on information operations for some moral reason. It would do so, if it was in the rebel position, because that is its most effective strategy. If it was in the position of controlling the federal government and dealing with red rebels, it would not hesitate—not even for a moment—to go all-out kinetic if it could. But we have seen the problems with that.

Now, what if the situation was a red rebellion against a blue tyranny?

CHAPTER TEN

THE SECOND CIVIL WAR: RED REVOLUTION

T he reality is that if a true civil war comes to America, it will almost certainly be red Americans against a blue federal government. And it will be against a blue federal government that has waived its right to loyalty and deference by embracing and escalating the kind of tyranny we have seen since the left lost its collective mind after America rejected Hillary Clinton.

The correlation of forces would be much different than in our red fed/blue rebel scenario. Again, there would be two basic types of conflict to consider—a low-level insurgency scenario and a multistate secession scenario. But, unlike in the red fed/blue rebel hypothetical, these would not necessarily be distinct scenarios. You might have whole states declare red, but in the rural areas of blue states you might simultaneously see a low-level red insurgency. That is, a bunch of rednecks with deer rifles (well, most would have something like an AR-15, but you get the point) out in the sticks could control a wide swath of territory and use that to spread easily into suburban and urban regions. If most of, say, Wyoming becomes a no-go area for the feds, that's a lot of no-go area, and a lot of its neighboring states would join in. Or several red states might secede straight away.

In contrast, an Antifa/BLM/street terrorist insurgency might support a blue state secession scenario, but it would not be the driver of it. A bunch of borderline sociopaths in black bandanas might take over central Portland, but that is not going to drive most of New York and California to announce that they are a new country. The blues are concentrated in the cities.

A red insurgency, assuming whole states with their governments did not secede, would not be concentrated in easy-to-besiege cities. It could encompass wide areas of territory, and such an insurgency could mimic the critical red fed/blue rebel victory dynamic because the red insurgents could control logistical access to the cities. Basically, a bunch of BLM communists could occupy Washington, D.C., and everyone in rural Virginia still eats. Yet if a bunch of rural Virginians with rifles decide that no food trucks move on I-95—and they could easily decide that—then no one in the District dines tonight.

To explore how this might go down, you need to consider the correlation of forces. In an insurgency scenario, who might the insurgents be? Probably pissed-off normal citizens pushed to the breaking point. Remember how at the Tea Party rallies there was always at least one guy in a tri-corner hat evoking the revolutionary era? A lot of Americans think of themselves as heirs to that tradition, and they are fully committed to the minuteman role. They see themselves as not only capable of standing out there at Lexington and Concord holding off the tyrant's cat's-paws, but of being obligated to do so.

The feds agree. Federal law has a name for the citizenry mustered to fight—"the militia." The "militia" is defined under federal law at 10 U.S. Code § 246 ("Militia: composition and classes"):

(a) The militia of the United States consists of all able-bodied males at least 17 years of age and, except as provided in section 313 of title 32, under 45 years of age who are, or who have made a declaration of intention to become, citizens of the United States and of female citizens of the United States who are members of the National Guard.
(b) The classes of the militia are—
(1) the organized militia, which consists of the National Guard and the Naval Militia; and
(2) the unorganized militia, which consists of the members of the militia who are not members of the National Guard or the Naval Militia.

Now, this definition would certainly get the liberals shaking, especially the fact that the militia includes seventeen-year-olds—hi there, Kyle Rittenhouse. It excludes the differently abled. It also excludes almost all women, and there is nothing that recognizes the 723 other genders. And beyond its total failure to validate the non-binary gender identity spectrum, this definition cuts off at age forty-five. Today, sixty-five is the new forty-five, according to people who are sixty-five—there are plenty of AARP-eligible guys out there who know their way around an AR-15 and will not tolerate being left out of the Big Game.

The bottom line is that there are many people out there who are potential warriors. Say the country splits down the middle population-wise. You are looking at about 165 million folks per side. Say 3 percent decide to participate in a red rebellion—and with 400 million guns in America, they are not going to find it hard to arm up. That's about 5 million folks under arms in the red.

Out entire military, active and reserve, is about 2 million.

And who would they be fighting if they were rebelling against a blue tyranny? Well, there is the blue part of the militia. There are a few who would do it. The Antifa types might grab some guns. What they lack in training or competence they likely make up in enthusiasm and bloodlust, but there are just not that many of them. Perhaps the liberal gentry could decide to train up. There is probably some number of them who are competent—blue falcon veterans and the occasional liberal whose disappointed father taught him to hunt before he moved to San Francisco—but not that many. In the red states, it is a point of honor to be able to participate in the defense of yourself, your family, your community, and your Constitution. In the blue states, it is a point of honor to allow working-class people to participate in the defense of yourself, your family, your community, and your Constitution, and to look down upon them for not knowing who Margaret Atwood is.

Then there are the troops. In this scenario, the blues control the federal government and therefore the military structure. The soldiers would have a choice—stay loyal or go home. The troops largely come from red areas, and the idea that a guy from Oklahoma would be enthusiastic about marching on his hometown of Lawton with a bayonet fixed seems far-fetched. It is even farther-fetched when you consider that in a real civil war scenario where they go to suppress rebels in a place like rural Missouri, the guy next to him might well get his head blown off with a .30-06 round by a guy who hunted deer in that county all his life. A war you don't want to be in against guerillas who have the edge on you is no fun.

As we have seen, an insurgency, if not snuffed out rapidly, could very well give rise to a secession crisis. But a secession crisis could also skip the insurgency stage in much the same way as a red fed/blue rebels scenario where the states band together to quit the country. How could that happen? The blue federal government could simply push the red states too far.

The threshold barrier, the obstacle that the red-state leadership would have to get over, is the allegiance hump. By simply holding the key positions in the federal government, the blue leadership would have a massive psychological edge against a red-state secession movement. The blues would have to lose their patina of legitimacy in order to allow the red states to take such a huge step. This is good, because it is a huge step, one that would shatter our country and likely lead to many deaths. It is not something to be done lightly, and would not be—at least on the red side.

But this is not so clear on the blue side because it is not so clear that the blue side has the same respect for the legitimacy of red elected officials that the red has for blue ones. George W. Bush was never acknowledged as a legitimate president by a huge swath of the elite left—this even became an issue for Terry McAuliffe during his quixotic Virginia election campaign in 2021. And Donald Trump was never truly acknowledged as the real president. The hateful windbag he defeated still mutters about his stealing the election from her, and the entire Russia collusion narrative her campaign manufactured effectively prevented Trump from fully governing for three years. Both Biden and Harris called Trump an illegitimate president. In a 2017 poll, 42 percent agreed.

It is not hard at all to see how the Democrats and their media minions might well refuse to accept the legitimacy of his reelection in 2024—or that of Ron DeSantis or another hard-core conservative, should Trump not go full Grover Cleveland. And this conclusion does not even require actual cheating or collusion. The Electoral College itself is illegitimate in the eyes of the elite, allegedly because of white supremacy or some other nonsense, but in reality because it allows normal Americans to counter the overwhelming electoral weight of big blue cities.

In contrast, the allegiance hump that red leaders, like red-state governors, would need to get over to engage in a revolt is much higher than that of blue leaders. What actions by a blue federal government might get the red leadership over the allegiance hump? It would probably not be a single action but many of them that, as we have discussed, compel the conclusion among red leaders and the populace that the system is irrevocably broken and that no meaningful paths exist for the redress of the legitimate red grievances. There would likely be a series of steps, with heightened pushback, and then a straw that breaks the proverbial camel's back.

It could be one of a number of things. Gun confiscation actions could spark it. It could be the deliberate refusal of the Democratic administration to obey the Supreme Court on some key matter. A climate cult–driven attack to suddenly destroy the fossil fuel industry and wreck the red-state economies—as opposed to the frog-boiling clampdown on it we have seen lately—could do it. It could be the imposition of some sort of fascist "election reform" measure designed to eliminate the scourge of Democratic candidates losing. It might be the refusal of the blue federal government to accept the election of a Republican presidential candidate—challenging the validity of the election was totally cool from 2000 to October 2020, then has been literally treason since, but as soon as whatever hack the Dems nominate in 2024 loses, the memo will go out making it A-OK once again.

We might see a number of red-state governors banding together and announcing that they and their states are out of here—this could come with or without a concurrent insurgency. But the challenge is that not everyone would be cool with that. Even deep-red states like Texas still have about 45 percent Democratic voters, who would not be thrilled with becoming some new country that enshrines the politics they hate. A negotiated national divorce scenario would presumably deal with this by giving folks time to depart and sort themselves out; if some sort of civil war broke out, the problem is that a whole lot of opponents would be behind red lines.

How large this fifth column is and what its impact would be militarily is the big question. The fact is that liberals are only mostly insipid sissies who do not have weapons like real men do, and some of them will be armed. What is not so clear is whether they can band together effectively to resist. Armed individuals can cause problems, and in the civilian law enforcement context these can be enormous. Remember the Boston bombing terrorists, including the one who got the dreamy *Rolling Stone* cover photo? Two schmucks with handguns locked down a whole city. Think of what a trained platoon could do.

But that assumes a peacetime, law enforcement mindset. Here's the thing about law enforcement—they are not combat troops, and they are not trained to accept casualties. Soldiers are. There is a planning matrix in the military that gives you the expected dead for every type of operation. You go in expecting to lose folks. The police never do that—the acceptable number of casualties is zero. But that mindset means that when a couple of untrained freaks with handguns go on a rampage, everything stops and the city shuts down. However, in the military context, these considerations are essentially irrelevant. A leftist with a gun shoots up some red forces then gets killed. Casualties happen; on to the next operation. To be a tactically significant force once the law enforcement mindset is shed, the leftists would themselves have to form into guerilla groups. This takes numbers, organization, and a hospitable battlespace environment, and it is unclear whether those can be achieved.

Say a terrorist force takes root in Austin. That's annoying; it's bad in an information operation sense to have any of your territory unsecured. But what does it achieve? So they block access to decent BBQ and SXSW? The red states can probably live with an uppity Austin until they get around to crushing the fifth column. Controlling a city is not necessarily tactically or strategically significant in the way that rural insurgents dominating swathes of the countryside and being able to shut down critical logistics lines is.

But banding together is one of the first things the leadership of Red America needs to get its loyal red citizens to do. The unorganized militia numbers in the millions. Once organized, these potential paramilitaries would be a key component of red-state combat power. Many have military experience; in fact, many have military experience from back when America actually won wars instead of getting handed strategic defeats by banditos driving white Toyota pick-ups around the Hindu Kush.

The red states would inherit a greater chunk of the current military if they seceded than a comparable blue-state secession because of geography—all those Army bases with those awful southern generals' names have southern generals' names because they are often located in the South. Today, the South is largely red. Moreover, the red states provide a disproportionate portion of military manpower, and when they are faced with a choice, a significant number of them are likely to go with the red. Moreover, the red states—with a population that is higher in veterans, hunters, and traditionally inclined males—are likely to generate significantly more paramilitary forces outside the regular military organization. Every man (and some women) with a rifle is a potential fighter.

The current senior military leadership will largely stay loyal to the feds. Leaving aside the allegiance hump, the generals and admirals at the higher levels of the military are fully integrated into the very ruling establishment that a red revolt would be against. The war colleges, where colonels are trained to be generals, are not primarily focused on running campaigns and winning wars but on socializing military officers to participate in "the interagency process." What this really means is that high-level military education is designed to make the generals fit comfortably into the ruling caste. A number would likely join a revolt, but most would stay with the blue government even if their political inclinations are centrist or even tepidly right-wing. The Curtis LeMay–style hard-right flag officers were long ago exorcised from the three- and four-star ranks, a phenomenon that closely tracks America's recent inability to win decisive victories.

What does it mean that most generals, as well as many field grades—the colonels and majors—are likely to stay loyal to a blue federal government? A lot of senior officers leading a lot fewer troops. Lower grades are not so invested in the establishment, and probably have little desire to fight other Americans over "politics."

As for the enlisted troops, the situation is a bit different. Most junior troops do a hitch of three to four years and get out. They do not experience the same pressure to conform in order to stay at least twenty years to get a retirement. Moreover, most enlisted troops (unlike all officers) did not spend at least four years in a college being indoctrinated. They primarily come directly from the patriotic precincts of America and, while they have experienced the influence of woke popular culture, they have not necessarily had to conform to the tenets of political correctness as civilians to be accepted in their caste in the same way the primarily middle-class members of the officer corps have.

So how does it work? How does a civil war happen? Because lighting that fuse is a huge step, personally and nationally.

There has to be a point when someone decides that he has nothing to lose. That's a big part of what keeps things in check now even as folks grow furious and frustrated—the idea that your life as you knew it is essentially over the second you pull a trigger. That's not a bad thing. We want there to be a huge sanction on improperly maiming or killing people. But people do maim and kill knowing the consequences all the time in the criminal context. It is doing so in the political context that is such a leap.

Most Americans are loyal to the country even if its leadership is so often garbage. To take up arms against the flag—even if the guy carrying the flag hates America and is doing it ironically—is not just a bridge too far. It's several bridges past too far.

Look at the so-called "insurrectionists" of January 6, 2021. These guys probably had enough guns that they left back home to clear the Capitol and hold it for a while, had they been actual insurrectionists. But they didn't do that because they weren't insurrectionists. The only shooting that day was by the Keystone Capitol cops. Sure, they threw some punches, but a brawl is very different than an insurrection. These people were profoundly loyal to the country, despite the legacy media's lies in service of the establishment. They were there because they thought the Constitution was in danger, not because they wanted to endanger it. Even unjustly held in squalid conditions in a federal jail, they still sang the National Anthem every night before lights out.

Many red-staters are vets, sworn to defend the Constitution. That would have to be what they thought they were doing.

Then there is the fact that if you pull the trigger at a fed and it does not turn into a successful revolution, you are done. Your life is over. You are going to jail forever; at best, you will be hunted forever. The second you take up arms, everything changes and your life is never going to be the same. Again, this is a good thing. We want to discourage this in all but the direst situations. It sets the bar appropriately high for the shot heard 'round the country.

If civil conflict comes, it probably starts during some tense encounter with federal cops that escalates out of control. There was almost one with Ammon Bundy's crew a few years ago, when the feds came to get them and a bunch of tacticool dudes showed up with their iron. Wiser heads prevailed, and the feds pulled back. But that could have erupted into violence.

It would not have started a civil war, though, because the conditions were not right. They are not right now either, thankfully. The procedural alternatives still exist. Elections, though imperfect, still take place. The courts, again imperfect, still sometimes rule fairly. But if that is no longer perceived to be true, and if a fearful combination of anger, ego, and testosterone causes someone in a confrontation to shoot, that may lead to a bunch of people being dead. And if the locals decide that the feds are not going to be allowed to come in to arrest the participants, then there is a problem.

Could such a rebellion be snuffed out with overwhelming force? Probably, but not certainly. If the word spread, including by social media before the tech titans figured out what was happening and shut down the #FedMassacre hashtag, maybe the whole region erupts. Suddenly there's a whole rural county where the feds dare not enter after their convoy to get to the crime scene gets ambushed. At Waco, the ATF hit the Branch Davidian compound and were initially shot to pieces by a group of amateurs. Four agents were killed. But Koresh's folks were in a central location. They could be surrounded. What do you do when it's a lot more people spread throughout a whole county? Or two counties? Especially where everyone in them has a gun, and knows every rock and gully, and has made the decision to fight?

When people see that resistance is not being smashed, it spreads. Maybe a sheriff announces he is banning feds from his jurisdiction. He is forming a posse of locals to enforce his order. You now have a significant number of armed combatants in a wide area. To secure a big rural county, you probably need at least—at least—a couple battalions of infantry. But just how many battalions are there?

The brigade combat team (BCT) is the main unit of action in the U.S. military. There are 31 active-duty brigades, and 27 National Guard brigades, so 58 total. There are 3 or 4 ground combat battalions per BCT, so let's say 130 battalions. Add some Marines and some military police units, and call it roughly 200 battalions. Many of those are stationed overseas.

America has 3,006 counties.

Do not forget that cities take even more units to control. To suppress the Los Angeles riots, President Bush ordered in one division—the 40th Infantry Division of the California Army National Guard, plus battalions from the 7th Infantry Division out of Fort Ord and from the Marines out of Camp Pendleton. This was at least four brigades' worth, at least sixteen battalions (including armor, cavalry, and artillery acting as infantry). So, it took about 8 percent of America's battalions, all to suppress one short riot, not an actual insurgency, in one city.

We have a lot of cities.

To truly secure an area, you need to have guys on the ground. But America has a lot of ground. This brings up a key problem. There just are not enough soldiers to control the United States, if by "control" you mean stick a guy with an M4 on every street corner. Even counting cops, the ratio of government gunfighter to citizen is already lopsidedly unfavorable to the government before you factor in desertions.

Soldiers need logistical support, and combat supporters dwarf the number of ground pounders. The "tooth to tail" ratio of support soldiers to fighting soldier can be as high as 10:1 (many are in units at echelons above the brigades). And remember that a soldier does not operate 24/7. Soldiers need to sleep, and eat, and shit, and shave. They need to refit and rearm and retrain. When you talk about a battalion, which is about 500 joes, you mean about 400 fighters in four infantry companies. For a while, you can sustain all of them ready for action at any one time. But they need downtime. If you go on and on—and insurgencies are infamous for going on and on—then you really will

But would the left care? Leftists' widespread social media glee over COVID deaths, at least until it became clear that it was not just the unvaxxed hicks dying, demonstrates a distinct dehumanization of red Americans by their alleged betters. If you look at the ridiculous hysteria over January 6, 2021, the elites' overwrought reaction becomes less and less funny. Why, if these insurrectionists are out to destroy Our Democracy, don't we have to fight them? They already killed unarmed Ashli Babbitt. Do you imagine they will develop qualms after the balloon has really gone up?

Add to this the fact that the blue elite is, in a word, stupid. It has demonstrated an astonishing capacity to choose the worst possible course of action in any scenario, whether it is a pandemic, riots, or the economy. These people are neither smart nor wise, and they also do not know or understand their fellow Americans. They could very well imagine that a brutal crackdown would break the spirit of their enemies instead of harden their resolve.

So they would almost certainly try, and early, before the ranks of the military drained and before the ammo—most of which comes from Red America—runs out. But what could they really do? Kill a few hundred or even thousand insurgents somewhere? There is an inexhaustible well of patriots to draw on to refill the red ranks—certainly every father, brother, and pal of one of the red rebels who gets killed in a blue operation is going to want to join the reds and get some payback.

And can the blue forces even rely upon their own forces for long? A lot of the red-inclined troops would desert. Others might stick around, but don't count on them to channel Audie Murphy. And some would be turncoats, feeding info to the rebels or engaging in acts of sabotage.

There is already an infrastructure for rebel governments in the form of the red-state governments. Where there is a government, there can be conventional forces. As we have seen, red states would likely inherit significant conventional forces relatively intact. That means, even early on, we could see actual conventional battles as either the blue forces sought to retake control of red land or the red forces advanced into blue territory to defeat the blue forces.

As the insurgents established tighter control within their areas, they would become more organized. Random groups of fighters would combine. A chain of command would develop. There would be more planning and logistical centralization. It would start looking sort of like a real military. And it would get ambitious. It would seek to carry out bigger operations, like taking a town. But, again, concentrating forces is risky because conventional forces can generally defeat insurgents when they go head-to-head. The guerillas have to be very strong, and the counterinsurgents very weak, to face off directly. As mentioned, the Viet Cong tried to do that during the Tet Offensive and they were slaughtered.

The blue states would be at a definite disadvantage in that their forces would be limited in number and hard to replace—do you see a lot of transsexual mime studies majors dropping out of Gumbo State to join the Army to fight guerillas in the Ozarks? But the blue side is going to have to build up an effective fighting force if it intends to do any fighting. The Antifa street punk stuff is all fun and games, especially since the cops are there to protect them, but war is different. These couch-dwelling losers are probably not going to make great troops, certainly not like the rough and ready farm boys and laborers who filled the ranks on both sides of Civil War 1.0.

The simple fact is that a generation that grew up getting participation trophies and protected from exposure to peanuts lest an allergic reaction make some kid in their class vapor-lock is going to have difficulty adapting to military life. And if you have a military where the troops are not adapted to military life, you have the German army.

Not the "invade Poland" German army that was scary and deadly, but the German army of today where they train with brooms instead of rifles. Oh, and they have a labor union, the Bundeswehrverband. That's the sign that an army is ready to kick ass—it's got a union. You can almost see the platoon shop steward telling the lieutenant that Private Gunter can't fire the machine gun because that's not in his job description.

The fact is that to create an effective military, the blue states need to give up their social justice pretensions. The deleterious effects of wokeness on our present military are there for all to see—rock-bottom morale, ships plowing into each other, trans troopers, ignominious debacles, and internal purges of people who want to fight instead of fret about pronouns. Now imagine this tendency running totally free, untethered to any residual red influence. How long until there is a political officer—a *zampolit*—in every company ensuring woke conformity at the expense of combat readiness? This is a recipe for defeat, and if the blue counterinsurgents were serious about stamping out freedom, they would have to dispense with much of this. But it's hard to turn on a dime.

Combine that problem with the next big issue and the blues face a real challenge. They will have those massively over-extended logistical lines. It's nice to hold cities, but if you do not also hold all the rural territory between the cities, as well as the routes to the places where you are getting your food and fuel (and holding those is a big question in itself), then you have a real problem. The stuff that keeps cities alive has to pass through Indian country, and even assuming you could convince civilian truckers to make that passage, the blue states would still have to devote a massive proportion of their forces to defending those routes. Even a small-scale campaign against those supply lines could cause chaos in the cities. Imagine the madness as soft urban professionals, unused to privation and largely disarmed, find themselves both starving and subject to the will of the strong and merciless. It's *The Road Warrior*, and there is no Mad Max coming to save you.

Meanwhile, in the red areas, they are growing food. And when they eventually win, they want payback. Perhaps they might negotiate a national divorce—sort of like the converse of a shotgun wedding—or perhaps they might just channel Michael Corleone and resolve to take care of all family business at once. They would not want to risk going another round with the enemy next door. As Cato the Elder might have said, "Blue America *delenda est*."

In short, a red rebellion—if it got going—would likely be unstoppable if it held out long enough. That's always the key to insurgencies—persistence. The best strategy for the blue states is to try to convince the red ones not to rebel, or to patch things up if they start to. In a fight, the blue states lose, even with the power of the federal government behind them. But the cost would be a mountain of bodies, and there is no assurance that the America that comes through on the other side is one that anyone would want.

What does a civil war look like up close? At first, small unit actions. Regular people will, as always, suffer. And, eventually, it might develop into a nearly conventional conflict as the victorious side chooses to reunify the country under its banner.

A half-dozen men in their old camo hunting clothes kept watch as Lou knelt by the metal tower's north pylon and slammed down the welder's mask he had brought from work. The acetylene torch was blindingly bright, and if there were cops or soldiers within miles it would have been easy to see them at work, but they knew from one of the sheriff's deputies that there were no patrols tonight. The blues were still licking their wounds from the ambush a few evenings ago and were staying inside the operating base built around the town police station.

Lou cut through the steel at two spots, then left the bubbling, glowing cuts to move to the next support leg. The power lines strung seventy-five feet above their heads hummed even as the crickets chirped. It would have been nice to do this with explosives. He had been a 12-Bravo combat engineer years ago, and if he only had some C4 they'd be finished already. But they did not have any, so cutting the supports was the next best thing. He again burned through the metal in two places and lifted his mask when he finished.

"Okay," he yelled. Two more of the group approached with sledgehammers as Lou loaded his gear into the back of his Chevy Tahoe. They waited until he drove a little way off, and then they began to pound the segments cut out of each leg with their sledges. It took a couple blows, but the pieces came free, and the huge tower groaned as the massive weight of the high-tension power tower shifted.

"Shit!" one of them yelled, grinning as he and his buddy ran out from underneath it. The tower groaned again and shivered, its support on two of the four sides gone. For a moment they were unsure it would work, but it did—physics was unforgiving and gravity did its job. The tower began to topple over, ripping apart the power lines in a shower of blue and yellow sparks.

It fell on its side with a deafening crash, the sparking cables starting little fires in the grass.

"We're outta here!" Lou yelled. The rest of the guerillas got into another pair of pick-ups. They took off down the dirt road, ecstatic. Many miles away, in New York City, the power would be off. Sure, the blues would get it fixed pretty quick, or bypass it, but the message was clear—the countryside belongs to the reds.

Lou's truck disintegrated in a fireball as the $150,000 Hellfire missile slammed into it. They had not even seen the drone. The other trucks scattered. They would escape. The expended missile left just 987 remaining in the blue arsenal; the missile was built in Florida, so obviously there would be no replacements.

It killed one guerilla. The next day, Lou's son and cousin both joined the resistance.

"Pizza!"

"I didn't order any pizza!" the woman said, opening the front door. There were two men there with big pistols in their hands. They pushed inside the house. Her little dog was barking madly. She shrieked.

"Shut up," the first one said, pressing the barrel into her forehead. She complied.

"Your husband flies F-15s," the man said. "They are killing lots of our women and children. He can either keep flying or desert. If he keeps flying, you tell him that the next time we come by, we're getting payback."

The woman couldn't speak. The men left, and she was shaking. She went to find her telephone.

The 155 mm artillery round hit next to the HEMTT truck rolling up Interstate 5 and set it ablaze. The infantry had cleared most of the forward observers the day before, encountering only scattered resistance from blue forces who had mostly retreated into Portland. The few howitzers the blue force had left were being dragged through the streets of the city and fired at preset targets, like the interstate which was now the 72nd Infantry Brigade Combat Team's main supply route to the front lines of the Second Civil War.

The tide had turned. What had begun as a rebellion by red-staters was now a conventional war. The reds had gone from secession to fighting on blue ground to reunify the country.

The commander watched from his main command post in a cemetery off to the east of the highway. The black smoke from the wreck twisted skyward. Other vehicles simply drove around it as it burned in the number three lane. The blues got lucky, the colonel observed once more, and his men in the burning HEMTT got unlucky.

Two more dead, he realized. How many was that lost under his command in just over a year of fighting? Hundreds? Thousands?

His exhausted brigade had been pushing north for a week now after sweeping through California. The blues had not stood and fought since Sacramento, hundreds of miles to the south, and they had paid for the mistake of doing so. After that, they had been in full retreat north. It was tactical insanity, in the colonel's view, that they had retreated into Portland. Divided by the Columbia River, the metropolis was a trap.

But this was a do-or-die fight for the enemy. Portland was a symbol of blue resistance. Losing it would be a devastating blow to enemy morale. Of course, that assumed the brigade could take it. Taking a modern city was no easy feat. It would require time to prepare for a ground assault. The 72nd had moved north up the I-5 and had dug in, sealing off the land routes in and out of the city to the south.

Now the colonel faced a daunting problem. His S2 estimated that there were five thousand enemy combat troops, conventional and irregular, in Portland. The irregulars were Antifa types armed with whatever guns the military could spare. Most were really just petty criminals. And most were on drugs. There were another estimated two hundred and fifty thousand civilians who had not gotten out as the red forces approached. Luckily, Portland was heavily anti-gun for decades before the Second Civil War. Those civilians would be largely unarmed, which was a relief. Blue forces entering red areas had paid a high price because every Bubba with a deer rifle took a potshot at the invaders. As Japan's Admiral Yamamoto observed about the risks of invading the United States, perhaps apocryphally, there was an American with a gun behind every blade of grass, at least in the red areas.

Still, his brigade was at only about 80 percent strength with four thousand troops—nowhere near enough to take a modern metropolis.

Of course, he had the paras too. The paramilitaries numbered another five thousand men and women, usually organized into bands of about one hundred under the command of a leader they elected and answered to. Many were ex-military; they used their own weapons. The most popular gun was the AR-15, a civilian version of the M4/M16 family of rifles his own troops used. Still, when you walked through the paras' camps, you would see all manner of firearms. Rifles, both hunting and faux assault, shotguns, and pistols of all types decorated these citizen-soldiers. American civilians owned over three hundred million firearms when the war started—in fact, trying to confiscate them had been the spark that lit the fuse for war.

The colonel welcomed the manpower the paras provided, at least when they cooperated with him. But they were stubbornly independent and only nominally under his command. He also feared their capacity for violence. Most of these paras were from rural California and Oregon. They had been subjected to the violent gun raids and the other excesses of the California and Oregon police states before the conventional red forces arrived to liberate them. The guerilla war in the Central Valley and the mountains had been bitter and merciless. Everyone knew about the Modesto Massacre.

The paras were not above some payback now that they were ascendant. The other day, twenty prisoners from a captured Oregon State Security unit had been found bound and shot in a parking lot. The paras' commander in the area denied knowledge of the atrocity—and denied giving a damn if the bastards who killed his brother had gotten a taste of what they had been dishing out to suspected reds prior to the liberation.

If it became necessary to storm Portland, the bloodbath before it fell might be exceeded by the bloodbath after. But then again, with the city cut off from food, and over a quarter of a million hungry mouths to feed, maybe they could be starved out. Except time was not on their side, and the colonel knew his military history. The people of Leningrad had held off a Nazi siege for over a year, albeit at a terrible price.

Another shell exploded on the freeway, this time well between vehicles. The brigade's artillery was ready this time; a fire direction radar calculated the location of the gun within the city and fed the coordinates to a firing platoon of M777 155 mm cannons, which adjusted and shot a counterbattery salvo over the hills somewhere inside the city. It was probably fifty-fifty that the strike would catch the enemy gun before it displaced, but it was certain to level the buildings in the immediate area of its firing position. More wreckage, more dead civilians if they weren't hiding in the basements, thought the colonel.

But Portland's buildings rarely had basements.

CHAPTER ELEVEN

THE CHINA CRISIS

Maybe we dodge the national divorce and avoid some form of civil war. But that does not mean that the barbarians will not appear at the gates anyway. And, of course, we currently have no gates because we have no walls—borders are racist, apparently. But threats loom from outside as well as inside.

Now there is an Asian powerhouse that is about to beat the U.S.A. in the drag race for supremacy and take home its pink slip. Our defeat is inevitable. We Americans are lazy and disorganized. They are centralized, disciplined, and efficient. They are not frivolous like we are. We took our economic dominance for granted, never even considering that the wily workers from the East are going to eat our lunch. Their economy is booming while ours stagnates. And, adding insult to injury, they copied much of our technology. They took what we created, made it better, and now we don't even make it here anymore. Many of our proudest manufacturing icons have moved across the Pacific, where they build stuff cheaper and better. Their centrally planned economic system will, no doubt, crush our disorganized patchwork of bickering, competing corporations. The smart people at the *New York Times* and elsewhere tell us that we have much to learn from our incoming overlords. We're doomed.

That could be about today and the People's Republic of China (PRC), but we also heard it in the early eighties. If you are old enough to remember, the era of *Miami Vice* and A Flock of Seagulls was also an era of extreme anxiety in America about the rise of Japan. Simply put, we felt that in many ways our country had lost its edge. After World War II, we had built the Japanese up and given them access to our markets, which they flooded with cheap and, initially, shoddy goods. You have to be old—not Biden old, but old enough to recall, say, K-Tel Records compilations—to remember when "Made in Japan" was a snickering sneer at something tacky and essentially disposable.

But intermittently functional transistor radios gave way to economy cars. The first models were no great shakes—the author's orange 1977 Datsun B210 had paper-thin fiberboard panels in the back cargo area with a thin veneer of off-white vinyl sheeting stapled over them—but they kept getting better. American cars kept getting worse. The unwieldy Big Three boats of the seventies were underpowered and bloated parodies of the magnificent road iron Detroit manufactured in the fifties and sixties. You still see glorious 1965 Mustangs rolling down the boulevard today; when is the last time you saw a breathtakingly ugly 1975 Mustang II moving under its own power? And people knew not to buy a car built on a Monday, when the United Auto Workers union guys were still sweating off their weekend hangovers as they toiled on the assembly line.

Bestsellers were written on the coming catastrophe. Politicians panicked. It was all over popular culture too. Japan was Godzilla and we were Tokyo.

And then the panic petered out. Japan, it turned out, was not invulnerable and not unstoppable. Many of its strengths were actually weaknesses. The highly centralized business sector, which far too many American economists pointed to as a worthy model to emulate, was actually sclerotic and inflexible. Socially, Japanese culture's unique issues caused significant effects absent in America. The work culture burned out men. Women had much more trouble thriving in the workforce than American women. Japan's birth rate collapsed. An aging population meant a shrinking workforce that had to focus a greater part of its efforts on caring for the elderly. Japan, again for cultural reasons, does not allow immigration, so the option of simply importing new workers (as we and Europe have done) is absent. There's no pulling out of the tailspin.

Today, Japan is not a poor nation by any means, but it is a dying nation. The old are ubiquitous, and the young are not interested in work or family. They are interested in boy bands, internet games, and bizarre manga porn. Its younger generation is filled with "herbivores," adult males who are "kind and gentle men who, without being bound by manliness, do not pursue romantic relationships voraciously and have no aptitude for being hurt or hurting others," according to Waseda University professor Masahiro Morioka. There's a recipe for societal collapse, a generation that cannot get up the motivation—or anything else—to reproduce.

Japan still makes a lot of good cars, and other stuff, but it is not going to dominate America or anything else. It's not even going to get laid.

The China situation today is the same, and also very different.

The PRC is the same in that Americans are perplexed and alarmed by the rise of Red China from backwards communist hellhole to a disconcerting mix of high tech and wealthy cities set against the old and poor villages of the countryside. You land in a big Chinese city and it is clean and modern and advanced, shaming our decaying urban infrastructure. Then you trek out to the hinterlands and they are still eating beagles.

What is absolutely clear is just how much junk we buy from them. China is our off-site factory with cheap labor and lax pollution standards, doing the work Americans just won't do. A never-ending stream of cargo container ships float across the Pacific to our West Coast ports packed with low-tech to high-tech goods bound for Walmart, Costco, and Amazon distribution centers. The COVID pandemic panic—besides revealing that China was playing God with bat viruses (likely funded by the geniuses in America's medical establishment)—made Americans aware of just how much of our manufacturing we have outsourced to the Far East. Masks, gloves, medicine—all of that is largely made in Chinese factories. So are our iPhones and many of our other electronics. If you wonder where America's manufacturing base picked up and went to, look toward the setting sun.

Of course, COVID also made America aware of the "wet markets," where you can shop for fresh pangolin chops and badger snouts in order to satisfy all your bizarre meat needs. That this kind of disgusting open-air abattoir exists side-by-side with high-tech stuff in modern Chinese cities reminds us that maybe China is not so thoroughly modern after all.

China also sends us people. These people, flush with cash and often favorites of the party, buy up American real estate as well as interests in strategic industries. They ship over hordes of university students—Chinese full-freight tuition money is crack to cash-strapped colleges. Of course, those selected students do not sign up for the kind of frivolous nonsense courses the spoiled Connecticut rich girls enroll in—they are studying STEM while our alleged best and brightest are surveying transgender themes in ancient Bolivian poetry. The party—because everything Chinese is, at its core, an extension of the Chinese Communist Party (CCP)—spends money to fund university research and gain access to cutting-edge technology. They outsource

their R&D, and largely steal it from us. We outsource our manufacturing, then pay to import it back.

The Chinese also know how to buy influence. Sometimes they
pay for it in cash, sometimes they pay for it in trade. Flatulent clown
Representative Eric Swalwell (D-CA) was tricked by an attractive
agent-ette into believing that she was putting out because he was
handsome and smart, as opposed to the fact that he was—inexplicably,
but his district is in California—adjacent to power. Dianne Feinstein's
driver was, famously, a Chinese agent. Whether he put out for the
Motherland is a question best not asked, at least not just before dinner.

But as comical as attractive girls granting mediocre men a bit of
attention and making them swoon is, the results are anything but
amusing. How many more American males who cannot score but for
the charity of foreign intelligence operatives are ensnared in similar
honey traps? Certainly Hunter Biden is—pity the flunkies at the
Chinese Ministry of State Security who have to screen the videos of
the Biden scion drunkenly tapping the countless commie cuties sup-
plied to him by his hosts during his visits.

Chinese influence in American society, and especially in the busi-
ness community, is deep and extensive, and it protects China and its
Winnie the Pooh–esque dictator from accountability. Repression in
Hong Kong? Oh well. Uighurs? Ho hum. Slave labor? Look, a squirrel.

Hollywood won't mention Taiwan lest its red masters frown. In
November 2021, JPMorgan Chase CEO Jamie Dimon publicly mused
that the United States would outlast the PRC; he got a call and back-
tracked ASAP. Silicon Valley titans—taking a break from lecturing
Americans on how to run their own democracy—eagerly adjust their
apps and search engines to facilitate Chinese social credit monitoring
and dissenter silencing. What NBA stars figuratively do for their
Chinese patrons is traditionally preceded by a fine dinner and fore-
play. Plenty of folks in the U.S. government dance to the Chi Coms'

tune as well. China has lots of friends in D.C., including the alleged current president.

But this problem of a nation's elite selling out their country to the highest bidder is not unique to America in the 2020s. Once again, ancient Rome provides an eerie echo. The great Numidian Jugurtha fought beside the Romans (before fighting against them later) and noted their penchant for being bribed. To get the Senate in Rome to settle a dispute back home in his favor, he spent lavishly buying support, observing that Rome was *urbem venalem et mature perituram, si emptorem invenerit,* "a city for sale and doomed to quick destruction, if it should find a buyer."

China is buying big-time. But there is a large difference between the Japanese boogeyman and the real Chinese threat. The Chi Coms have hot rocks, and they appear to have moved past the United States in hypersonic missile technology. Japan, besides being nuke-free—they really took the whole Hiroshima and Nagasaki thing personally—was at least an ally. Its limited military was never going to be turned against the Americans. In fact, one of the reasons Japan could spend to modernize its economy so quickly was that the Americans were largely picking up the tab for its defense against the nearby U.S.S.R.

The Chinese were not always a threat to America. They got the bomb in the sixties, but their missile force was relatively small, especially compared to that of the Russians. Until recently, the People's Liberation Army (PLA) was big, but it was outdated and unwieldy, and still based on masses of infantry. At one time, that was a threat. The United States fought the Red Chinese in the Korean War after Chairman Mao, afraid that General Douglas MacArthur was not going to stop the United Nations offensive at the Yalu River, ordered the PLA south in what they call the "War to Resist Americans and Aid Korea." The sheer mass of the Chinese offensive sent the American and allied forces reeling back south. The Chinese were not exceptionally great fighters—more on that in a moment—but there were a lot of them. As has been observed, quantity has a quality all its own. The mass assaults were terrifying, without finesse but brutally effective if the defenders were not in good defensive positions. If the Americans or allies were in a good position, however, it was a slaughter. American artillery positions were buried in empty shells while infantry company machine guns glowed red as they spewed hot lead at the never-ending hordes. Remember, the American military is a logistics machine. As long as that was up and running, we would kill every commie bastard they sent our way.

America lost about fifty-four thousand men in the three years of the Korean War. The PLA lost nearly a million men, yet still today claim it as a victory even though the war ended with the opposing forces at about the same positions as they had held when it started.

Obviously, the Chinese have a different perspective than we do, and the communist government is not about to allow any local revisionists to ask how a 20:1 kill ratio translates to a check in the "W" column. In fact, in the fall of 2021, the biggest budgeted Chinese movie ever, *The Battle at Lake Changjin*, was playing to record audiences. We know Lake Changjin as the Chosin Reservoir. Chi Com audiences were going nuts cheering a movie about killing Americans. At the same time the Chinese were caught up in a patriotic frenzy, the United State Air Force announced its new policy allowing officers to add their preferred pronouns to their signature blocks on official documents.

Modern Hollywood would never make a movie celebrating Americans killing communists, but unlike our ruling caste, the Chinese are not ashamed to love their country. Nowhere is their perspective more different than regarding Taiwan. After the Chinese civil war, in which the communists eventually prevailed, the remaining anti-communist forces hopped over to the big island of Formosa off

China's east coast and created an anti-communist redoubt. Red China considers Taiwan its own, and this is not merely a pose but as close as the officially atheist state has to an article of faith. Think of how we might feel if, say, New Jersey was occupied by rebels. Well, perhaps not the Garden State, but the point remains. We would want it back. And we would not rest until we got it.

This is not to say the Chinese communists are right. Communists are never right and possess no moral standing to be right about anything. But that is how they feel, deeply and unequivocally, and you do need to understand your enemy and how he thinks. That particular sentiment comes from Sun Tzu, an ancient Chinese military thinker whose classic book *The Art of War* still sells in America today to everyone from unwoke military officers to Wall Street douchebags. It offers a glimpse into how our enemy thinks.

Sun Tzu offers countless memorable aphorisms, many misunderstood and easily misapplied. His influence on military thought is undeniable, however. Sun Tzu's driving principle is to seek advantages over the enemy that allow you to prevail quickly and with minimal losses. He advocates extensive reconnaissance and spying, psychological and information operations to influence the enemy, and deception to shape the battlefield to your advantage if you do have to fight. But you should not fight except when there is no other choice; one of his most famous contentions is that the greatest victory is the win obtained without battle. Chinese policy toward America and its allies today reflects all of these ideas; the Korean War campaign, not so much.

While Sun Tzu is certainly in the top ranks of influential military thinkers, the Chinese themselves have a pretty mixed military tradition. They fought a lot of wars in their many thousand-year history, from battling other Chinese to steppe nomad hordes to Americans and even Vietnamese in the late 1970s (the Vietnamese won). But they are not known as a particularly great warrior nation, not like the Romans or the Spartans or the aforementioned steppe warriors.

The Chinese had wealth and organization, and they often leveraged that to obtain what arms could not. They had problems with the nomadic raiders, so they built a network of giant barriers, collectively called the Great Wall, that ran for thirteen thousand miles. When those raiders from the north got restless, the Chinese tried to crush them with punitive expeditions, but chasing horsemen around a barren wasteland was a bad idea. Instead, the Chinese opened trading posts, selling the nomads silk and other luxuries and generally wrapping them up inside the Chinese economy. Once their enemy was intertwined and dependent, war became impractical. If you can't beat 'em, buy 'em.

Sound familiar?

When they did fight, and the Chinese often did fight, their victories came through size and organization, and they built an ancient empire. Administration was where they excelled. Of course, a well-organized empire without a great warrior tradition is an irresistible target. The Mongolians and other raiders eventually conquered them; later, the European powers would take what parts of China they wanted, and Japan seized much of it before and during World War II. Moreover, the Chinese had nothing like a great naval tradition, and still do not.

But none of that matters much. The idea that the Chinese were meh warriors in the past does not mean that the new People's Liberation Army is a pushover. It is not. It is no longer the cumbersome blob of screaming conscripts that American soldiers and Marines mowed down on the Korean Peninsula. A couple decades ago, the Chi Coms drastically cut the size of their military, getting rid of the mass formations and making the force smaller but deadlier by equipping it with new technology. An astute observer will note that this began not long after America demonstrated its precision guided strike prowess in Desert Storm and, later, over Serbia. The Chinese are no fools; they saw the parallels between their mass conscript army of marginally trained peasants operating outdated equipment and Iraq's mass conscript army of marginally trained peasants operating outdated equipment. They decided to compete with America on its own turf, which seemed hilarious at the time. A generation later, no one who has been watching the transformation of the PLA is laughing.

Nowhere is this more apparent, and scarier, than in the PRC's strategic expansion east into the South China Sea and the Pacific. China's goal is area denial—it wants to keep America afraid to come in close to the coast where it can defend Taiwan if Xi chooses to invade, and it wants to establish its own hegemony over these critical trade routes. As America dithers, it is pushing forward.

Today, the Chinese fleet is bigger than America's. The People's Liberation Army Navy (PLAN) has approximately 355 ships and submarines. The United States Navy had almost 600 ships under Ronald Reagan. It barely has 300 today. Of course, that does not take into account the U.S. ships laid up being repaired after ramming into each other because seamanship has taken a backseat to wokeness in today's fleet. The USS *Bonhomme Richard* caught fire tied to a pier in San Diego—allegedly, an aggrieved seaman started the blaze—and had to be scrapped because the fire could not be put out. After-action reports indicated that the crew did not conduct its firefighting training—it should go without saying that fighting fires is pretty important on a ship—but is there any doubt that every single sailor had been put through his/her/xir trans awareness training?

The sad fact is that if China and America fight—and history indicates this is a near certainty—then a lot of young Americans are going to die, albeit fully aware of the impact of white privilege and the patriarchy. The fact is that it is difficult for the Navy to fully accept the new reality that today our sailors are not only outnumbered and outgunned, but perhaps also out-led. Since the victory over Japan in World War II, the American fleet has treasured its legacy as the world's preeminent sea power. It knew how to fight and win in the water in ways no one else (except the Brits) understood. China, the upstart, has no such legacy. For a long time, as China floated new destroyers and frigates, that was going to be what kept us ahead.

But history again echoes the present. The Romans knew nothing about naval operations; they relied on their allies to do the sailing. But the Carthaginians, descendants of those legendary mariners the Phoenicians, had those traditions in spades. During the first Punic War, it became obvious that a lot of the fight would be on the water, so the Romans took a captured Carthaginian *quinquereme* and copied it. It then trained up a navy, and added a few tweaks to the mix to maximize its advantages. This included the *corvus*, a device that was essentially a spiked boarding ramp that could be dropped onto the deck of an enemy ship. The Romans might not have known an anchor from a mizenmast, but they knew everything there was to know about land combat. The *corvus* allowed them to fight a ground battle on the water. This is asymmetrical warfare—creating strength and putting it against an enemy weakness. Despite a number of grievous losses, the Romans still won the war.

So, the hope that the fact we have been doing naval operations in the western Pacific for almost a century will guarantee us victory is a hollow one. The Chinese might not be as good at seamanship as we think we are—whether we still have that edge is in doubt—but they are enthusiastic and there are a lot of them. Like the Romans, they help themselves to our intellectual property so we cannot rely on having a technological edge. And like the Romans, they fight asymmetrically. They do not have the massive supercarriers we do, but they do have carrier killer ballistic missiles designed to ensure that our precious carriers do not dare come close enough to the PRC to get their air wings within striking distance. Basically, by being able to send one of these multibillion-dollar ships to the bottom with five thousand crewmen, they have effectively neutralized the Navy's foremost striking power for the price of a few rockets.

A quick and ugly conflict in the South China Sea that results in a PLAN victory is not going to cause a fundamental change in America. As we saw earlier with regard to the Romans, history demonstrates that great powers suffer disastrous defeats, recover, and go on without falling. But China's ambitions are not necessarily limited to hegemony in the western Pacific. After the humiliations of the last few centuries at the hands of the European imperialists, and taking into account Chinese nationalism born of pride in an ancient culture, there is a sense that now is China's time to take its rightful place as the preeminent nation on earth. Chinese students all know about the "War to Resist Americans and Aid Korea," and they not only think they won but that they were the good guys. In contrast, American students learn from their unionized public school teachers that their country was built on slavery. Maybe a few students have seen reruns of *M*A*S*H*. When they think of China, they think of how that's where iPhones come from.

The Chinese people are being prepared for China to displace the decadent and feeble United States, and the American people are likewise being prepared for China to displace the decadent and feeble United States.

The question is whether the Chinese Communist Party's goal would be to see the United States simply become a second-tier nation or something directly dominated by China. As a second-tier nation, America would still run its own affairs—as long as it did not cross China—and would merely lose its influence. But the PRC might not be able to live with that for long, because a second-tier nation might one day dream of returning to the first tier. Remember the Third Punic War and Cato the Elder's insistence that Carthage be destroyed. Carthage had been beaten already, but that was not enough.

The United States might well enter second-tier status through its own mismanagement and profligacy. China might well make a play to dislodge the dollar as the world's reserve currency and otherwise leverage its control over resources to take America down a peg. Would America resist this economic warfare? A country whose elite has grave doubts about its own legitimacy is vulnerable to a confident and assertive opponent. One strategy for China is simply to allow the current trends to play out, and in a couple decades America would find itself displaced and impotent. It would fall, relatively gently, and continue on in a recognizable but weaker form.

Or China could strike and make the fall happen much sooner. As we have seen, a naval defeat in the western Pacific alone, whether in one battle or a short war, is probably not sufficient to create the kind of fundamental transformation of the kind we have been considering. A defeat along the lines of the Japanese defeat in World War II, which led to the fall of the imperial system and a transformation into a very different country (militarily, economically, politically, and even culturally), might. But could China pull off that kind of comprehensive victory?

America did. Japan collapsed before the first American set foot on mainland Japanese territory and the USS *Missouri* slipped into Tokyo Bay to receive the surrender. It would not necessarily require the storming of the city walls and the salt-sowing of the destruction of Carthage.

China is building hypersonic missiles that can strike throughout the continental United States. It is important to remember that this is nothing new. Since the late 1950s, the Russians have had their missile fleet aimed at the U.S. homeland. Those of us who grew up before the

Berlin Wall fell remember the feeling of having a thermonuclear gun to our head. The kids today do not have that feeling, but the Russian gun is still right there at our temple. Now there's a Chinese one aimed at the other temple. Our very limited missile defenses are mostly designed to take down intercontinental ballistic missiles from rogue states like North Korea or, if Biden's track record of failure holds, Iran. They don't work against hypersonic weapons.

The hypersonic weapons give the PRC the ability to conduct a first strike on our missile fields in North Dakota and elsewhere, and to take out our much-shrunken bomber leg of the triad too. The problem is that they come so fast that they abbreviate the decision cycle for a counterstrike. The attack warning comes, and there are only a few minutes to get the National Command Authority (NCA) go-ahead to launch. The current NCA is Joe Biden. This is a man who spends a good deal of his day looking for his lost slipper. Yes, he could probably handle the deliberations necessary to choose between a rerun of *Matlock* and *Murder, She Wrote*, but who would trust him with making a quick decision about launching nuclear weapons?

Unfortunately, millions of American voters did. And the Chinese have got to be wondering what the hell they were thinking.

With the hypersonics inbound, it is use-them-or-lose-them for the land and air legs of the triad. Lose them and that leaves the sea leg, the boomers. The *Ohio*-class missile submarines number fourteen, with twenty-four Trident D5 missiles with at least four hydrogen bombs each. Not all are on patrol at all times, however. The good thing about the subs is they can hide in the oceans undetected—we hope. If the Chinese find them, adios to the third and last leg. But technology might provide a way to find them. So might cyber warfare that breaks into American computer systems and retrieves the deployed subs' locations.

If the Chinese can strip away America's nuclear force, then it is game over. The same with a set of nuclear detonations that fry our above-ground electric grid with electromagnetic pulses and set us back two hundred years. Either way, they would be in charge, and if the surviving Americans get uppity, well, then an American city turns to glass as a lesson in the price of resistance.

But the Chinese would not want to roll those dice; the stakes are too high if they fail to take out all our nuclear assets. Instead, their play would most likely be an asymmetrical attack on the homeland designed to embed Chinese influence in the United States government.

Cyber, as discussed above, provides one of many asymmetrical capabilities that the enemy could leverage on the United States. Everything works on connected computers in the United States—logistics, health, finance, manufacturing, everything. If you imagine that the Chinese have not comprehensively indexed our key points of vulnerability, you might believe Swalwell scored with Fang Fang because of his sexy good looks and winning smile. You cannot go a week without some ramshackle bunch of punks in the suburbs of Moscow injecting ransomware into the computer system of some big company or institution that should have known better than to be vulnerable. Imagine what the PRC's legions of hacker could do once given the green light.

Other tools include anti-satellite weapons. The bad guys already have them. How much of daily life today relies on Global Positioning System (GPS) satellites in medium Earth orbit? Most of it. Ditto all our communications and a host of other capabilities we take for granted. America is not hardened. Spoiled by nearly a century of unchallenged dominance, we have created a Garden of Eden. We just never thought to build a figurative (or literal) wall around it.

They have human capabilities too, unlike us. Our glorious intelligence community saw its entire China network rolled up a few years ago—it's not clear exactly how that happened—and there is no reason to believe we have rebuilt it. The Chinese tend to shoot spies. Chinese spies here tend not to get shot, and many eagerly play the racism card against a credulous Uncle Sucker. China's human assets are not only the Chinese sleeper agents and spies that infest our institutions but the Americans already bought by Beijing. When a crisis arises, they will act. The sleepers will awaken and cause chaos where they have been planted. The collaborators are more insidious; using a willing media and supported by fellow travelers, they would pressure the U.S. government to drop its defenses and accept the new status quo.

With the lights out, nothing moving, no water or food flowing, and a bunch of establishment voices demanding that they "negotiate" and "compromise" with the Chinese, what does a senile Joe Biden or an utterly incompetent buffoon like Kamala Harris do?

Whatever Xi tells them to do.

Perhaps he demands close oversight immediately, and decides to rule not through lackeys holding the old constitutional offices but with a governor for China's newest province. Or perhaps he is kind enough to let us maintain what remains of our republic, though with an acknowledgment of Chinese hegemony. In that Hong Kong scenario, Xi promises we can go on running our own affairs. He just alters the deal when it suits him, and warns us to pray he does not alter it any further.

The scenario is scary because it is so manifestly plausible. China does intend to displace America. Our current ruling class is composed of the corrupt and the clownish, and usually both at once. Our country is not hardened in terms of infrastructure or, more importantly, attitude. We have not been threatened, really threatened, in so long that it is hard to make the mental leap and accept the hardships that come with understanding that there are bad people out there who wish us ill, not the least of whom is a communist dictator with a creepy resemblance to Winnie the Pooh.

But the scenario is not hopeless. We made the mistake of thinking that Japan was invincible a generation ago and failed to look closer at its vulnerabilities. China seems mighty in part because it has built up its capabilities in recent years, but also because our own leadership's failures have been so frequent. Yet China has problems too, big ones.

First, it is a communist dictatorship. In the short term, that is an advantage because it allows for centralization of political and economic power to focus on supporting the junta's objectives. In America, we fight among ourselves about policy, and our business leaders are usually focused on maximizing their individual, as opposed to collective, self-interest. That often causes chaos in the short term. But over the long term, the calculus changes. The ability to mobilize a nation toward one single objective only lasts for a while. You can only suppress dissent for so long. We saw over thirty years ago what happened at Tiananmen Square. Is it likely that after three decades of exposure to the rest of the world, which is much freer than China, the Chinese people have become less aware that they are subjects?

The Chi Coms make no bones about the exchange they offer their people—freedom for stability and prosperity. Sure, you can buy people off for a while, trading them material comfort in return for submission, but in an aging dictatorship, you can only keep rival power bases suppressed for a while. With Xi consolidating power and showing no signs of departing the stage, even within the CCP you will see the pressure building as upward mobility slows and stops. With no way to advance within the party (because old men are holding all the plum spots), you will naturally see attempts to advance outside of the party course of honor. Palace intrigue in China is nothing new, nor are mass revolts.

People will suck up this reality for a while if they are getting rich, and many have gotten rich. But most have not. The wealth disparities are striking, and this has always caused unrest in Chinese history—the communists made much of the oppression by landlords and landowners. So, you have a people culturally sensitive to this phenomenon now staring it in the face again. For every Jack Ma, there are a hundred thousand construction workers, sweatshop drones, or wet-market bat wranglers.

Xi must keep delivering prosperity, and that means Xi must keep delivering growth. But economies cannot boom forever, and a bust creates the chance that these other tensions will explode. We are more frequently seeing economic panics and scares in China, especially in the massively overbuilt real estate market. COVID-zero policies that lock down cities do not help either. The government seems to have been able to keep the defaults from spinning out of control, but while a communist dictatorship can dictate a lot, it cannot dictate a good economy forever.

Perhaps a permanent mercantilist system of extracting and repatriating wealth from abroad can ameliorate the risk. With its Belt and Road Initiative, that is what China seems to be aiming at. It arguably has one in the form of the massively unequal trade with the United States. China has become America's outsourced fabrication facility. But what if that stops? What happens if a populist president slaps a 25 percent tariff on everything made in China as a way to repatriate our manufacturing base? What if we get cagey about our debts? America and China are tied together economically, all right, but the relationship brings to mind the old saw about borrowers and debtors. If you owe the bank $10,000, you have a problem. If you owe the bank $1,000,000, the bank has a problem.

And speaking of problems with collecting on loans, what happens when the Third World borrowers China has been shoveling billions to in an effort to buy influence and power decide "Nah" when those notes come due? Is Xi going to repossess Burkina Faso and auction it at the courthouse?

You also have a problem if you invested billions in real estate in the United States, since it is really hard to pick it up and take it home if the Americans decide to expropriate it from their enemy. Chinese economic entanglement with the United States is a two-edged sword, and it could cut the Chinese badly if swung. The Chinese need the American market, meaning Americans to buy their goods, and this is one reason the hyped electromagnetic pulse issue is perhaps overwrought. Putting aside that we are probably still competent enough to return the favor and wipe out all of China's electronics with our own high-altitude nuclear detonations, the last thing China wants is America mired in a new Dark Ages unable to buy its junk. Think of the PRC as Cleavon Little in *Blazing Saddles*, holding his six-gun to his own head to escape being lynched by the residents of Rock Ridge, who are like the Americans fretting over the threat of an EMP attack warning, "He's not bluffing! He's crazy enough to do it!"

But does America even need to have China make all its stuff? We could build new factories, but could the PRC get a new market for its stuff? A break with China would be a big economic problem for America, but for China it could be terminal. America can likely weather an economic storm, because a good economy is not the cork in the bottle of social unrest in the U.S.A. We understand we are promised freedom, not perpetual good times. But for China, it is the opposite. Their social contract demands serfdom for financial security. And if that social contract gets breached, China has a problem. China has quite a history of rebellions—its leaders are terrified of civil unrest. That's why they sent tanks into Tiananmen Square instead of waiting until the protesters got bored and went home.

194 WE'LL BE BACK

Moreover, there are other social currents at play in China. They say hard times make hard men, who make good times, which makes soft men, who then make hard times. China is hitting the soft-man phase. Rising prosperity and the smaller families under the one-child policy designed to fight overpopulation (it was a disaster, and the PRC ended it in 2015) have created a significantly softer young generation. Don't look for these guys to get up from their video games to take another Long March any time soon. The *Study Times*, a government publication, warned, "Soldiers from the one-child generations are wimps who have absolutely no fighting spirit." The party recently directed that broadcasters must "resolutely put an end to sissy men and other abnormal esthetics."

It's never good when you have to launch a campaign to butch up your populace. While America's naval traditions might not be decisive in an actual conflict, they can be revitalized with a refocused leadership that tosses out the woke nonsense and focuses on warfighting. And while you do not want to rely on an enemy's ineptitude, the PLAN has not demonstrated that it understands how to operate all those new frigates and cruisers in a complex combat environment, something that America at least has a record of excelling at within living memory.

The Chinese themselves are worried about it. Not one Chinese soldier currently serving has fought in a war. Most senior American soldiers and plenty of enlisted troops have—though that assumes they learned the right lessons, something that is not at all certain. Combined arms operations—integrating various battlefield operating systems from various branches of the military—is extremely difficult. The Chinese have never had to do it with lead flying. America has, a lot. Though the Chinese are cunning enough to try to erase that advantage asymmetrically by using electronic warfare and cyber to disrupt the communications that make our joint operations possible, stopping us from doing it does not help them to do it for themselves.

They have a nice new military, but how will it work in action? American equipment is, at least, battle-tested in large part. This is not true of the Chinese arsenal. America has its military corruption issues, especially in procurement. But so do the Chinese, much bigger ones, and not just in terms of bribes related to equipment and supplies. There is also massive bribery within the PLA ranks, including the selling of ranks. Of course, American officers now buy their ranks by selling their souls to the false god of wokeness, so maybe all this is a wash.

And America may have more up its sleeve. Remember all those unidentified flying objects the Navy recently released footage of shadowing our warships and warplanes, often in U.S. military training areas? Are they aliens? Probably not. Are they Chinese or Russian? Doubtful. Are they... ours? America was unaware of the F-117 stealth fighter until after it was deployed during the Panama invasion in 1989. Who knows what else we have up our sleeves at Edwards Air Force Base and Groom Lake, a.k.a. Area 51?

Yes, our infrastructure has a lot of vulnerabilities to Chinese cyberattacks, but we have quite a cyber right hook of our own. Moreover, the U.S.A. gets the cream of the crop worldwide moving here to help. And China has plenty of fat, juicy cyber targets itself. Think of the havoc an American electronic attack on the systems controlling the massive Three Gorges Dam could wreak.

What is required is America's taking seriously the threat and taking precautions to mitigate our most dangerous exposure. Obviously, that means we need to elect an essentially serious leader instead of having a glorified sock puppet who calls a daily lid at 11:00 a.m. every day so he can nap. And that's when he's not back in Delaware, likely getting reinvigorating transfusions of the blood of children.

The fact that our current president is unfit to lead provides Xi a dilemma. If he acts now to seize Taiwan, or perhaps even to knock America out of its place as the leader of the world, he faces an inept opponent who may not resist at all. But Xi must balance that against the fact that it is uncertain whether his forces have the power to confront America at this moment should Biden choose to resist. And whoever follows the senile commander in chief is almost certain to be more dangerous to Xi's plans.

So what would it look like, worst case, if China acted?

Upon the first missile warning, the USS Ronald Reagan went to general quarters, along with its escorts, as it cruised north of the Philippines in international waters. The combat information center (CIC) reported the flash traffic to the captain, who was sipping black coffee out of his "THE CAPTAIN" mug on what had been an ordinary day.

He had no orders yet to launch a retaliatory strike with his air wing, but that would have been a secondary consideration anyway. The first priority was to defend his ship from the DF-21 ballistic missiles launched from the mainland that the air defense system computers calculated were coming their way. Off his bow on either side were a fleet of destroyers, cruisers, and other warships that filled out Carrier Strike Group 5, but the Chi Coms were not going to be targeting those. It was the carrier that was the enduring symbol of American power, and its F/A-18 and F-35 fighters made it more than just a symbol.

The huge ship was maneuvering now, though it was unclear how much that would help. An ensign said something like "INDOPACOM reports that the PLAN is moving on Taiwan," but while that provided some context it did not provide any assistance in his current situation.

It was really up to the Aegis missile cruisers and destroyers. The USS Antietam *was on its last deployment, being scheduled to go into the Fleet Reserve upon return to the United States. But the Navy had spent some money on it for this last run in upgrading it to fire the RIM-161 Standard Missile 3 (SM-3) missile; with luck, it might even be able to take down a DF-21.*

The AN/SPY-1 radar identified the three targets burning in from above and generated attack solutions against the missiles. The captain of the Reagan *looked over to the starboard and saw the deck of* Antietam *suddenly engulfed with white smoke as the SM-3s shot skyward one after the other. More missiles launched off the* Chancellorsville *on his port side—maybe it was overkill, but missiles were expensive, while a carrier and its crew of five thousand were priceless.*

"One hit!" someone from the CIC shouted. "Two inbound!"

The captain's face displayed no emotion as the men cheered around him.

"Two, that's two!" came over the speaker.

The captain allowed himself a sigh.

"Wait, there's—"

The captain saw a flash of white, not even a cognizable shape but more of a streak coming down from the sky into the middle of the flight deck and disappearing into a black hole.

Then the explosion came, orange and black, throwing the captain off his feet and scattering his sailors across the bridge. The noise was indescribable, the boom and the shearing and breaking of metal. Klaxons sounded and the radio chatter died as the power went out.

The captain struggled to his feet, pulling himself up to look down through the bridge window at the orange fireball erupting out of the hole blasted outward from below. The flight deck was eerily empty—every man and aircraft on it had been blown away into the ocean like leaves in a wind. The flames were at his height now, feeding on fuel and ammo below.

There was no question that the USS Ronald Reagan *was out of this war; the only question was whether he could save it from sinking.*

The lights in Los Angeles flickered and went out. The citizens grumbled, muttering about their useless governor whom 60 percent of them had nevertheless voted to keep in office. His green energy policies had shut down the reliable sources of power for the state, making blackouts more common than they had been in decades. Most people thought nothing of it, assuming it would come back in a few minutes, until they noticed their cell phones were out too. The texts worked though. And even when the reports of the war in the western Pacific came through via people texting one another, few people thought to wonder why the Chinese would take down American communications but leave the text system up.

Later, they understood one reason the Chinese cyberattack had left the text system untouched. Everyone began receiving texts such as: "Attention! The people of the People's Republic of China have no quarrel with their friends the American people. Your warlike leaders have launched an unprovoked attack upon the PRC. Demand that they negotiate in good faith to stop the conflict before the PRC is forced to exercise its full might!"

Captain Eric Han of the United States Air Force showed his ID, and the security police waved him past the crush of vehicles at the gate to Whiteman Air Force Base. A graduate of the Air Force Academy, Han's parents had been living near San Francisco when he was born in the late-1990s, meaning he was a U.S. citizen. His father was an executive with an import-export company, and his mother stayed home to raise the children. Besides Eric, one brother was a nuclear research scientist at Lawrence Livermore Laboratory, and his sister was a programmer with Google. None had any trouble getting a security clearance, as none had ever been in any kind of trouble, and by then their parents had obtained U.S. citizenship themselves. Their mother was a true "tiger mother," refusing to accept anything but straight As (both Han's siblings went to Berkeley), demanding they excel in extracurricular activities, and inculcating in them a deep and abiding patriotism.

But that patriotism was to the People's Republic of China, their true country.

Being assigned to Whiteman Air Force Base in Missouri as an operations officer (Han's eyes were not good enough for him to fly) was perfect. He had occasional contact with classified material, but was heedful of his instructions to do nothing that might bring him under suspicion. Rise in the ranks, he was directed by his mother, who never said it but who Han believed was an officer in the Ministry of State Security (MSS). Over the years in the USAF, he had encountered several other sons and daughters of PRC immigrants. Nothing was ever spoken, but they always extended him career assistance.

The text he received tonight would change everything. Obviously, the Chinese attack on U.S. naval forces in the western Pacific and the cyberattacks across the country meant war, or at least a brief skirmish. According to the news, the USS Reagan *was on the verge of sinking, and if that happened the United States might not be able to back down in the face of China's public demand, delivered though the Xinhua New China News Agency, for "a truce and negotiations to settle the new allocation of power following America's unprovoked aggression."*

He was waved through the base's internal checkpoints by security police in full battle rattle and parked at the spot at the far end of the lot overlooking—through a chain-link fence with a sign warning,

"AIRFIELD—NO ADMITTANCE—DEADLY FORCE AUTHORIZED"—the long tarmac. Down by the aircraft bunkers there was a whirlwind of lights as the crews prepped the base's prized aircraft.

He counted six aircraft, B-2 Spirit bombers being prepared about a quarter mile away down the tarmac. There were twenty left in the USAF inventory, as one had crashed in 2008. With their stealth technology, decades-old but updated since, these craft could penetrate enemy air defense systems and take the war to the Chinese homeland. That was what they were being prepared for now, and that was what could not be allowed to happen.

He got out and went around to the trunk of his Camry. Inside was a nearly four-foot-long bolt-action rifle with a large scope and a box of .50 caliber ammunition. He had known this was a possibility, but even when he bought the Barrett Model 99 and later practiced with his American "friends" at the range on weekends, he never really thought it would come to this. Yet it had, and Captain Han did not shirk his duty when the coded text came through. He took the rifle and ammunition to the hood of his sedan, loaded it, and placed the crosshairs on the engine cowling of the first B-2. The report was like a thunderclap. He pulled back the bolt and ejected the shell, then slid in another. He settled the crosshairs on the next aircraft and fired. When he had fired on the sixth aircraft, he then returned to the first one. The half-inch round would do incredible damage to whatever it hit, and B-2s were notoriously delicate. They did not explode or catch fire. The rounds just tore apart their innards.

He kept firing even as the blue and white security police SUVs roared towards him. He had been an investment by the MSS over the last three decades, one that they had hoped would pay off when he pinned on general's stars. But the elimination of 30 percent of America's strategic stealth bomber fleet was an even greater payoff.

The president seemed even more confused than usual, sitting at the head of the White House bunker's situation room before a bank of video monitors. His national security advisor (NSA) explained again.

"The Taiwan government has ordered its forces to cease resistance to the invasion, sir."

The president stared, uncomprehending. "I'd like some soup," he said.

The NSA licked his lips. "Sir, Taiwan has surrendered."

"Surrendered?" demanded the president. "What about our Navy?"

"Sir, the chairman says we have to pull back to the east and get out of range of their missiles. We do not have enough forces left to continue this fight." What the NSA did not explain was that the Reagan was dead in the water, that a dozen smaller ships had been sunk with massive loss of life, and that Kadena Air Force Base on Okinawa was out of operation due to ballistic missile attacks. American Ohio-class cruise missile subs—boomers converted to fire waves of conventional missiles from underwater—had launched strikes of their own, but with most of the satellites down it was impossible to get solid battle damage assessments. With much of the bomber fleet out of action, that was probably the last arrow in America's conventional quiver.

"I want to talk to Xi," demanded the president. "He knows me. We can talk this out."

In fact, the Chinese had demanded that the president get on the line with the general secretary of the Chinese Communist Party Xi

Jinping, but the White House staff had decided not to tell the president for fear that he would order them to put the enemy leader through. The president was…not prepared for that kind of face-to-face encounter.

"Sir, I recommend we accept that the conventional war is over and focus domestically. Water and power are out in all major cities; it's essentially Chinese ransomware," the NSA said. An aide came in and shook his head. The vice president was not coming to the situation room. Apparently, she had decided she wanted nothing to do with this disaster. Yet, she was the only possible alternative to a president who was manifestly unfit to handle the unfolding crisis.

"Can I get some soup?" the president yelled to no one in particular.

"Mr. President, I need your authorization for the secretary of state to communicate with the Chinese government."

"Yes, we should talk. Work this out. Maybe get my son involved. He knows the Chinese very well."

The NSA ignored that tangent, and would have even if that son had not been arrested wandering nude though New York City high on something thirty-six hours ago. This latest embarrassment was yet another thing he had kept from the commander in chief.

"I will tell the secretary that he is authorized to talk to the Chinese government," the NSA said, making sure the aide keeping the minutes noted the president's approval. Whatever happened was going to be historic, and he wanted to ensure that his own ass was fully covered for posterity.

"You do that. We need to work this out. Negotiate. I mean, a war is an environmental catastrophe," the president said. "You know, climate change?"

"Yes, Mr. President."

"Can I get some soup?"

"I ain't turning in my guns, and I ain't living as a Chinese slave," Abe Hanson had told the crowd in the Fort Wayne Veterans of Foreign Wars hall. Many of the audience cheered, but the actual veterans of foreign wars were a bit more circumspect. They had some idea of what the route they had chosen looked like.

Three months ago to the day, the president had gone on television to announce that the sudden war with China, which came out of the blue to most regular Americans, was over. The power came back on, and therefore the televisions, because the Chinese allowed it. The president did not say so, but his prepared script—which he had trouble reading off the teleprompter—made it clear that the Chinese still had their hands round America's throat, and that they were prepared to squeeze if defied.

"This new reality calls for new thinking," the president said, staring as if seeing the words for the first time. *"We need to cooperate with the People's Republic of China, to recognize its rights and dignity, and to understand and accept our own limitations and take responsibility for the wrongs and aggressions we have inflicted around the world. America must accept this new reality."*

It soon became clear what this *"new reality"* would be. America would be allowed to govern itself, in a fashion, but the guardrails were clear. China was calling the shots, couched as suggestions but not open to debate regardless, and America needed to accept its new status.

Many Americans, still under the impression that the Constitution was in effect, protested this arrangement. The "National Security Law" passed unanimously by the reconstituted Congress (many legislators were disqualified from service—the Chinese ambassador handed the Speaker and majority leader a list of those to be expelled) outlawed "misinformation, lies, and slanders regarding the United States or its allies, such as the People's Republic of China," and set appropriate sentences for such treasons. Dissent was no longer patriotic.

MSNBC and CNN slipped seamlessly into the new paradigm; in fact, it was hard to detect any change at all. Fox was removed from the airwaves, to the delight of controversial intern manager Joe Scarborough and others who were willing to toe the new party line. The FBI was enlisted to arrest troublemakers, a job it undertook with gusto. Camps for reeducating hooligans sprang up throughout the West.

Life got tougher for normal folks, who saw gas prices rise even more, but the Chinese were careful to ensure that the economy did not collapse. After all, America was a key market for Chinese goods, and at its suggestion, the new Congress imposed tariffs on all non-Chinese imports. To ensure that "disruptions" were minimized, unions were barred from striking without the permission of the government.

The large corporations adapted, and they were happy to work with the government to assure "market stability." Smaller companies found themselves at an even greater disadvantage than before; the new policy was that large entities were "more efficient" than a large number of smaller, harder-to-control ones.

In Hollywood and among the rich, little changed. Both groups were used to kowtowing to the Chi Coms (that term was banned as "disrespectful"), so both were allowed to continue the way they had before. "I love how America is now working with instead of against the Chinese government," hophead comic Seth Rogen announced on heavily regulated Twitter. However, when marijuana was recriminalized at the suggestion of the Chinese, who accurately assessed that pot "made workers dull and lethargic," he kept his fury to himself.

The order to turn in all firearms, cheered as long overdue by the largely unchanged ruling caste, met with immediate resistance. Some *of it was armed. Most was simply a refusal to comply. The Chinese were furious that the American government was only able to confiscate a minute number of weapons, and pushed for "sterner measures." The sterner measures led to stiffer resistance.*

"It's time to fight," Abe Hanson said, holding aloft his AR-15. And they would, for years, against collaborators and even Chinese forces sent in when the American security services could make no progress. They even fought on after the Chinese made an example of Oklahoma City; in fact, the rebels adopted the mushroom cloud as their symbol of vengeance against their hated foreign occupiers, and especially against the quislings who had once called themselves Americans.

CHAPTER TWELVE

BROKEN AND BARREN

We have seen some of the ways that America as we know it could end with a bang, but what if we choose to end it with a whimper? It is a choice, after all. What if we embrace decline and ride it like a toboggan all the way down to the bottom, where people are eating the zebras at the zoo like they do in Caracas?

Maybe, like old soldiers, we just fade away.

This is not outside the realm of possibility. Civilizations don't have to collapse violently. They can just crumble. If you look at Japan, they are on the verge of dying out. The Europeans are way below replacement level too. Even the French and Italians, famous for love, just aren't making it the way they used to—all that ennui is killing their sexy. America, especially after the COVID nonsense started, is at or below replacement level as well. The year 2021 saw the smallest organic population growth the country has ever experienced. If we were not importing, by choice or otherwise, zillions of Third World newcomers (formally invited or otherwise), we would be shrinking too.

What does it say about your civilization that a huge proportion of its members have little or no interest in whether it continues? Nothing good. It's the ultimate expression of existential exhaustion. There's just no will to go on. In Europe, they forgo kids and take their vacations in Ibiza on the beach in those creepy little thongs, then come home to Stuttgart and stare at the television until there's another vacation. That's not living. That's existing. But that's what a lot of people do.

They just are, and then when they aren't anymore, who cares?

And that leads to all sorts of other problems. Consider the trillions upon trillions in debt we have piled up. It's not for anything tangible. Even the trillion-dollar "infrastructure bills" include just a few bucks to fix some roads, but a bunch of free money to be spent on transitory nonsense like "tree equity" and appeasing angry weather gods. The left babbles about "investing" when it advocates running the printing presses, but an investment demands a return. What is the ROI on giving free money to layabouts? They just return for another handout.

By 2021, America was $30 trillion in debt. That's a lot of dough, 100 Elon Musks' worth. And if it's all owed then there is someone, somewhere, who wants it back. We can shuffle the decks and print some more dough, but eventually someone is going to say "Gimme," and the debtor is going to pull his pockets out, and then it's going to get real.

And it may get real sooner rather than later. In 2021, the effective interest rate on the national debt was something near zero. We still backed up figurative trucks of money to pay the interest load, but what if interest rates go to, say, 8 percent? Don't laugh—we are within living memory of 18 percent interest rates following Jimmy Carter, the Joe Biden of his time (albeit less senile and gropey). Imagine the entire current budget taken up by interest. Well, that might be a problem.

America's whole economic edifice could come down, and if it does, count on the whole world coming with it. We saw a preview in 2008 when a bunch of ruling-class types nearly managed to tip everything over. We actually got through it fairly easily—it was especially easy for the guys who caused it because they got bailed out—but it was a taste of the future. And despite that taste of the future, our appetite for budgetary junk food has only increased.

What do we get for the money? Is America still a shiny, modern exemplar for all mankind? Do you see $30 trillion in infrastructure out there? No, you see very little new being built and not enough old being fixed. Los Angeles today looks much like Los Angeles thirty years ago. Sure, there is a nice new convention center, but it is surrounded by homeless wandering around like the Monroeville Mall zombies in *Dawn of the Dead* (in which George Romero really called what is going on with our society between shots of heads detonating). There are some new skyscrapers and a subway too, but the city itself, including most buildings and (vitally) the freeways, is pretty much the same one that Bruce Willis saw when he looked out the window of the Nakatomi Tower (the old Fox building out in Century City) in 1988. And that's true all over the country.

We did not invest. We squandered our money, the fiscal equivalent of spending all our borrowed cash on hookers and blow.

We pay people not to work. We pay people to be here illegally. We pay people to get useless degrees. We pay schools not to teach kids. If they are government workers, we pay them a lot for their retirements.

We pay and pay and pay, and all we get is more people wanting more money for doing less.

It's quite scary what might happen when this whole house of cards comes tumbling down. It will happen, but who knows when? It might be five years, or it might be fifty years. But it will happen, unless someone along the way is willing either to pay it off—ha!—or accept the economic body blow of simply saying, "Hey, you know all that national debt? Sorry, whoever is currently holding it, because we are repudiating it." Talk about a moral hazard problem.

"Well, we just negated all the debt we owe. Now, please lend us more."

Of course, no one thinks that the bill will come due imminently. If they really did, they might act differently. The people voting for the people who perpetuate this insanity have it in their heads that they are not the ones who are going to have to pick up this check. One might think they would care that their kids will be, except there are a lot fewer people with kids now. Instead, we invite in foreigners without mentioning that they and theirs are going to get stuck with the bill. Surprise!

That kind of does serve the illegal aliens right, though.

Our fiscal profligacy is just one example of our societal apathy toward the future. Another is demonstrated by our declining adherence to religion. Much of Europe is essentially post-Christian. The churches are mostly empty; the beauty and glory of Christendom is a museum instead of a living faith. Notre Dame burned down, and it looks like it will be rebuilt not as a bastion of faith but as a local tourist attraction.

The churches themselves, outside of places like Poland, where they believe in something beyond soccer, are broken. The Church of England, for example, is a tired institution more concerned with the scripture of the modern woke than with the Word of Jesus. You get the impression the whole religion part of religion is something of an embarrassment to many of the people who have taken over the old institutional churches abroad and here in America as well. Priests and preachers fear to speak the Truth, instead waving it away as some sort of mere story that vaguely supports a watered-down catechism that boils down to "Love yourself and be nice and heed the com- mandments of your local diversity, equity, and inclusion consultant." The grace of God is replaced by the grace bestowed by the woke on the people most eagerly parroting their precepts. Of course, the woke do not bestow grace but damnation. They are the true fire-and- brimstone fundamentalists, and don't look to any mainline church to oppose them.

Millions grow up without faith, meaning the civilization is without faith. Christianity ignited the Renaissance and the Enlightenment (even if the institutions themselves were sometimes not big fans). Look at the great works of art, the ones you think of when you think of European history. *David*, the Sistine Chapel, a thousand others, all impossible without the Judeo-Christian tradition. Now think of something similarly great and transcendent created in the last century.

Keep thinking. Hard, huh?

Modernity is an artist-huckster mounting a urinal on a wall and watching the swells coo. That's Europe today and that's what America may become, something mundane and low. What you hear is the moaning of an exhausted civilization too tired to get out of bed.

But there is still energy in Europe, and in America.

There is the energy of Islam. On the day the United States military left Kabul in disgrace, a Taliban-oriented Twitter troll—and they say America accomplished nothing in its twenty-year war—by the name of "Malang Khosty" tweeted a particularly potent meme. The meaning was clear despite its grammatical shortcomings. On one side was the legend "America kids show," and on the other, "Muslims kids shows." Beneath the "America kids" label was a cartoon GIF lifted from Nickelodeon's "Blue's Clues Pride Parade Sing-Along." It fea- tures a smiling drag queen alligator waving a rainbow flag, and a pink dolphin with a little dolphin in some sort of LGBTQ march. Under the "Muslim kids" label was a GIF of a bunch of Saracen warriors on stallions charging the infidel crusaders.

It misses the point to observe that our Afghan enemies—and allies, for that matter—famously have their own sexual proclivities. What matters is the painful truth. American kids are growing up in a frivolous culture that leaves them utterly unprepared to exist in a world full of people who are many things, but not frivolous. The Muslim kids subjected to this propaganda are learning that their job is to defeat their enemy, an explicitly Christian one. Of course, no mainstream American cartoon would promote Jesus stuff; the Muslim kids' show features one of the fighters getting down for some prayer, presumably after vanquishing his Western foes. In a war between folks concerned with scimitars and those concerned with pronouns, bet on the ones who go with steel over stupidity.

Many of the peoples welcomed into Europe to do the jobs Europeans no longer wish to do brought with them that faith. We have seen decades of trouble with Islam's extreme forms. Islam itself is largely immune to the kind of establishment social contempt that Jewish and Christian communities face; the ruling caste is giddy at the chance to belittle both those religions, but its own code of behavior prevents it from doing the same to Muslims. Protected from the outright hatred of the elite, Islam has grown, and even its most radical adherents seem to get a pass. That is not as true in France, however, because the French are the French, and perhaps wokeness unacceptably limits the ability of the French to be rude to those they consider their inferiors, which is everyone.

There is still the energy of evangelism and true belief, as in the Orthodox Jewish communities and those of the non-mainline Christian sects. Battered by COVID, they still survive. Who thinks that the ability to break the habit of church attendance was not viewed as a welcome fringe benefit of lockdowns, which let liquor stores and strip clubs function even as the government aggressively closed temples and churches?

But could there be another Great Awakening, a wave of religious revival in America or even Europe? In past waves of Christian fervor, the society at least paid lip service to Christianity as the unofficial state religion, so it never really felt the current full-court press of government, media, Hollywood, and such all combining to resist religiosity. In the past, you would not be denied jobs or opportunities for being faithful, while we see that going on now. So a true religious revival would seem difficult. If it arose in America, perhaps we would see it in the rural and red areas. The idea of Jesus sweeping the blue cities seems hard to imagine, but with God all things are possible.

The fiscal insanity and the petering out of the teachings of Peter and Paul are, perhaps, symptoms of a greater problem. Perhaps our civilization is just exhausted.

We in the West had a good run for a couple thousand years. Sure, the exact power center moved from Rome to various European capitals to Britain to America, but it was always within the same context of what we call the West. The rest of the world followed our lead. What we did not conquer outright, we influenced and changed. Today, all cities look, basically, like Western cities. Most governments look like ours. The technology is ours. We won.

And perhaps that is the problem. What's the challenge left for the West in general and America in particular? The stars? Maybe, if we survive that long and work up the motivation to actually do it. But in a terrestrial sense, what is our purpose? Even a few generations ago there were places on the map that were essentially blank. No more. Every mountain has been climbed, every jungle trekked, every sea sailed. We are out of firsts. Instead of "The First Man to _____," maybe you get "The First Differently Abled Lesbian Hindu of Color to _____." That's not the same.

Where is the course of honor like the Romans had? You are a promising lad, and you go serve with the legions somewhere, then serve as a questor, then an aedile, then a praetor, then a consul. You see the world. You gain glory. But we are glory-free today. Military glory is out. The Romans had no shame in crushing an enemy, including an enemy whose only crime was that it had booty and vulnerability. We look upon military victory as, at best, a necessary evil. This idea of some triumphant American general marching his troops and his captured foes in chains down Pennsylvania Avenue, his face painted red and someone whispering "Remember, thou art mortal" in his ear, is inconceivable. At this juncture, the idea of a triumphant American general at all is hard enough to imagine.

Maybe you can be a TikTok star. Or a YouTube star. Or maybe get a reality show. This is what our people have instead of glory, and no wonder we are failing.

We despise the values and attributes that bring glory. Masculinity is toxic, we have learned from toxic feminists whose miserable, frivolous existence would be impossible in a world not created by "toxic males" and defended by "toxic males" from males who actually are toxic.

Aggression, risk-taking, and stubborn independence are, when controlled and utilized by disciplined people, the keys to greatness. They are also beaten out of our kids in government schools run by government employees who hate the way masculinity creates dominant men rather than submissive neuters. Our kids are told that to fight back against a bully is the same crime as bullying itself, and they are punished instead of rewarded for standing up to evil. The warrior spirit is relegated to a few select castes—cops, soldiers—who do the dirty jobs society needs done and often get grief for it. But for the rest, the warrior spirt is verboten. Leave it to the professionals. Don't be a vigilante. Why would you need a gun? That's for government-controlled specialists, not mere citizens!

No wonder our young men retreat to the virtual world of first-person shooter video games where they can, at last, be what every man truly wants to be and should be allowed to be—a hero.

No wonder the elite wants to take those away too for fostering violent impulses and leading to bad thoughts.

Our society is dying out for lack of families. Maybe when we tell men not to be men we should not be surprised when they aren't. And isn't it interesting that where we see big families—or at least lots of children—it is often in explicitly religious communities, or in other communities where masculinity is celebrated? Evangelicals tend to breed. Football players, who battle for our amusement, often seem to have scores of kids (not necessarily via traditional families), as do gang members who fight and die according to a twisted male code. The men who don't? The urban metrosexuals who have never gotten in a fistfight.

The cultural war on men includes the war on gender identity. Those who wage it would love to eliminate the whole idea of men, and they are doing a fair job of it. But lurking outside our ridiculous society are men who have no intention of becoming neutered. They cannot be shamed into submission. Once we have ruined our men, they will slip in to fill the void, and that will not be pretty.

Women fare no better in our society. Young women are told by all the smart people to prioritize their careers during their years of greatest fertility. These biological clock–deniers are the same people who tell them to believe in "science." A huge number of women spend the years when their bodies were meant to be reproducing going into debt for a college degree and then toiling away for corporations, as if Goldman Sachs or General Motors will be there for them at their bedside when they are eighty-seven. By the time they decide to have kids, they might be able to squeeze out two before the alarm goes off, if they are lucky. If they aren't, they find that "their body, their choice" actually means their body makes the choice, and they ran out the clock.

Or they just decide not to reproduce, either because they can't find a worthy man or because a kid would cramp their style. And kids do cramp your style. There's no doubt about that. Raising kids is a succession of wonderful moments—when they get out of diapers, when they don't need a babysitter, when they can finally drive themselves places. But a society where people refuse to undertake the hassle of having kids is a society that is going to die out.

The multiple trends that lead to slow decline—economic malaise, cultural exhaustion, and the infusion of outsiders—are not unusual or unprecedented. Rome finally fell—the big fall, with the subsequent Dark Ages—after these trends had gone on for hundreds of years. The fall of the Roman Empire did not happen quickly, and there were tentative comebacks when decent emperors started putting things back in order, only for the trends to continue over time. Rome debased its currency and Rome stopped expanding. It became stagnant, inwardly focused, with people competing over dividing up the scraps instead of creating or conquering anything new.

The Romans themselves just stopped being Romans. Rome even stopped being Rome—the capital in Italy was moved to Ravenna. The real power was far to the east in Constantinople. At the end, the western empire that had ruled most of the known world was in chaos, with its re-barbarizing population living off the corpse of what came before. The legions were manned by people who did not necessarily speak Latin; at the end, some German warlord simply plucked the final emperor—ironically named Romulus Augustulus—off the throne and that was that. Rome did not fall as much as it faded away.

So what happens to America if this is our fate too?

Perhaps we muddle through when the accountants have their revenge and all that public debt comes due. But it is hard to see the economic system surviving that and becoming more efficient and prosperous. Instead, the answer is likely to be what the answer from our garbage ruling class always is—more power to them. The free market will get the blame, as if our corporatist economy can truly be called one today, and so the economy will go under tighter control of the very people responsible for the sorry state we are in. The prosperity we experienced at America's peak will fall out of living memory. People will not know a time when the supply chain worked, or when you could get rich, or at least prosper, if you worked hard. As in the seventies, America will just stumble on, poorer and without hope of renewal.

Socially, the ruling class—left to its own devices—is unlikely to gather the will to make the changes necessary to avoid the civilizational exhaustion we face. It will not come to a consensus that we need to return to a dynamic society that builds and creates. Dynamism implies change, and the people in charge do not want change. The status quo may not be optimal, but that is not their criteria. Their own power is. It is better to rule a fading nation than to risk being ousted as the leadership clique of a vibrant one.

Moreover, in the absence of actual religion, we have a leadership class that believes in its own secular myths. To change course from "Men are just girls with penises, though of course women can have penises too if they want them" to "Men need to be men" would just be too great of a leap. The same with women. Imagine a conscious attempt to return society to a pro-fecundity model. Not only are all the cultural messages the opposite, but our society is designed to facilitate the opposite. At eighteen, when women are entering their prime childbearing years, we take four years right off the top for college. At least at one time, college was where people met their mates—the Mrs. Degree was a thing. But if you get engaged before getting your diploma today your peers will think you are at a minimum insane, and possibly seditious. Next, they are expected to go out into the workforce, and they have to. Those college loans for that Marxist pottery degree have got to be serviced. Even if you did get married, where would you live to raise kids? You can't afford a house. There are no starter houses anymore.

And who would you date? Some man-child who lives in a world of video games and internet porn? Only a madman would try to date someone at work these days, so where does a nice girl meet a guy? Online? It's too easy to swipe left—thanks to dating apps, we are a society of first impressions. When they interact electronically, women and men do not get the chance to rethink their first impression. It empowers unreasonable, bright-line rules. Not over six feet tall? Swipe. Not a great job? Swipe. Photo not quite hot enough? Swipe. It's like all of America's dating scene now is as shallow as Los Angeles's in the nineties.

But this presumes a desire to create families, and that presumes a desire for more than just the next bender or the next promotion or the next vacation to some adults-only resort. Where would that come from? In a late-stage civilization, the goal is just to keep existing. But to recreate a vibrant civilization and snap out of decline, you would need a societal purpose.

How would that get turned around? Perhaps it could be, but it would take a grassroots movement, like a Great Awakening, because it could certainly never be imposed from on high by the current elite. We will discuss that later, but in the meantime, what would this fading away look like in practice?

Britney lived with her cats in Chicago, and on June 13, 2062, she celebrated Mr. Fiddles's seventh birthday. Her other cats, Romeo and Socrates, watched her light the candles on his cake. She had bought them little hats, which was quite a sacrifice since her Social Security payments did not go very far at all.

Her bachelor's degree hung on the wall, and there were pictures of her and her friends out partying back in the twenties. She had had a career as a diversity consultant for a number of different companies, retiring recently after the last one went out of business. Now she read a lot and spent time with her pets. She used to keep up on current events, but it was exhausting. All the news was bad.

On June 15, 2062, she tripped over Mr. Fiddles and hit her head on the edge of her coffee table. She bled out, and when the police—warned of a smell by a neighbor—did a welfare check a week later, the cats had eaten a good part of her body. It was the second one of these cases the cops had seen in the last week.

CHAPTER THIRTEEN

THE AUTHORITARIAN TEMPTATION

But maybe America will not go quietly, slowly dying out and leaving no one to bury its corpse. Maybe there will be a backlash.

If America is to continue as a going concern, there are three options for its future, just three:

1. America embraces the Constitution and returns to being a republic with some democratic characteristics such that all Americans can participate in their own governance, and which once again zealously defends and promotes basic natural rights of the type set forth in the Bill of Rights.
2. The right controls America.
3. The left controls America.

Option 1 is the preferred option, and we will get to that shortly. Option 3 is the option that our current establishment has selected and which it is trying to make a reality. As we have seen, this is unacceptable to those of us who are not leftists, which is the vast majority of us.

Which leaves Option 2.

We want Option 1, we won't accept Option 3, but we could live with Option 2 if we had to.

What would this Option 2 be like? What happens when the right controls America, and not in some apologetic way where it tries to build bridges and sing "Kumbaya" and generally return to normalcy, whatever that means? No, we are talking about right-wing control where the agenda is the conservative wish list and there is no stopping it. Checks and balances—adios! This is about wielding will and power—the will and then power to enact and run things the way liberals only dream of in their nightmares.

First, we should figure out what to call this vision of an unapologetic right-wing America. Uncompromising right-wing control of the country would imply that we Americans have given up on restoring America to what it was and are seeking something new. Like the old Roman Republic—or even the Old Republic in the insufferable post-1983 *Star Wars* movies—the old American republic would be replaced by something different that responds to the weaknesses and failures of the past paradigm. Does this constitute a "fall" in the sense that what comes after it is something, in the words of Woody Allen describing his bizarre transformation of a minor Japanese gangster pic into the brilliant dubbed comedy *What's Up, Tiger Lily*, "wholly other"?

Probably not. When the Roman Republic "fell" after a century in free fall, Augustus did not announce, "Hey, we're now an empire and I am the king of the empire—I guess that would be the 'emperor.' Yeah, I'm that." In fact, there was no word for "empire" or "emperor." Augustus would have been hailed as *imperator*, but that venerable

title regularly went to victorious Roman generals and did not necessarily mean the head of state. Of course, Augustus was not really a
victorious general himself—his pal Agrippa usually did the general-ing
for his sickly buddy and was happy to play second fiddle to the
adopted son of newly minted god Julius Caesar.

What Augustus did, and what is important to understand about
a scenario where the right wing unapologetically assumes total control, was not draw a bright line between the past paradigm and the
new reality. Historians did that later. He did not dismiss the Senate
and sit inside a palace, surrounded by courtiers, issuing commands.
When he granted an audience, he did not demand that petitioners
grovel and kiss the hem of his purple robes. That only came into
fashion a few hundred years later, starting in 284 under Diocletian.
On the surface, Augustus changed nothing.

Well, except for making himself the First Citizen, the *princeps*.
This changed everything. The institution became known as the *principate*, and the *princeps* was basically an emperor in terms of raw
power, but Augustus and the rulers that followed were careful to
observe the traditions and institutions of the old republic. There were
senators, whom Augustus pretended to listen to as they droned on,
and there were consuls, whom he picked (and, occasionally, he picked
himself). The not-emperor (wink, wink) worked through a simulacrum of the old *mos maiorum* institutions in a simulacrum of the
republic.

But the change was real and the change was permanent. Everyone
knew it, too. There were occasional mutterings about restoring the
republic during the early *principate*, but that usually came to naught.
When Caligula got knifed by one of his soldiers whom he had publicly
humiliated—probably not a great idea to insult the guys around you
who have weapons—there was a short window where some folks tried
to go back to the old ways. But the Praetorian Guard liked the new

ways, since a savvy *princeps* paid them well and did not insult them publicly, and the guys with the swords told the guys with the togas, "No, here's Claudius, and we know he's deformed but he's *princeps* now and you guys probably want to confirm our choice right now."

When the choice was the old republic and a *gladius* through your liver, or Claudius and business as (now) usual, the senators chose expedience over nostalgia. Probably a wise choice.

So, we are not talking about some right-wing ruler (or junta) announcing that America is now an empire and he's the emperor, any more than a left-wing ruler or junta would announce that America is now the United Soviet States of America and we now have a chairman. Likely he would rule through the current institutions. He would just have absolute control over the institutions, free of those nagging checks and balances that make governing such a hassle. There would be elections, but there are elections in North Korea and Chicago too. Likely, we would have the same country name—the United States of America—but a very different country.

The presidency, by its unitary status, would be the focus, and we would expect the ruler to occupy that position. He would effectively control the Congress and the courts as well. He would do it as head of a party—in this scenario, likely the Republican Party, but there is a small chance a new one might rise up to fill the role of the party of the right. In that way, he would seem, superficially, to be just a really successful politician. His commands would not be anything so vulgar as orders and decrees. They would be carefully and deliberately enacted through the processes outlined in the Constitution. Things would simply always turn out how he wanted them to turn out.

His rise would come as the result of a backlash against the left, and it would be propelled by a sense that the institutions, left to their own devices, would frustrate the true intent of the framers and the people. He would call himself the restorer of American democracy (which sounds better to American ears than "restorer of the republic," even if not technically correct). He would observe the rituals and symbols of the old United States, yet his reign would be distinguished by the unbridled use of his power. He would ignore the norms and unofficial rules of American politics that have so far restrained the conservatives but, to their mind, not the left. Checks and balances? Nah, it's an emergency. We'll get back to having those later.

And later never comes. His supporters would see him as cutting through the obstacles to enact the necessary reforms to restore America to greatness. His opponents would call him an authoritarian. And they might have a point.

Now, their promiscuous use of language in the past would definitely raise the specter of Chicken Little. They called Trump an "authoritarian" throughout his tenure, and it is truly hard to seriously apply that title to The Donald. Trump respected the institutions, unlike many of his supporters. He proposed laws, got many passed, and mostly undid executive orders of other presidents as opposed to issuing a flurry of decrees of his own. When the courts shot down his actions, he acquiesced. Congress impeached him twice. No one has ever been as checked and balanced as Donald J. Trump.

Even at the end, after the fundamentally unfair—from a combination of traditional cheating, unlawful election law changes, and the informal intervention of the entire establishment in favor of the basement-dwelling incompetent who falsely promised "normalcy"—2020 election, Trump still kept within the rules. Yes, he later listened to the insane ramblings of the likes of Lin Wood and bought into the coming of the Kraken, but on January 20 he packed his gear, did the duffel bag drag to *Marine One*, then choppered off to Mar-a-Lago and (at least temporary) retirement.

If Trump was an authoritarian, he was a really, really bad one. But he was not an authoritarian in any serious sense. An authoritarian does not color within the lines. And an authoritarian, when faced with institutional resistance, levels the offending institution. Then he posts the figurative head on a pike for all to see and learn from.

Trump played by the rules, for all the credit that brought him.

The left suffers from the problem common to those who create new rules. Their new rules will come back and bite them. Here, the new rule is that norms and mores and traditions that slow you down in the short term may be waived. We've discussed examples of this previously—the corruption of the justice system, the indoctrination of students with leftist race effluent, and the ideological purging of class enemies from the military are just a few. Compounding this is the active participation of nongovernmental institutions. The regime media has discarded objectivity, Silicon Valley tech titans have taken it upon themselves to limit the range of tolerable speech, and Big Business has signed on to promote the leftist narrative.

All these things would have been verboten a generation ago—or, at least, no one would have admitted to doing them out loud. Now they shout their norm-abortions. And the consequences are inevitable. The conservative victims of this onslaught will grow to reject the idea of norms at all, viewing them as what they have effectively become—a set of constraints that apply only to conservatives and prevent conservatives from using all their power against opponents who feel free to use every ounce of their own power to get what they want.

What the left will call an "authoritarian" is basically someone who will play by the left's rules in pursuit of conservative objectives, dispensing with checks and balances in the pursuit of power. He might well be celebrated for it by the right. Such is the fallout of leftist rule-breaking.

The norms 'n' rules crowd on the right is shrinking into a small rump subset of conservatives that includes the likes of the editors of *National Review* and, well, Ben Sasse maybe. Other conservatives moved on completely as the right began to lose its taste for norms. Some used the end of norms as cover for defecting—despite their protests, they were less concerned with the end of the old ways than the end of their sinecures in the old order. Bill Kristol's shabby crew of grifters abandoned the conservative cruise ship; today, that bunch is effectively left-wing. The Lincoln Project types are practically enrolled in the Frankfurt School, which is conveniently the one school that they are allowed within a thousand feet of.

As the left rejects the norms by embracing (with varying levels of success) such previously unthinkable initiatives as filibuster repeals, court-packing, speech limits, and open borders, the right is rejecting the unilateral disarmament that is pretending the norms are healthy and vital and must be scrupulously observed regardless of what the other guys do. Trump's election, of course, was a breaking of norms in the sense that he was, well, Donald Trump. But that was done within the rules, and it was less a calculated pursuit of conservative objectives than a cry for help. "Listen to us, we're serious—look who we've elected!"

But the leftist establishment did not listen, nor could it. The logic of the left was always authoritarian because the authoritarianism is part of the fun. It's a delight to torment and command others without restraints—if COVID taught us anything, it is that there's a little dictator inside every frigid Karen scolding normal people for not wrapping a cloth around their three-year-old before he jumps on the jungle gym.

Conservatives tend not to get off bossing around others. The leftist catalog of conservative faults includes selfishness, but "selfishness" is really a focus on dealing with their own business and letting others do the same. Telling others what to do is not part of the joy of conservatism. The left cites abortion as such interference, but to the extent that telling someone she cannot kill her baby is bossing her around, that exception hardly disputes the rule.

An authoritarian of the right will almost certainly come to power as part of a backlash toward leftism gone too far. It will be reactionary in the truest sense of the word—it would be a reaction to the failure of the left. When would it arise? When inflation gets to Weimar levels and a Big Mac is $22 while a gallon of gas—assuming you are still allowed to drive a gas-fueled car—hits $25 a gallon? When crime is so bad people are huddling in their homes as the hordes of thugs left unprosecuted by Soros-bought district attorneys roam the streets? When America's military is crushed by an enemy sneak attack that occurs while our troops are attending their mandatory Non-Binary Gender Appreciation Day celebration?

This could come through a crisis, such as one we have described, but most likely it will come via a wave election. It would have to be a massive Republican victory—again, the GOP is the party of the right and the most likely vehicle for such an electoral victory. If you look at the situation in the run-up to 2024, with a manifestly senile jerk in the Oval Office presiding over an endless pandemic, tail-spinning economy, military humiliation, and rising anger, you see the seeds of such a transformative election.

The American people will demand that their candidate "fix it," and the man they choose to do it will nod and proceed.

The Romans had a fix-it-man procedure called, not surprisingly, the dictatorship. When everything was going to hell, they would appoint a guy for six months with near total power. He was above the law, unaccountable, and empowered to cut through the clutter of process to make things happen. And then he was supposed to lay his power down. Cincinnatus did. He served, and then went home to his plow—almost certainly he inspired George Washington, who could have been king but instead returned to Mount Vernon. But Julius Caesar became dictator for life. If a true authoritarian is not a dictator, he would be perilously close.

Keep in mind that there is an authoritarian fantasy on the left. Writers such as Thomas Friedman admire how the Chinese communists do not have to consider the petty complaints of mere stakeholders when imposing their vision. Joe Biden's fellow travelers feel the same way. They are outraged that their razor-thin Senate majority—based entirely on Kamala Harris's wandering over to cast tie-breaker votes—does not allow them the same nearly limitless power as FDR had with a huge majority. The left sees limits on its power as a crime against progress; limits on conservatives are blessed by Gaia herself.

A right-wing authoritarian simply would not care.

What would an authoritarian do? The most important characteristic is that he would wield his power without restraint, ignoring checks and balances. It is not so much that he might exceed his enumerated powers, though he might well do so. If norms won't stop you from doing something you really want to do, then rules on an old piece of parchment probably won't either. But a United States president, the unitary executive, has enormous powers at his fingertips without even tearing out of the envelope. He just has to push the envelope.

The first thing is personnel. The government is not elected officials. No, they come and go—regardless of who they are, they do go, and that is truly their distinguishing characteristic. But the distinguishing characteristic of civil servants is that they don't go—ever. And why would they? The money is ridiculously good for the effort required. Far from being impecunious do-gooders sacrificing for the American people, these toxic layabouts have managed—often through union contracts—to set themselves up quite nicely. They stay, the elected officials go, so who has the real power over the long haul? Call it the deep state if you wish—it is really more of the deep states, with dozens of little fiefdoms scattered throughout the bureaucracy—but it is real and it is a problem.

It also has a reputation, which it does nothing to undermine, of being invulnerable. You can't fire a civil servant, goes the conventional wisdom. But that is not so. They can be fired, though it takes some effort. But they can also be neutered. A civil servant who is ordered to his new position in Nome, Alaska, will certainly complain, but unless he packs up his stuff and hightails it there, he is insubordinate. And that is grounds to boot him.

There was once a senior commander of the California National Guard who had such issues with the bureaucracy. He was told that low performers could not be fired, so he would fire them anyway and have them walked out of the building with their junk in a banker's box as they threatened to get a lawyer and sue. And he would answer them, smiling beatifically, "Yes, you can sue. I have lawyers too, dozens of them, all being paid by someone else to defend the case. And you might win. But by then, I will be retired, and you will be old."

One thing people who are not lawyers do not seem to understand is that all it takes to file a lawsuit is a filing fee and a word processor. "But they will sue!" seems to work for many folks as a kind of trump card that stops an action in its tracks. But it need not, and a president who realizes that it matters not at all if the government's lawyers must fight one more lawsuit by some aggrieved oxygen thief at the Department of Agriculture who has been holding up one of the president's initiatives, or ten, or a hundred, or a thousand of them. By the time they come back to work, if they ever come back, the president will be gone and they will be old—and a bunch of things they were delaying, disregarding, or undermining will have happened.

Or, or course, a powerful president could ram civil service system reform through the Congress. The left would scream that this would turn the civil service into a patronage system with ranks full of the president's personally picked cadre of enabling bureaucrats. And that would be true. Entirely true. That would be the goal. Instead of a long-term, left-leaning bureaucracy, it would be one full of conservative-friendly appointees. The left would accurately assess the objective. And a right-leaning authoritarian would not care.

Not caring is a powerful weapon that is sorely unappreciated. Besides the fear of procedural consequences, such as lawsuits, other conservatives have been terrified of public opinion. But does that truly matter, especially if the authoritarian is actively reforming the electoral system to one based on securing the vote from Democratic manipulation? Photo identification would be mandatory, as would in-person voting on Election Day only. Absentee votes would be greatly limited, like to deployed troops and coma victims, and counting would be closely observed in blue cities by an army of active and aggressive federal election watchdogs.

Naturally, the outcry would be deafening within the legacy media. But then, if a tree falls in the wilderness, does anyone see it if CNN broadcasts it live? There are do-it-yourself pedicure shows that out-draw CNN's ratings, so what that collection of clowns, potatoes, and sex pests says matters little. Moreover, the legacy media has largely destroyed its own credibility anyway. Let them scream that securing elections is an attack on democracy. They have been doing that for years. Nobody cares.

What matters more is what the tech titans do. With control over search engines and social media, these Silicon Valley boys and girls wield an unacceptable level of power which they have managed to protect both by liberally showering dough onto Capitol Hill and by hiding behind the conservative principle of free enterprise to retain their lease on the public square.

An authoritarian right-winger would not adhere to such alleged principles. He would be about power, and he would not hesitate to exercise it. The first step might be to convene a summit with the titans soon after inauguration and then, behind closed doors, tell them there is a new sheriff in town and this one is not playing around. There are whole battalions of lawyers paid by Uncle Sam to litigate anti-trust violations. And there are others to investigate civil rights violations against Christians and others whom the Palo Alto pagans disapprove of. Will the feds win? Maybe. But hey, those lawyers are on the payroll, and they might as well be suing everyone in Cupertino. And perhaps the algorithms they use are of interest to China and other enemies—better designate them as national security items to limit their use. And this is even before the Congress starts passing new laws.

Now, they might well protest that the president is using his power against political enemies, to which he would answer, "Yes, I am. Good catch." Then he would have a question of his own: "Do you still want to be my enemy?"

Understand that this treats our nation's norms like Brazil treats the rainforest, clear-cutting it and setting the debris on fire. This is not business as usual. This is not within the spirt of the Constitution, as any reasonable reader might understand it. It is unchecked and unbalanced. But this is well within the new rules of a norm-free paradigm.

Adios to academia. Cut it off from money and derail the student loan gravy train.

The military? Say goodbye to diversity, and pretty much all of the generals and admirals appointed under Obama and Biden—and Trump too.

Antifa? BLM? The new FBI director would refocus the antiterrorism mission on actual terrorists instead of on conservative dissidents. You know, like Antifa and the liberal millionaires who fund it.

And his politicized Department of Justice—because the new rule is that the DOJ is the president's enforcer—would follow suit, starting with subpoenaing all of the text messages from your favorite Joe

Scarborough guests. We would finally see Eric Swalwell's Fang Fang chats. Pity the guy who has to wade thought what every creepy, weird stuff Ted Lieu and Adam Schiff have been texting with their buddies about.

The authoritarian will be charged with solving problems. Dealing with the bureaucracy, with the media, and with the opposition are just supporting efforts in that. The real key is results. Augustus may have taken away the ability to rise to true greatness from the Romans, but he gave them a long peace and a lot of prosperity. Cheap gas and low crime are our bread and circuses.

Obviously, the authoritarian would reject the entire climate hoax and administratively order exploitation of American energy resources—including nuclear. Like Augustus, who found Rome a city of brick and left it a city of marble, an authoritarian could cut through the red tape of environmental hooey and build a network of modern reactors that would power America for generations.

He would seal the border and deport illegal aliens—oh, and they would again be called "illegal aliens." Due process would consist of "Pack your stuff and get on the bus—next stop, Tijuana!"

He would handle the true homelessness problem by dealing with its root causes—derelicts are either on drugs or on drugs and nuts. The nuts go to asylums, the addicts to treatment or jail. This is not cruelty; cruelty is letting madmen and junkies in throes of delusions and addiction die on our streets. Nor should asylums be snake pits. Conservatives have a vision of limited government, but that reasonably includes compassionate care for the insane and the hopeless while they cannot live in society. And it's also compassionate to everyone else too. If conservatism becomes so entangled by alleged principles that it cannot provide normal people with secure streets, it has lost its reason for being.

Some might point out that this is a federalism issue, and homelessness is an issue for the states. But notions like federalism could get in the way of delivering a life-enhancing improvement to his people, and this would not deter the authoritarian.

And he would deal with crime. He would restore the common-sense notion that the cause of crime is criminals, and lock the root causes up for good. He would also turn the feds on the enemies of the regime, investigating them until a crime was detected, after which it would be prosecuted to the maximum extent allowed. The new rules the Democrats pioneered sure are a bitch.

Authoritarians are tolerated as long as they deliver results. The idea that these types of issues are not federal issues is not going to stop him from addressing them—and harshly. But if you can reject the limitations of federalism, what else will you reject? Maybe the freedom to utter insurrectionary words and deeds. After all, the left demonstrably wants to undermine the checks and balances of the Constitution to seize total power. Does it make sense to allow that? We have been told by the legacy media that insurrections are bad, so is it wrong to treat them that way? Should leftist insurrectionists be allowed into positions in and out of government where they might undermine the Constitution? Should they be allowed to express opinions to that effect? Is it wrong to use the power of the government to stop that threat in its tracks?

The logic of the authoritarian is that it is not.

So is it really wrong to ban inflammatory speech? Is it wrong to disqualify brother-touching anti-American ingrates like Ilhan Omar and Marxist morons like Alexandria Ocasio-Cortez from office? After all, they would trash the Constitution and ship you off to the gulags in a heartbeat given the chance. And if not barring them and their ilk completely, is it wrong to administer the elections in such a way that the People get the right answer?

Again, the logic of the authoritarian is that it is not.

And what if the Supreme Court stepped in to stop the authoritarian? Might he just wonder, as Stalin did about the pope, about how many divisions John Roberts has? What if Congress put up a fight, not just the tiresome pinkos but the respected members? Might a White House staffer show up with some embarrassing data mined by the National Security Administration and suggest they fall into line lest it leak? You know, like the kind of leaks that started the sequence of events that led to the prosecution of Lieutenant General Mike Flynn?

Or, if they won't play ball, might they get a knock on the door from one of those SWAT teams that took down desperados like the elderly Roger Stone? Does anything limit the power of the authoritarian once he begins to use it?

The logic of the authoritarian is that there is no limit. Power is the only principle. The authoritarian logic is that claimed necessity trumps the rules.

But then, taken to the extreme, there goes the Constitution. While the *deus ex imperator* fantasy is fun—it's always entertaining to imagine a world without constraints—the reality is not so delightful. Yes, an authoritarian can make the trains run on time for a while, but that kind of regime has to derail eventually. The authoritarian scenario above assumes an authoritarian whose sole purpose is conservative change. After all, he would only be using his power for good, right?

But what are the chances of that? Did human nature suddenly change when Ronald Reagan came along?

Every *imperator* is not going to be Augustus. Even Augustus was not Augustus in that sense—sure, he sought to do great things and he did do them, but not for their own sake. He was interested in his own greatness. One of his most famous legacies is a long litany of his achievements, "The Deeds of the Divine Augustus," that he had sent around the empire. He chose the name "Augustus" (granted, he was born Octavian, which sounds like Rome's equivalent of "Newton" or "Melvin") and had himself declared the son of a god, all of which gives you an idea about where his head was at. He turned down the title "dictator," but he never gave up dictating.

Notably, though some solid performers showed up occasionally, the Romans never topped Augustus. So, unless America is blessed with an endless series of men even greater than Augustus, the authoritarian fantasy is probably not going to pan out in the long term. Nor would we want it even if it did.

"My Justice Department will not tolerate perjury," the president said into the mic. "Which is why Mark Zuckerberg is in custody." In fact, the FBI raid on his home had dragged him out of his palace in his underwear in cuffs. His security team, mostly ex–special forces, had stood down when the convoy arrived to serve the arrest warrant for lying to Congress about Facebook's censorship policies. It was the same team that had busted the head of YouTube the week before.

"There are some who say that this administration is intimidating its political enemies?" one reporter asked.

"I don't speak to the New York Times," *the president said. He nodded and three Secret Service agents hustled her away. The other reporters watched, but none spoke up.*

"This is an emergency," the president said. "Our very democracy is at stake. There are some that demand we coddle the criminals who terrorize our streets, that we subsidize un-American ideas in schools and universities, that we allow illegal aliens to freely remain in our country. We will no longer tolerate it. The American people elected me to solve these problems. I will do so."

"Many people say you are exceeding your power as president and acting without the authority of Congress," another reporter said. "Do you believe your actions are undemocratic?"

"Nothing I do in the defense of democracy can be undemocratic. I was elected to fix this crisis. For too long, we tolerated division and hatred from the media, from the corporations, and from the other party. That ends now. I was elected to unify this country, and I intend to do so."

"Well, then I guess you can close the school part of your organization," John Stewart told the Harvard chancellor. "After all, you basically are a hedge fund that occasionally teaches some classes to spoiled rich kids."

"But if you seize our endowment, we will—" the chancellor began.

"What?" asked Stewart, cutting him off. "Can't your rich kid students pay their own freight? I mean, it's harder since we banned red Chinese students, but I think you can manage." Stewart had worked for Senator Ted Cruz before being brought into the Department of Education under the new administration. He relished his new role as Undersecretary for University Liaison.

"This is unprecedented! You can't interfere with how we choose to teach!"

"Why not?" Stewart asked. He was genuinely curious. He had helped draft the new curriculum guidance the department had sent out. It included "Civics and the American Way" as a required course for any university receiving any federal funding. And it banned all critical race theory and Marxist coursework, with one exception. "You know, you can still have a course on 'The Failures of Marxism' if you want."

"*This is an attack on our academic freedom!*" *the chancellor said, but not loudly. It was more in resignation, since the protests at the other colleges being informed of the new rules had totally failed. And, as he felt he would fare poorly in prison, he did not wish to be one of the administrators being held without bail on charges of "interfering with federal administration activities."*

"*Oh, that reminds me,*" *Stewart said.* "*First, there are several cancelled professors you'll need to hire back. And second, my Education Department's Office of Academic Diversity will need to approve all future hiring decisions to ensure you are complying with the new ideological diversity mandates.*"

"*You're going to destroy Harvard,*" *the chancellor sputtered.*

"*I know,*" *Stewart replied.* "*But then again, if you cooperate with us, like you did with the left, maybe you can keep your school and your job. Maybe.*"

The federal marshals in riot gear cleared the protestors out of the way, and not gently. Any of them that had shown the least resistance were zip-tied and hauled away in black vans to be charged with assault on federal officers. The U.S. attorneys were seeking that these rioters be held without bail; all were being charged with felonies. Word would soon get out that there was a price to rioting, and the criminality would fade. In Portland, over three hundred people had been arrested and charged with crimes that carried more than five years in prison before the trouble there ended. The federal prison system was now largely full of drug traffickers and spoiled kids shocked to be doing a stretch for the same thing their older brothers and sisters had done in 2020 without being charged at all.

With the activists out of the way, the feds descended on the homeless encampment. The inhabitants were herded out and triaged. The obviously insane were hooked up and hauled away to the mental

*health facilities—actually, large encampments out in the sticks—
where they were assessed and treated, mostly with medications. The
straight-up drug addicts got a choice, then and there: rehab or incar-
ceration. The rehab encampments were also out in the sticks. The
ones with warrants were sent to jail—if the local authorities would
not take them, the feds held them using some of the new laws passed
by the Congress that criminalized homelessness under an expansive
view of the Commerce Clause.*

*The inhabitants having been shipped off, the contractors came in
and loaded up the entire encampment for disposal. This one was in
Los Angeles, where the mayor had promised no cooperation with the
federal initiative right up until he was arrested for interfering with
federal officers. The people of Los Angeles, except for the die-hard
liberals on the Westside, were happy to see the streets cleared of the
drugged-out zombies and junkies, as well as the petty (and not-so-
petty) criminals who had defiled the city.*

*As one man said to a TV interviewer, "Yeah, it seems kind of
harsh, but now my kid can play outside again."*

The authoritarian fantasy, and it is a fantasy in the sense that it's
nothing more than an expedient to address the monumental problems
the left created or refuses to solve, is a concession of failure. It says
the Constitution does not work and we need to abandon it. In that
sense, it tracks with the three options. We want the constitutional
option, but if that's not happening, we will resign ourselves to doing
the best we can. It certainly beats the other alternative, submission to
leftist tyranny. Perhaps, if there is to be tyranny, it's better to be on
the side of the tyrant.

But is everything an authoritarian would do necessarily wrong?
We have seen that the key to authoritarians is that they ignore formal
and informal rules. But some formal rules have outlived their purpose,

and some informal rules are unequally applied. The formal rules that need changing can be changed. The informal ones are tougher. To accept a double standard is to accept defeat. There is no moral obligation to submit to the tyranny of others in order to prevent the risk, down the road, of tyranny by your own side. This is the challenge when the other guys have decided to abandon the rules—you have no good options to deal with them. You can continue to play by the old rules and risk serfdom, or you can abandon the rules and hope to change course down the road. The Romans hoped that. It never happened.

But perhaps there is a middle ground.

CHAPTER FOURTEEN

AMERICA COMES TO ITS SENSES

Sometimes there are happy endings. So, what if we decided to reaffirm and recommit to the values of the founders? What if we somehow decided to return to normality—not pre-Biden normality or pre-Trump normality but the normality in which many of us grew up or lived our early adult years. Something like that interregnum between when Reagan hosed the muck of the seventies out of our economy and the nineties, when we were the unchallenged superpower?

You know, prosperity and peace. *Pax America II: The Revenge.*

Sounds great. Let's do that!

Except things are not so simple. We cannot just wish away the last couple of misbegotten decades. The international correlation of forces is what it is. Domestically, we would have one hell of a hangover following the drunken spending spree and the hollowing out of our manufacturing sector since we were at our pinnacle. Nor can we wish away the fact that our friends on the left—many of whom would love to ship us off to gulags, but worry about the environmental impact of

242 WE'LL BE BACK

dotting the Arctic tundra with work camps for dissidents—require a divided, angry, and poor populace from which to draw power.

So, the odds against this result are formidable, but it does not mean we should not aim for it. It seems the result that is least likely to change America fundamentally for the worst. And it might actually be durable, though history does seem to be a series of people forgetting what happened the last time and making the same damn mistakes over and over again.

America coming to its senses means a struggle, a peaceful one within the political battlespace. It means discarding some old norms and bending others, but this is a natural and necessary response to the discarding and bending of norms we face. The key is not to succumb to real authoritarianism, the willful rejection of the checks and balances that the Constitution envisions. Hardball, yes. Dictatorship, no.

But we cannot let the authoritarians win.

Let's look at what is going on. As of early 2022, the Democrats control the White House in the sense that Joe Biden lives there when he is not in Delaware wrapped in a shawl in a rocker slurping mush. Nancy Pelosi has a literal handful of votes to spare in the House, though she has intermittent help from Liz Cheney (Dick's worst legacy, which is saying something) and her personal Mr. Smithers, Adam Kinzinger. In the Senate, Chuck Schumer is tormented by Joe Manchin and has to rely on Kamala Harris to break ties, assuming he gets every one of his Democratic members to sign onto the Squad-approved legislative electoral suicide notes he keeps trying to pass. How precarious is your position when it relies on Kamala Harris's coming through for you? How sad are you when everything depends on the judgment of someone who dated Montel Williams?

If historical trends continue, the Democrats will get wiped out in 2022 on that basis alone. But when you add the absolutely terrible job they've done since the alleged 2020 election, then you have the makings of a ballot-box Cannae. They will almost certainly lose the House and, if trends hold—the polling provides a bleaker forecast than Michael Moore's A1C—there will be a Republican Senate majority.

And then from January 2023 to January 2025, the weight of the Democrats' already shattered agenda will be on the slumped, frail shoulders of Joe Biden. So, basically, stay out from under the high windows at the Democratic National Committee headquarters, lest you be squashed by plummeting pinkos.

There are a few things you can rely upon. The sun will come up in the east. You will be expected to pay taxes. The third season of a given Netflix or HBO series that began promisingly will suck, mostly because the plot will get woke. And Joe Biden will make Jimmy Carter look like Ronald Reagan.

Biden has to fail. Besides being stupid, which probably gave him a solid head start on his senility, he adheres to an ideology that not only never succeeds in bringing prosperity or freedom but cannot do so if it wishes to continue. Things will get worse and worse, and all the legacy media tap-dancing in the world is never going to convince Americans that 20 percent inflation is a good thing and proof of a booming economy. He is going to screw it up, and there is going to be a huge opening for a Republican in 2024. And, hopefully, it will not be a terrible Republican.

This is true whether Biden bows out of the election or, because the last twenty years have been a flock of black swans, chooses to run again. If Kamala Harris picks up the banner, perhaps she will inspire and excite not merely the woke Democrat base but tens of other millions of Americans. Or, as is more likely, she will appall and repel tens of millions of Americans and lead the Democrats to electoral oblivion.

So, there is a huge possibility that the Republicans will take power again after 2024, but will the next few years be such an unmitigated clusterfark that it will permanently scar a generation of Americans and make them utterly unwilling to risk electing another liberal Democrat? FDR famously won the loyalty of millions of Americans, despite the fact that he extended the Depression. Ronald Reagan was one of them. He only became a Republican later. The fact is that this terrible, terrible era could so poison the well for Democrats that perhaps we could see a few decades where a liberal just cannot win. Is it likely? No, because there are a lot of stupid people in this country. But it could happen.

We will discuss the attributes of a conservative leader who might rebuild and reinvigorate our country later, but the key point here is that this all requires a change of heart in a critical mass of Americans. Is that possible?

Yes.

The last couple decades have been characterized by the opening of the Overton window and the throwing of so much of what is good about America out of it. We have agreed to government interference in our lives to a degree never even considered before. The pandemic panic is an obvious example. Who would have thought that so many Americans would willingly agree to extend two weeks to stop the spread to two years to…do something? It is unclear what, since by then COVID appeared endemic, but a lot of people—mostly liberal—eagerly went along with it. Well, at least for other people—photos on social media of various high-profile, mask-wearing dudgeon people not wearing masks in public became an aggravating cliché. And often there would be servants in the photos, all of them clad in mouth thongs.

Other kinds of submission to an overweening government include injecting the venomous ideology of critical race theory into schools and other institutions. Yes, there was pushback, glorious pushback like that of the people of Virginia who rejected another four years of Democrat Terry McAuliffe and his pro-indoctrination agenda, but it was terrifying to see just how many people eagerly accepted this kind of propaganda.

Then there was the trans craze, where Americans were expected not only to accept that men could transform into women (or vice versa), but to pretend that it was real. Merely not protesting the nonsense was not enough—it had to be celebrated and the gender imposters had to be welcomed into every nook and cranny of society. The most obvious manifestation was second-tier boy athletes suddenly discovering they were girls and then proceeding to utterly destroy the actual women they competed against as girls. It happened again and again, as real women were beaten by bigger and stronger males who took some estrogen and a new name and proceeded to use their male bodies to set records. The women, their hard work made moot in the name of validating the delusions of a few boys, were expected to celebrate their loses and exclaim, "You go, girl!"

It's crazy, but there are millions of Americans who think this is all A-OK.

But will America's patience for this ridiculous nonsense wane? If we are too far gone to achieve a critical mass to slam the Overton window shut again, then we might well be headed for one of those terrible scenarios we have discussed. Hopefully, we can do it without going full authoritarian.

The elite is not noticing the unrest because the people whose patience is being lost are not the people dwelling in their bubbles. In the liberal bubbles, the conformity is rigorously enforced. You cannot be a member of the clique unless you sign on. You lose your privileges if you dissent—you lose your chance for the right school (careful what you post on Instagram—they're watching!), you lose your job, you lose your friends. But outside the bubble? There are changes that they never saw coming.

We have seen bizarre and shocking changes in the coalitions that make up the two parties in the last twenty years, ones that would have previously been utterly unthinkable. The Democrats abandoned the white working class for the woke white-collar and various minorities, confident that the emerging Democrat majority would include all those black people and Latinx people whom they had counted on for so long.

Except a lot of those black and Latinx people were also working-class, and the same miseries inflicted on the white working class were also being inflicted on the other shades in the rainbow of people who work with their hands. Black people driving to a construction site pay the same for gas as white people, and they have no interest in a three-dollar-a-gallon surcharge because a bunch of Marin County swells think we need to keep it from getting a degree hotter in a century.

And as for the Latinx people, what the hell is "Latinx" anyway? This clunky moniker perfectly encapsulates the liberal delusions about a people the left condescends to when it considers them at all. First off, how do you pronounce "Latinx"? Is it "Latin-ex"? "La-tin-ex"? It's not a Spanish word; it's a college ethnic studies seminar word, designed to differentiate credulous suburban girls who are getting their woke on as Wellesley sophomores. This jargon, of which "Latinx" is but one example ("gender-fluid" and "non-binary" are a couple of other examples), is specifically designed to set the user apart from the unenlightened. These magic words identify fellow members of the secular clerisy of wokeness to one another, like a secret hand-shake for people who think shaking hands is a manifestation of structural ableism.

Only the woke use these words—Hispanics famously reject "Latinx" so thoroughly that consultants are begging fellow Democrats not to use it because it risks further alienating Hispanic potential voters. But this is on purpose. Using exclusive jargon fulfills a primary goal of wokeness, which is to make the practitioners feel special and virtuous. Remember that a huge part of all this nonsense is acting out the personal psychodramas of the damaged people who subscribe to the tenets of wokeness. It's all about the feels, not of the oppressed, but of the purported ally.

Hispanics do not play this game. In late 2021, a cold terror began to spread through the Democratic consultant class as polls began to show that Hispanic—again, most definitely not "Latinx"—voters were about tied in their support between Democrats and Republicans. This was an earthquake within the consultant class. Since the aughts, the Democrats had been counting on importing millions of Hispanic voters, legally and illegally, with the assumption that these voters would become loyal Democrats. But that has not happened the way they hoped—it was far from that simple, but the Democrats would have known that if they had thought of "Hispanics" as human beings instead of a convenient ethnic pigeonhole.

Hispanics were supposed to support open borders. But poll some Hispanics whose families immigrated legally and their sympathy level for illegals pegs in the red. Many Hispanics are working-class, and they suffer the same class antipathy from the Trader Joe's set as the white working class. But then most Hispanics consider themselves "white" in the sense that, yes, their grandfather came from Columbia or Jalisco, but now they are just another bunch of Americans. This is heresy to the left, which considers racial identity and clear racial categories as sacrosanct. How can people *not* want to stay in their lanes?

But why would anyone? The left needs Hispanics to be "others" because that allows the left to leverage that artificial difference for power. Yet, millions of Hispanics have no interest in being "others" or anything else except Americans. As the left would say, they have embraced "whiteness," but that is only because what they call "whiteness" has zero to do with skin tone. It has everything to do with accepting traditional American values.

This is why you see diversity consultants list concepts such as "hard work" and "colorblindness" as characteristics of "whiteness." They are not, in any objective sense. But by sticking a color label on basic American values and norms, they seek to drive people in other ethnic groups away from racial harmony. The problem is that not all folks are saps or suckers, and they refuse to play along. They want to work hard, take care of their families, and live in a colorblind society, and they will vote for the candidates who agree. That is why they are moving toward the Republicans.

When the Democrats put all their chips down on racial strife, that was a big risk. And it looks like it is not paying off. Americans disappointed them by choosing not to hate each other because of race or ethnicity.

Throw in the cultural affectations about gender, and that's going to drive away every American without a ruling-caste secret decoder ring. People simply are not going to take it, even in areas formerly thought of as liberal. These cultural issues are devastating to the left. That's why Republicans are constantly reminded and warned by the trained parrots of the legacy media that the GOP must not address them. The Republican Party, with its too-high percentage of fools, often concurs. And it is never the officially deplored working-class types, the Lauren Boeberts or Marjorie Taylor Greenes, who heed these boundaries. It is always, always the rich guys, the guys who care about what goes down at their country club, who go along with the hustle.

The GOP is becoming a working-class party, and that may be a key to turning this all around. After all, the failures America has suffered since the fall from the heights that our working class—in building, supplying, and defending America—brought us to did not bubble up from the grass roots. This was top-down failure, the best and the brightest botching it all.

An America that focuses on the frivolous and foolish fetishes of the ruling caste is a failed America. Our elite is concerned with the weather, with gender, and with racism that stopped existing in substantial quantities a half century ago. And that performative concern is inextricably tied to its own desire to obtain and keep power.

But an America that is based on the concerns of the working class is an America that is necessarily addressing real issues and building a stronger country. Normal Americans want strong families. As we have seen, the family is under attack, and our birth rate is shrinking. Normal Americans love their country. They do not want to hear about how it sucks, particularly when many of their families came from places that *really* sucked. And especially when many of them fought for this country in stupid wars the ruling class started.

Normal Americans want an economy where you can work and support your family. Bizarre tangents like the panic over climate change—a hoax in which perilous predictions prove false and deadline after deadline passes without Armageddon, yet the doomsayers say on—serve only to increase the cost of energy and limit the freedom of normal citizens. They are the ones responsible for the fact that the new washing machine you bought last year works significantly worse than the washer your parents bought from Sears forty years ago. No one in Manhattan or San Francisco needs a big V8 truck, and most of these nannies don't know anyone who does, so they insist that you do not either. But lots of people in America do need a big V8 truck. The quasi-religious campaign to shrink America's carbon footprint (which has shrunk, even as China's has grown) is yet another attack on the working class.

Every time a working man's paper straw melts into an unsuckable tube of goo, it's another reminder that the elite despises him.

So, with a working-class party united to demand a focus on normal issues—and forgoing the weird obsessions of a bored and idle ruling class—combined with a Republican Party that is resistant to such obsessions, we may well have a shot at returning to normality. Imagine—patriotism, prosperity, and peace, just like we used to have. That does make a compelling vision. Especially in comparison to the liberal elite vision, which is eternal racial/ethnic/gender conflict over an ever-shrinking pie in a country that can never grovel and apologize enough.

The challenge is that so many people have become emotionally invested in their own wokeness. It fills their souls, taking up space where some actual faith should have been instilled when they were kids. America's troubles are spiritual as well as political and cultural. While vibrant communities of faith exist, the war on religion in the name of COVID—the First Baptist must lock down, but not Barney's Booze-o-rama and Uncle Busty's Gentleman's Club!—caused grave damage. Many churches will collapse as Americans have fallen out of the habit of regular worship. To succeed, we are going to have to work to revitalize religious faith. If we don't, we will have a bunch of people with empty souls vulnerable to having them filled up with all manner of pinko nonsense.

America has had Great Awakenings in the past. Whether another revival arises or not is out of our politicians' hands in the sense that it cannot be astroturfed. It must come from the people. But our politicians can block political and cultural efforts to suppress it. Politically, the left will launch even more attacks on churches if it senses a revival. Such attacks were unforgivably aided and abetted by establishment hacks such as John Roberts during the COVID era. With most of the religious folks in the working class, the religious will make up a key element of any coalition that returns America to its former greatness. The ironclad protections the Constitution provides for the free exercise of religion must be honored, and when our politicians pick judges, anyone who thinks that religious considerations are just another factor to consider, despite what the First Amendment says, must be excluded.

Culturally, the left will respond to any traditional religious revival with the same venom it always has. It's always those uptight Jesus people who won't let Kevin Bacon and the kids dance. Perhaps we need to engage that stereotype more aggressively from our bully pulpits. Of course, it would also be nice if some Christian celebrities were not such transparent charlatans bringing disrepute on the faith. Regardless, faith is a powerful weapon against the godless communist future our enemies seek—you can tell because of how much the godless commies hate faith and the faithful.

We're down, but we are not out. Americans still retain their innate common sense, unless it was sucked out of them via matriculation at some Ivy League conformity factory. We can still win. The Constitution has not failed. We just need to bring enough of America around to our way of thinking.

CHAPTER FIFTEEN

WHO WILL CARRY THE BANNER?

The Great Man theory of history is long out of fashion, since the Marxists who currently dominate the academic study of the past prefer to focus on alleged trends and currents that—surprise!—always flow right toward validating *their* wish list. The study of great men refutes the notion that the individual is meaningless, that we are just flotsam and jetsam floating along through history without agency. But commie nonsense aside, great men do exist, and they do change the course of mankind. Normal people know this instinctively. The popular history books that tend to be most successful are biographies of great men.

A United States of America without Washington, Lincoln, Roosevelt, or Reagan would be a very different America. It might not even be a United States of America at all. Now, this is not to say that regular folks play no part, that they are mere footnotes. That is to misunderstand the whole premise. Great Men are great because of their interaction with the regular folk. Their greatness starts with their vision, but it truly manifests in how they lead, influence, and inspire regular people.

America has always been blessed with Great Men at the key crossroads in its history. It's got quite a remarkable streak—every time it looks like we are about to career over the cliff, someone great appears to grab the wheel and yank us back onto the road again. It is tempting to see this phenomenon as due to the favor of a higher power, that God blesses our nation with the right man at the right time. But if this is so, we must consider whether, as a nation, we have proven ourselves still worthy of His blessing today, when we need a Great Man once again.

One certainly hopes so.

And we do need a Great Man now, one of vision and one of resolution. As we have seen, the stakes are high, and avoiding a catastrophic fall will take clear sight and a steady hand. Joe Biden is not even a caretaker president—he can barely take care of himself. But the inept James Buchanan preceded Abe Lincoln. Will we be granted another Lincoln? The odds are against it. Civilizations do not get granted more than a handful of Great Men, and we have had more than our share in just under 250 years.

Maybe we can make do with a Good Enough Man.

But what is beyond doubt is that the next president needs to be a Republican and he must be a conservative. And not either of those labels in name only, either—that is part of what has got us here. Rather, we need a new kind of conservative Republican, one unafraid to exercise power, one not restrained by arbitrary conceptions of what a conservative Republican can do, but still aware that to rebuild America for the long term we cannot succumb to the expedient of true authoritarianism in the short term.

What he needs to do is win, indisputably, the fight we have found ourselves in. The next phase of that fight begins in 2024. The alternatives we have reviewed are simply too grim for us to contemplate anything less than victory.

But while we have examined many hypotheticals so far in our journey through the past and the future, 2024 is close enough that it is not a mere hypothetical. We know the key players today. And while someone new might emerge in the meantime that we never saw coming—can you say, "Glenn Youngkin"?—the man or woman who will win the GOP nomination in 2024 is almost certainly someone we already know about, and whom the chattering class has already chattered about.

It has to be someone who can do the big things we have discussed. To fail to do them simply puts off the confrontation over the future of America to a later date when we might not necessarily have the advantage. Based on Biden's sorry showing as our alleged president, 2024 is the perfect battlefield for us. Like Hannibal walking the ground at Cannae before mauling the Romans and nodding to his lieutenants, this is where we want to fight.

The question, then, is who is the individual who can do these things, and therefore change America's trajectory from ruin to power and prosperity again?

Let's start with the obvious, the eight-hundred-pound Orange Man, Donald Trump. His choice to run or not will so thoroughly dominate the campaign that some would simply not bother considering alternatives if he chose to run. This is probably true in 2022. But he may not choose to run, and in 2024 the facts on the ground might not make his victory in the primaries so certain. Moreover, he would be seventy-eight on Inauguration Day 2025. Does he want to spend most of the rest of his active life running again, maybe losing and being utterly humiliated, or winning and spending four years as a lame duck? Perhaps, but perhaps not.

Regardless, the fact is that Trump could win the general election. The utter failure by every measure of Joe Biden's inept administration—he wanted to be FDR but he ended up being a gropey-er James Buchanan—has made it possible to imagine that Trump can pull off Grover Cleveland's stunt. By the time this book is released, he will not have announced anything, unless he is seized by madness or decides he is definitely not going to run for some reason. Look for a decision in the spring of 2023. A master showman, Trump will certainly attempt to keep up the speculation—and his freedom of action—for as long as he can. He knows his fans are not going anywhere.

But are his fans going to vote for him? There are plenty of people who voted for Trump as the right guy back in 2016 but are not so certain he is the right guy right now. By the time November 2024 comes along, it will be eight and a half years since he descended from the elevator in June 2015 and announced what everyone—including, perhaps, him—thought was a quixotic campaign for the presidency. That's a long time, and it may well be that the Trump act is wearing thin even on those who appreciate what he did in the face of an entire establishment's trying to destroy him. Alinsky Rule Number 7 is "A tactic that drags on too long becomes a drag," and even his biggest fans must concede that the Trump circus, including his inexplicably self-defeating tangents, can be exhausting. The dumbest thing the establishment ever did was get its Silicon Valley allies to lock him out of social media; after all, absence makes the heart grow fonder, particularly when this implies the absence of bizarre tweets that step on the day's themes or focus on some private beef when they could be rallying the troops.

Trump did a remarkable job, and toward the end of his term he seemed to fix many of his personnel issues. This time, he has a whole cadre of experienced administration operators to call on to fill out the

Trump 2.0 administration, as opposed to having to rely on Republican establishment hacks. That's good. His performance after the election was bad, though, including his emotion-driven dalliance with the Kraken-releasers who never released anything except their credibility. If his reelection is about payback for what was indisputably an unfair and disgraceful election, he will lose the nomination.

We conservatives, who have nowhere to go but the GOP and so will stay and make up its grassroots base, are looking toward the future. Is Trump the guy to navigate the challenges we have discussed here and set up a realignment that will truly make America great again? No one thought he would do as well as he did. If he had not, and we were following the nightmare of a Hillary Clinton regime starting in 2016, we might be well into the worst-case scenarios we discussed here by now. After all, someone like Clinton—but not her savvier husband—has the unearned arrogance, the bitter contempt for her opponents, and the messianic narcissism that might create the conditions for one of those fraught scenarios.

Could Trump save us again? Lots of people who supported him as president in round one think it's time for a change. They fear he can't, or won't, learn from his mistakes. But he does understand important parts of the puzzle. His vision for this country is simple and correct, all about making America great again and putting America first. These are proper objectives, but do they reflect that he understands the true nature of the threat? Trump is an establishment guy in the sense that he would rather win it over than burn it down. No matter how often the snarling, slobbering beast bites him, he still can't get it through his head that it's Old Yeller. In 2021, he gave interviews to guys like Bob Woodward and Jon Karl, who promptly vivisected him in their books. He still accepts establishment credentials as validation, though the results were guys like Rex Tillerson, James Mattis, and that gnomish narcissist Tony Fauci.

What will it take for him to see what time it is?

Leaving aside whether he can win in 2024—he has a definite ceiling as well as a definite floor to his support—is he the man who sees the peril ahead and has the energy, the focus, and the will to steer our ship of state off the collision course with the iceberg that lies right ahead?

Or do we need a flat-out visionary, preferably one steeped in the kind of understanding of the Constitution you get from the Claremont Institute or Hillsdale College? Yet, he must also have the conservative woke warrior spirit, an understanding that the Democrats today are not merely opponents but are in thrall to an ideology that will not be satisfied as long as we retain our liberty, livelihoods, and—in the case of some of their folks who say out loud what is not meant to be spoken—our lives.

What we loved about Trump was that he fights. But we need someone who not only fights but who understands the enemy and is committed to its defeat. Maybe that is Trump, but maybe it is someone else.

The challenge for a conservative is the conserving part, the idea that we dare not tear down. But we must not fear creative destruction. We have seen that our institutions are rotten and rickety, preserved by the conservatives out of habit and by the left out of self-interest. The left will let them collapse when they have served their purpose in the war for power, but we conservatives seem to habitually back them simply because they exist. Why do conservative politicians vote again and again to hand money to academia when it is basically America's Wuhan lab of ideological pathologies? We need a guy who not only will, but can, effectively make the case that not only should Harvard not get a dime of government money but its massive endowment—it's basically a multibillion-dollar hedge fund conducting some classes in some of its real estate holdings—should be taxed, if not seized outright.

Who might be up for it, whether or not Trump runs?

There is no shortage of potential candidates who want to ignore the realities. Some Republicans are essentially conservative quislings, conservative in all but beliefs, actions, and conservatism. They think everything is fine, or would be if we only did more of what our enemies want. There is an appeal to people who will tell you everything is fine 'n' dandy. Maybe they even believe it. These folks, the Mitt Romneys and Larry Hogans, delight the left. They will sit silent as they are pummeled, because fighting back is ungentlemanly or something. And if they do win, the worst case for the left is that they tread water. They will never, ever even try to turn back the march through the institutions. In fact, they will sometimes march right along with the left, eager to score a biscuit. Remember how Mitt Romney joined a Black Lives Matter march, an organization run by literal communists? And who believes, even for a second, that if this schmear of human Miracle Whip was ever somehow elected president that his marching comrades would not be screaming about how he's the second coming of Mussolini?

That's the bottom rung of the Republican ladder. A step above are the safe establishment types, the Jeb!s whose consultants prepare them a list of conservative words and phrases that they read on Fox News in order to satiate the rubes. But their real bosses are in the C-suites. They are the ones who get creeped out at conservative parents upset about critical race theory, mostly because their liberal friends seem so upset about the sanctity of school boards. They think conservatism means their rich friends get a tax cut and some Third World hellhole gets bombed. They talk a lot about Ronald Reagan, and have literally no idea why Reagan was popular. If they were even alive and aware in the '80s, there is an approximately 100 percent chance they referred to him as "a cowboy" and wished he wasn't so confrontational.

This is where you find Nikki Haley and her ilk. She started an advocacy group named—this is not a joke—"Stand for America." Think of how many poor saps sat through the three-hour focus group for fifty dollars to validate that entry in the Encyclopedia of Hack Clichés. The website is missing an eagle image, but of course there's a flag. Her consultants' level of contempt for the base is so intense that it's almost hilarious how they can't even see that they should try to hide it.

The next rung is the earnest establishment types, the folks who mean well but just don't get it. Tim Scott is the front-runner here. He's a nice guy, a good guy, a guy who legitimately wants to reach across the aisle and work with our Democratic opponents. This is disqualifying. We need to win, which means they need to lose.

Marco Rubio is another establishment type with flashes of basedness. He's shown a willingness to work with the Democrats on important issues for the American people, like immigration. It'll be hard to forgive that.

Then you have the establishment rebel, a contradiction in terms personified by Chris Christie. He has carved out a unique space for himself both by his aggressive style and his vulnerability to embarrassing memes involving beach chairs and bridges. Christie barks loudly, but he won't bite. He's a proud moderate—he would call it "sensible" or some other soothing descriptor, by which he means he's never going to disrupt anything. His appeal, the establishment thinks, is that Christie is one of them, but he knows how to spout off the way those hillbillies outside I-495 like to hear. There are literally no actual conservatives who want Chris Christie.

There's also Kristi Noem, who…no, she's gone. The thing about conservatives, the abused wives of American politics, is that you get one chance. She blew it with her transgender/girls' sports sellout. It's sad to see her fail so needlessly, but we dodged Nikki with a lasso. It is good, however, to have a figurative head to mount on a spike. Think of it as a teaching moment for the 2024 candidates.

There are the senators, like Ted Cruz, who will have more money than Crassus. He is certainly conservative woke. And he certainly does not care what liberals think. These are good qualities. But does he have the charisma? Can the Cancun tourist undo his January 6 blunder? He came close to losing to that furry in Texas in his last Senate run in 2018. He would probably have to drop out of the Senate race to run. A tough call for Ted.

Rick Scott of Florida is a solid guy who likes to fight, but his compromise on guns in the past might hurt him. He's getting more based, though. You could do much worse.

You then have the Trump-ally band of candidates, and there are lots of good folks here. Tom Cotton is bright, but he's very young. Mike Pompeo has slimmed down and hinted he will run even if Trump does. His big handicap is that he is Mike Pompeo. Robert O'Brien is a diplomat who is very smart, and he can reach out to both the establishment and the base. These guys all know what time it is.

And there's the alligator state's governor. Ron DeSantis, our nation turns its lonely eyes to you. His wife's health is a concern, and he needs to get a smashing win in the 2022 governor's race, but if he goes for it he is a front-runner. He simply does not care what the media or the establishment thinks—not even a little. Take that, Disney groomer-enablers. He is also absent from social media (though his team is killer on it), and his selling point is that he just *does*. DeSantis heaps accomplishment on accomplishment, turning his state from a symbol of fascinating insanity to the go-to spot for fed-up blue-staters.

But do any of these guys beat Trump for the nomination if he runs? Well, someone has to choose to run to find out. As noted, Pompeo might be open to it. Others have peremptorily declined. The Republican love for Trump is wide, but how deep is it, especially considering the stakes? Trump draws the media fire, though anyone who runs as a Republican is going to be Hitler, so that's not really a consideration. The challenge is that a lot of people hate Trump. They shouldn't—they should choose mean tweets, peace, and cheap gas over the alternative—but they do. And that means a general election with Trump in becomes close because he's Trump.

This is all amusing speculation, except the stakes are Mount Everest–level high. We have seen what is coming. This is not a time to indulge ambition. This is not a time to indulge personal resentments. This is a time to win so we can keep this country from going over a cliff. We've peeked at what lies at the bottom of the chasm. Avoiding that is more important than soothing any of these people's egos.

So, we need a winner. But we also need a warrior. For too long we figured that once we won an election we could sigh and go back to other things. That's what got us into this mess. There are no other things. We need to take our country back. And that means years of peaceful struggle designed to avoid the unpeaceful struggles that are some of the fearsome alternatives.

It means rethinking conservatism to defeat the current threat. Conservatives must get over their fetish for conserving. A gangrenous leg gets lopped off. Our whole society is full of septic limbs.

Unlike the left, we do not seek to remake society into something new, but rather something old and proven by time. The Constitution, and all it entails, is the key. But America must change from a country where we take our founding principles for granted and let them be disregarded to one where we zealously guard and nurture them. And that starts by defeating the ascendant left.

If we do not begin remaking society into one where all the heights of power are not occupied by leftists, America is going to become more and more unstable until it collapses. The chances that we are going to become the first society where Marxism is tried and it "works" are nil. We either win, or it all goes to hell.

CHAPTER SIXTEEN

THE DECISION POINT: 2024

A conservative victory in the 2024 presidential election is a necessary step, but is not sufficient to ensure that America will rise again. It seems likely that the GOP will have Congress back if current trends hold. The Democrats are facing a fateful combination of historical headwinds, GOP-dominated redistricting, and alleged President Biden's apparent intention to have Jimmy Carter hold his Billy Beer in terms of showing just how steeply approval numbers can nosedive.

The Supreme Court is unlikely to go left anytime soon—the only way conservative veterans Justices Thomas and Alito are leaving the high court while the Delaware dementite is in office is feetfirst. But to truly change course, conservatives need to regain the executive branch. The president works with the Congress to pass legislation, and he nominates judges. These are vital tasks. But the presidency provides an energy to power change that the other branches can't muster. Certainly the executive order function is important, but so is guiding the execution of policy. It's not enough to issue orders or even sign laws if the permanent bureaucracy can simply stall, undermine, and generally wait out the president. To save the country—that is, to manage the coming changes so that they result in our being, stronger, richer, and freer, instead of weaker, poorer, and more serf-like—we need a president who is not only conservative but who knows what time it is.

He must be woke, if you will, but conservative woke. He must clearly see the correlations of forces today and must have a vision of America tomorrow. Then he must aggressively execute a campaign to make that vision a reality while remaining within the Constitution. He needs to understand that this is a struggle for the country's future, and that reflexive support for institutions that betrayed us and rules that no longer exist ensures a leftist victory.

We cannot afford a Harrison Bergeron president artificially weighed down and handicapped by amorphous and obsolete norms and rules that keep him from soaring on the dance floor.

And all the while, he must honor the checks and balances of the system and resist the temptation to become an actual authoritarian— although he needs to resign himself to the fact he's going to be called an "authoritarian" no matter what he does. Ignoring or mocking the haters is essential to keeping his promises—that's Trump's lasting lesson. Focus on the objective and attack, attack, attack.

The establishment will not like it. It will fight back. It will not give an inch. He will have to fight for every millimeter, starting at 12:01 p.m. eastern time on January 20, 2025. And not everyone is up to that. Not everyone is ready to face that reality. Some want to live in a fantasy world of reaching across the aisle to build bridges and so forth. But when it comes to building bridges over the River Kwai or in D.C. today, you can either be Alec Guinness or William Holden.

Don't be Colonel Nicholson, hesitating to push the plunger and blow up the bridge.

We need the right person for the job, someone who understands at an instinctual level that this rumble is for all the turf. It's not about abstract principles or pleasing donors. It is certainly not about enjoying the role—far too many Republicans seem to want to be president simply so they get to be president. It is not enough to be; our candidate must do.

As we have seen, everything depends on it.

We need a candidate who gets that, who feels the gnawing fear that, if he fails, all this—the freedom, the prosperity, the ability to live as citizens—goes away. Because that is exactly what is on the line. If we fail in 2024, then one of those terrifying scenarios we have seen, or something like them, comes true, and then America changes for the worse, perhaps much worse. This is our last chance to stop the decline that started back in the Persian Gulf the moment after America hit her peak and that has continued, with a few temporary rebounds, through this day. Don't fool yourself; it can get worse. As we have seen, we have come nowhere near hitting bottom yet.

We need focus in our next president, a clear-eyed vision of what he wants to achieve in his four, hopefully eight, years. The big-picture strategy, in broad strokes, must assure our place at the head of the world order—we need to eschew the "New World Order" stuff that is code for "America is not in charge anymore"—and begin the domestic reset of America to serve the needs of the great American working and middle class that is spread across the land, not the very wealthy and the liberal gentry clustered in blue enclaves on the coasts.

There are plenty of specific policies we need to pursue with gusto. Internationally, we need to build and man enough ships to control the oceans. We need to revitalize the nuclear triad so China, Russia, and—if Biden keeps true to his penchant for disaster—Iran understand that if the thermonuclear fastballs get pitched, they strike out forever. We need to rally our existing allies by showing them that we are not going to cut and run the next time things get hard, and to build alliances with key new allies like India. But we also need to recognize our limits—as a practical matter, Americans are done sending their kids and cash off to Whogivesadamnistan to sort out thousand-years-old beefs between near-savages. At some point, all peoples need to choose, chaos or civilization. And now so do we.

Domestically, the specific policies are important. A social media user's bill of rights, the defunding of the FBI, the end of student loans, and the closing of the borders and deportation of illegal aliens—these support the greater strategy. And that is to move America away from centralized economics, centralized power, and centralized thought, and toward individual responsibility and truly free enterprise, not the kind of "free enterprise" that allows mega-corporations to leverage lobbyists to lock out uppity upstarts.

When the next president leaves office in 2033, God willing, we want—among other things—corporate power restrained, working- and middle-class Americans economically and physically safe, the government smaller and weaker, and academia unrecognizable from what it is today. This is big-picture stuff, and having a big picture is important, but it's the details that win or lose the battle. And the president can't do details—at least not all of them.

A president needs a team of like-minded folks who understand his vision and are loyal to it—behind him. There are about four thousand presidential appointees, four thousand handpicked leaders spread across the bureaucracy who can each ensure his domain (be it an entire department, say, the Department of Agriculture; or a small part of one, say, the Undersecretariat for Sorghum and Legume Affairs) conforms to the mission. That's a lot of appointees, so you need a bulging Rolodex. But here's the thing—if you are an outsider to the establishment like, say, a New York real estate magnate and reality show host known largely from newspaper stories about his incredible streak of insanely attractive female companions when you get elected, you will come into office essentially Rolodex-free.

Jeb! Bush would have had a Rolodex—every slot would have been filled before he even put his soft, girlish hand on the Bible. But, of course, that Rolodex would have been filled largely with establishment timeservers eager for a new CV entry whose loyalty, if to anyone, was to Bush. What are the chances they would have been committed conservative ideologues ready to disrupt the dominant paradigm?

About the same chance as Jeb! had to get elected president.

An establishment president will have an establishment administration. Members of the Republican establishment have as little interest in pillaging the status quo like Atilla the Hun as the Democrats do. You don't gain power as a bureaucrat by cutting your budget and closing up shop. Establishment people want to perpetuate their own power. They don't want to come to D.C., spread fear and chaos, then go home. Hell, they live in Georgetown. That *is* their home.

Donald Trump showed up in Washington and had exactly zero friends there. But he had fake friends, establishment types who saw his election—regrettable to them as it was, because you know they were dying for a dose of Vitamin Jeb!—as their opportunity to take a turn padding the old resume.

His Rolodex being empty, Trump had to rely on the Republican establishment's Rolodex, which was packed with the kind of people whose unbroken track record of failure had led the voters of the GOP to nominate a guy like The Donald in the first place.

And personnel was Trump's bane. Yeah, he got shafted by the press and plagued by lies about Russian collusion and all the rest. But every problem he had could have been solved, or at least ameliorated, by having a loyal, competent, and based ("based" being "woke" in Conservatese) conservative team in position. Look at the collusion scam. Jim Comey, that paragon of integrity, was already playing him even before he was sworn in. Did Trump keep him? Yeah, for too long, and then he replaced him with another guy who all the D.C. people assured him was a paragon of integrity, Chris Wray. Said paragon turned his G-men into the personal Stasi of the liberal elite, raiding with SWAT teams and hassling moms worried about CRT, all while missing an endless series of mass killers whom, it turned out, the FBI knew about.

Trump nominated Jeff Sessions, another paragon of integrity, to head the Department of Justice. Sessions was dopey enough to take the paragon-of-integrity crap seriously and, like the sap he was, let himself be manipulated into recusing himself from oversight of the Russian hoax. That led to another paragon of integrity, Robert Mueller, being appointed special counsel to hamstring the Trump administration for a couple years. It turned out he was a paragon of senility whose team knew the Russia thing was a lie yet kept the ball rolling because a perpetual scandal served the establishment's purposes.

So many paragons of integrity, yet so little integrity. The lesson for the next president is *no more paragons*. If the establishment gives a thumbs-up, that's a thumbs-down.

And then there is the military. Name a general who did not shaft President Trump—just one. Trump, sadly, suffered from the delusion that a constellation of stars and a chest full of fruit salad is a *Good Housekeeping* Seal of Approval. Never be impressed with generals, particularly ones who can't point to a war they won while being generals. Even Mike Flynn, a nice guy framed by the FBI, screwed up. How? He trusted the FBI. The next president needs to ensure that his generals have all earned a ribbon for Valorous Conservative Service in the Bureaucratic Wars with multiple oak leaf clusters.

The other generals Trump had in his inner circle simply decided that the president was wrong about the foreign policy the people of this country elected him to pursue, and they substituted their own policy preferences—again, these are the guys who never won a war as generals. Many of them were personally brave, like H. R. McMaster, a VII Corps hero of the Gulf. General John F. Kelly lost a son in Iraq. James M. Mattis was a good Marine division commander and a terrible secretary of defense who proved the Peter principle by, among other things, falling for the Theranos nonsense spewed by Silicon Valley vixen Elizabeth Holmes.

Even the worst chairman of the Joint Chiefs of Staff ever, Mark Milley, served bravely as a junior officer and was, according to baffled troops who served in his unit, a good battalion commander. But they were all total failures at their jobs in the Trump administration because none of them could swallow the bitter pill that was deference to the commander in chief. They fought his proposals, and they lied to him about what was really happening. It was a disgrace. Woe to any junior officer in these generals' commands who treated their expressed intent with the same contempt they treated their boss's.

The Trump administration was chaos early on, with far more leaks than even the usual administration suffers, and many of them about the president himself. Remember the ridiculous first secretary of state, Rex Tillerson? Where did he come from? Not from Trump's inner circle, or even outer one. He was recommended, and Trump appointed him. And he was a disaster. So was Defense Secretary Mike Esper. Where did Trump find these nimrods, and more importantly, why did he not 86 them after their first failure?

Trump got personnel under control after three years; by then, he had established a mostly loyal cadre of appointees (though the Democrats did what they could to slow or stop his ability to nominate people to fill the positions requiring confirmation). Following John Bolton—who got appointed even though everyone knew his views on useless foreign wars were 180 degrees off from the president's (The

Moustache loved wars)—Robert C. O'Brien came in and was arguably the best national security advisor in American history. All he did was help end, you know, the seventy-year-old Middle East conflict. Ric Grenell, as ambassador to Germany, took America First and rubbed it in the Eurotash's faces before going over to be acting director of national intelligence and starting to drain that cesspool.

Think of what they could have done with another four years . . .

Of course, that raises the issue of election security. Play it again, Sam—the establishment let Trump down. Without relieving him of his responsibility—the commander is responsible for everything his unit does or fails to do—Trump relied on the GOP establishment to ensure that the legal and other aspects of voter security were in place in 2020. They were not in place, not even remotely. Your author received a call the day after the election to come to Las Vegas to help in the legal effort—note the "after" part. Nevada was one of the six corruption battleground states, and when your author rode into town he found a GOP lawyer.

"A."

As in "not plural."

Look, he was a very good lawyer, and he brought his dog along, which was nice, but one lawyer in one of the top six Democratic shenanigans target cities? That's not a serious effort. It barely qualifies as an effort at all.

The clusterfark that was the GOP's 2020 election litigation response is a book of its own. Suffice it to say there was evidence of actual, traditional cheating—we found a dead guy who voted within a couple hours, so the question was not if there was cheating but how much. More important were the massive extra-legal changes to the elections laws slammed through improperly on the grounds of COVID, all things that should have been fought by well-funded and organized GOP election lawyers weeks and months before November

3, 2020. And then there was the third leg of the triad of cheating, the informal rigging of the establishment and media to weight the scale for Joe Biden. The institutions gave not a second thought to dispensing with their neutrality and jumping in for the leftist with both Gucci-clad feet because they feared no consequences.

The next GOP president should not allow those who should be on the sidelines to think they can come onto the field without being tackled. Trump was not sufficiently feared because he did not effectively use his power to punish his enemies. Right now, the giant corporations who backed Biden are sitting sipping their Rémy Martin XO brandy and smoking their Montecristo cigars as they gaze through their monocles at the workers toiling in their fields, serenely confident that the moment the domesticated GOP takes power again, it will come loping to their mansion door with a new package of corporate tax cuts in its mouth, ready to be petted by its master.

That better not happen if the Republican Party does not want a full-scale revolt among the base.

The next president must put down a marker. To cross the conservatives is to pay a price. You are not going to get many of the fat cats to do the right thing by appealing to their altruism. Instead, target their lizard brains and their pain receptors.

No one feared Trump. That was the problem, for early on he failed to wield his power ruthlessly in support of his vision. Every Army commander knows that you need to firmly take command on day one. You can't start in soft and huggy and then harden up. You can come in hard and ease back on the throttle when the unit is performing.

There is a difference between using your constitutional authority and being an authoritarian.

People respect strength and will conform when faced with it. It does not require the full "authoritarian" example we discussed, but it does require a focus on rolling back the liberal invasion of the institutions by refusing to accept their legitimacy at face value and using power to limit or eliminate the power of left-corrupted institutions, sometimes by taking down the institutions entirely.

So, what does this look like in practice?

At 11:59 a.m. on the crisp, cold morning of January 20, 2025, the president-elect arose to stand before a pouting Justice Roberts, who held the George Washington Inaugural Bible in his gloved hands. During the campaign, the president-elect had made his position clear: "You will not see another John Roberts from me. You will not necessarily see another Federalist Society nominee from me either. You will see committed conservatives who understand that the duty of a Supreme Court justice is to ensure that the Constitution as written controls. And that always means a proper justice will be a conservative." The media nearly collectively wet itself over that comment; when asked, as he was a dozen times, about whether he was "going to require a conservative political litmus test for Supreme Court justices," he replied, "That's exactly what I mean."

And he never backed down, moderated his statement, or apologized.

The chief justice had been so scandalized that he felt compelled to issue a press release on behalf of the Court explaining the importance of the Court's remaining apolitical. Democrats were delighted; the president-elect simply said, "I will never appoint another John Roberts" to massive applause at a rally. But where the chief justice wore a frown on the frigid platform, the president-elect was smiling. Among other things, he knew that within a week Justice Thomas would announce his retirement in order to travel the country in his RV. The judicial appointments team, which had more political operators than lawyers, was already vetting a replacement, one who was chosen in part because he did not attend Harvard or Yale.

Nearby, newly sworn-in Vice President Ric Grenell smiled. The veep always swore in first.

As he placed his hand on the Bible, the president-elect heard a vague mumbling from the front row. "Look at the pretty birdy, Dr. Jill," the soon-to-be ex-president muttered. Kamala Harris was absent. She said it was because she would "not condone the false installation of a racist following a rigged election." It was a stand universally hailed by the mainstream media, as doubting election results had recently morphed from treasonous to the height of patriotism. In truth, Harris was angrier at the former Oval Office occupant for hanging on all the way to the end and running out her clock.

"I do solemnly swear that I will faithfully execute the Office of President of the United States, and will to the best of my ability, preserve, protect and defend the Constitution of the United States," the new president said, removing his hand from the Bible. Justice Roberts offered his hand, and the forty-seventh president of the United States shook it. It was limp.

His speech was short and clear—the president told the country he intended to keep his promises and then departed to the White House after cursory congratulations of various levels of sullenness from the other pooh-bahs on the platform. Few Democrats attended, as his election was being hailed in the press as the greatest and most serious attack on "Our Democracy" since the last one. When asked at a recent press conference—he gave a lot of them—how he "could legitimately serve as president when surrounded by the election controversy and when tens of millions of Americans doubted the validity of the results," he replied, "Watch me."

The documents the new chief executive had directed be prepared for immediate execution were present on the Resolute desk when he arrived in the Oval Office. He would not have tolerated anything less. His first potential chief of staff had made the mistake of second-guessing his directions, and his replacement learned the lesson the bureaucrats throughout the executive branch would soon learn. This president meant what he said, and he would not hesitate to exercise his power to ensure his intent was carried out.

The busts of Lincoln and Churchill he had directed be returned to the Oval Office stared at him as he began signing the papers. The firing of Christopher Wray as FBI director, the firing of every general on the Joint Chiefs of Staff, the firing of Dr. Anthony Fauci—they went first. Their acting replacements were already identified; the computers and official cell phones of the fired personnel were already being secured by federal marshals in case any investigations became necessary—and they would be.

He signed the military orders next. The first was a strategy document clarifying that the number one strategic threat to the United States was neither "climate change" nor "domestic white supremacist terrorism," but enemy states like Red China, Russia, Iran, and North Korea. The strategy guidance also specifically identified "radical Muslim terrorism," in keeping with his promise to "call things by their true names when I am president."

Next came the orders banning critical race theory–type training and programs throughout the government, as well as directing that the occupant of every federal job with a title that included any of the words "diversity," "inclusion," or "equity" be terminated. Many canned functionaries would sue over their lost jobs; well, that's what DOJ lawyers were for. And on the subject of the Department of Justice, he executed an order firing every United States attorney and another order requiring that the attorney general personally sign and approve any investigation of any kind involving administration personnel. That order, of course, would send the media into orbit, but his people leaked it to Fox first before the leakers embedded in the department could. He would set the narrative, portraying it accurately as a means of preventing deep-state officials from trying to frame members of his team the way they had done to those in the Trump administration. His new AG was an old friend, and he would, of course, be the president's wingman. The new AG would never recuse himself.

Next were the January 6, 2021, pardons. He signed them, pardoning every individual charged except those working as FBI informants. He skimmed the pardon message—yes, the key part was included: "There can be no dual system of justice in America. Because leftist Democrat-allied protesters were not treated identically, justice demands these pardons." He smiled. Just wait until the media found out he was directing the DOJ to settle the civil rights claims of these people for millions of dollars.

Then he began signing the border emergency bills. The new deportation policy was to deport every illegal alien and increase internal enforcement. Sure, some Hawaiian judge would enjoin it but, again, that's why the DOJ had so many lawyers. He signed an order banning federal contractors from hiring illegal aliens as well. And the construction of the wall would begin again immediately.

The idea of hitting the ground running like this, with a tsunami of pre-drafted orders (his team had been working twenty-hour days since November to prepare them while also dealing with the passive-aggressive resistance to the incoming administration), was stolen from Barack Obama's crew. They called it "stray voltage"— you put so many controversial things out there at once that your opponents cannot figure out which to focus their ire upon. Any one of these would have been a whole news cycle of performative outrage by the mainstream media had it happened by itself. Now, with dozens of initiatives, each "a grave threat to Our Democracy" or, at least, "clearly racist," launched at once, the outcry became just noise.

There was a method to this massive assault. The initial terminations and executive orders were designed to neutralize the ability of the institutions to continue their remaking of the country, an attempt to stop the bleeding. The coming legislative initiatives were designed to undermine the lost institutions and force those that potentially had value to reform without leftist domination. He had been working with Mitch McConnell and Kevin McCarthy on the agenda since even before the election. McCarthy did not have the same challenge as Cocaine Mitch—he could deliver a majority every time. Much of what needed to happen in the Senate would have to come via reconciliation—McConnell was not lifting the filibuster. But a good deal of filibustering could be avoided with some focused hardball on vulnerable Democratic senators—the president made it clear that the favorite programs of those acting as obstacles were on the chopping block.

Regardless, the president was intent on structural change. This meant ruthlessly eliminating subsidized liberal bastions like NPR, which was to be defunded despite the screams of the Volvo set. There were numerous other subsidies for leftist agencies and nongovernmental agencies as well—they would be identified and defunded. A flurry of orders and guidance from the Department of Education took aim at academia. The universities found themselves under investigation for lacking "ideological diversity," which became a condition of the diminishing federal aid they received. And rules conditioning funds on campus free speech and on a one-administrator-to-ten-students ratio helped break the left's ideological hammerlock on America's impressionable college students. Forcing the schools to accept liability for a portion of defaulted student loans (the president would have eliminated them all together, but even some squishy

Republicans resisted that) disincentivized the ridiculous race, gender, and ethnicity studies fad, since people working at Starbucks were unlikely to pay off their useless degrees. Enrollment in STEM majors, however, surged.

The backlash was entirely predictable, but once again multiple moves happened all at once, diluting the Democratic response. The Overton window was open, and the president was going to defenestrate institutional Marxism. In fact, the president's newly appointed chairman of the Department of Homeland Security's Disinformation Governance Board, Jack Posobiec, formally listed "Marxism" as "dangerous misinformation that makes Americans unsafe," along with "critical race theory," "climate change hoax propaganda," and "claims that mutilating children is an appropriate remedy for gender delusions."

There was some violence in the streets of some blue cities, mostly purported to be over the allegedly stolen election. The media eagerly pushed the most ridiculous conspiracy theories even as the courts swatted down Marc Elias's countless lawsuits. But the president was having none of it. The FBI was reoriented—painfully, with many agents associated with past persecutions and fiascos handed their walking papers—toward dismantling leftist militia groups. Antifa rioters found themselves in federal lockups for crossing state lines to riot or organizing violence using electronic communications. There were no mass dismissals of criminal charges; the fun stopped, as did most of the street violence, as soon as the mob saw its buddies looking at hard federal time.

The New York Times, 60 Minutes, and the rest of the mainstream media could barely get the time of day from the administrations. Bob Woodward asked to be allowed to observe for his next book; the one administration official who actually told him anything of substance was fired and found himself persona non grata in the Republican world. Loyalty was enforced ruthlessly. Sure, there were leaks, but *nothing like the torrents from the prior Trump administration. Friendly media got the good stories; if you wanted to know what was going on in the administration, you had to watch Fox or read the reporters from Townhall.*

While working to dismantle the leftist hold on the institutions, the administration focused on high-impact policies to ensure its popularity. The lodestar was Trump's tried-and-true principle of "promises made, promises kept." Getting gas prices down by abandoning policies to address the nonexistent climate crisis was one initiative. Keeping food prices low through federal subsidies was another. Some critics on the right claimed that these were not conservative policies, but the president was looking at the big picture, and he understood that pure politics sometimes had to take priority over pure free-market principles. That was also illustrated by his "millionaire's tax," a sharp surtax on those making over $5 million a year that proved very popular with most Americans, though not with those making over $5 million—but they were mostly Democrats.

It was not all success. There were setbacks, initiatives that could not get sufficient support on Capitol Hill, and occasional corruption within the administration. But the economy recovered, America's enemies realized that the new president was a serious man and not a doddering clown, and slowly the left was forced out of its sinecures in the institutions. Sure, there were casualties—the woke NBA's loss of its antitrust exemption devastated the sport, but Major League Baseball and the NFL both got the message. There was no more kneeling and no more China stroking. Corporations that pushed a woke agenda got a friendly call warning them that the world had changed. It was okay to be neutral in the cultural political battles, like they had been before, but they needed to understand that to side with the conservatives' enemy was to be the conservatives' enemy.

And this president did not hesitate to turn the enforcement power of the federal government on the conservatives' enemies. No one learned that lesson harder than the social media companies. The passage of the Social Media User's Bill of Rights Act, which required strict political neutrality, enforced by private lawsuits to recover staggering punitive damages against companies silencing individuals, was just the start. The Algorithm Transparency Act forced the largest search engine companies to reveal exactly how they manipulated search results (again, enforced by greedy lawyers suing over violations), and the characterization of granting internet visibility advantages to particular candidates as a political contribution helped convince the moguls to return to neutrality lest the conservative government punish them further.

The president did not shrink from using his formal power—after all, the left had not shrunk from using its formal and informal power. Complaints that his doing so violated some abstract conservative principles were unavailing. "My conservative principle is that American citizens must be free, secure, and prosperous," the president replied to those critics. The checks and balances restrained him, but he certainly pushed the envelope regarding the informal norms.

America looked the same, but the feel was different than under Biden and Harris. Crime was down, as Democrats in blue cities realized they needed to move right to have any hope of competing for votes. The economy was booming. But mostly, the institutions were staying out of people's faces in a way they had not for a decade, having been either razed or terrified into retreat by conservatives exercising power without arbitrary limits. The institutions had started that trend—they had taken aim at normal Americans with such initiatives as their critical race theory nonsense, their climate hoax, and their COVID hysteria. They experienced no pushback as they exceeded

AFTERWORD

Looking back on that day in the Saudi desert in February 1991, when America was at the peak of its power and the world gazed upon us in awe, I find it difficult to square that moment with the present. We were invincible then, and now we are still contending with the consequences of being recently 'vinced by a bunch of seventh-century savages. Our president then seemed competent—we were not yet fully woke to the reality of the Bush clan—while today the occupant of the White House, assuming he has not been replaced by his hideous political consort, is a senile joke for whom any event where he doesn't soil himself is a triumph.

Nevertheless, I am an optimist, and I believe America will rise again, albeit with scars.

What has happened in the last three decades will leave a mark. All the norms that were shattered cannot be pieced back together again so easily. The rules we thought we had agreed upon about personal freedom, property rights, and the relation of government to citizens have been rewritten for short-term convenience. They will not go back to what they were. Imagine the response the next time the American Civil Liberties Union, which once earned grudging respect even from its enemies for being so consistent that it defended the rights of Nazis to spew their nonsense, tells us we can't take action against commie college professors intent on indoctrinating our kids. It will be something to the effect of, "Aren't you the guys who wanted to mandate the vaccine because the Democrats wanted to? Maybe you should sit down and shut up."

So, when we say America will rise again, we need to understand it will be a different America. And we also need not mourn the America that is gone. It was not perfect, though—like dead Republicans always cited by the mainstream media to chide breathing ones—old America will gain that proverbial strange new respect as the outlines of the future America become clear. It will be a more partisan and more ruthless America. Power will more often prevail over process. Perhaps the best we can hope for is a kind of federalist cold war where some states abort babies with abandon and others don't, where in some states hobos wander freely leaving their spoor and needles on sidewalks, while in others they can't.

That kind of cracked federalism might be a least-worst case, but we have seen plenty of worse cases. There was really nowhere to go but down back then in 1991, and the optimist in me hopes, seemingly against hope, that today there is nowhere for us to go but up.

Of course, that is wrong. We can certainly go down further, for leftism has no bottom. As we have seen, there are myriad ways it could get worse, much, much worse. And yet, as we have also seen, there are ways it could all get better.

I think it will get better. I have to believe that we will get through this, that America's era is just beginning, and that the mediocrities and morons who are bringing us low will not prevail. The mere thought of it is hateful. We cannot let these losers win. But I cannot pretend that my optimism is based upon any actual evidence. Should you examine the evidence, the rational conclusion is pessimism. Instead, my optimism is purely a gut feeling. But then, so is diverticulitis.

To the extent that that constitutes optimism, color me optimistic. Yes, it could all go utterly bad, but optimism remains our only reasonable choice. To accept that we are headed for one of these dooms we have reviewed or some other fate that we have not yet imagined is to shrug and sit waiting for the asteroid to hit. We could decide that there is no hope and no reason to fight, but then the prophecy would fulfill itself.

Conservatives have a knack for pessimism. This is likely because conservatives recognize the imperfectibility of man and thereby understand that those same endemic flaws will necessarily infect the institutions we create. The United States of America is, after all, a nation of men—and women, and that's all, because there is nothing else—and we conservatives accept that about the best we are going to get out of any government is going to be mediocre.

But pessimism is exhausting, and boring, and worse, it is self-defeating. When you talk to a pessimist, it's nonstop assurances that it's all over and we're finished and the like. Maybe it's just easier to make your peace with the coming collapse than to confront it. But whatever it is, it is not helpful to the project of preventing the worst-case scenario.

Better to go down fighting, because the hell with them. The hell with the people who got us here and their garbage ideologies and their desperate need to force our submission. They get nothing, not our obedience, our cooperation, or our complicity in turning this country into a historical footnote or a cautionary example that Chi Com college kids can study to learn what not to do.

Pessimism might be realistic, but realism is not helpful in tough spots. You have to believe you can win. And, of course, you might actually win—the 150 or so Brits of the 24th Foot did at Rorke's Drift in the face of 4,000 Zulus and their assegais. Of course, we remember them because their win was so improbable. There are lots of Rorke's Drifts in history, and in most of them the guys in the Zulus' position killed everyone. We don't talk about them because of course the 4,000 guys with spears annihilated the dudes they outnumbered thirty-to-one.

We talk about the outlier because what probably should have happened didn't happen. And what probably should happen to our country is that it fades into insignificance, either by subjugation or through chaos or simply by way of monotonous decline. That's what history would tell us is likely to happen. The great powers shine and flicker out. Why should we be different?

But we are different.

We are not quite at the surrounded-by-Zulu-impis point. Nor are we quite fully down the *cursus horribilis* of ancient Rome. There are some echoes and parallels, but no Gracchi have been beaten to death by the establishment yet. Lesser-known folks, the occasional Ashli Babbit, yes, and that might well prove a foretaste of what will come. But it hasn't come yet.

We still have some ability to be heard, whether through elections or the courts, and some access to platforms, be it books or Fox News or various social media. And, of course, we still have our guns.

The point is that this is not over. There's another election coming, another fight up ahead. We will lose some, but we will win some. We're never going to know the end of the struggle. Freedom is a perpetual fight with the people who can't stand that we have it. But what we have here is something undeniably special—though our opponents regularly deny it.

The United States of America is the greatest nation in the history of mankind. Its foreign enemies are clumsy and evil, with huge problems we overlook because we are too fixated on looking at our own. And our domestic enemies are unaccomplished in inverse proportion to their self-regard. They are not genius supervillains; they are ridiculous fanatics who think they can tweet us into serfdom.

I cannot imagine that America will ever fall to the puny likes of them.

What I can imagine is us, the patriots, bringing America back to where it was in February 1991, and then taking it beyond.

ACKNOWLEDGMENTS

I want to thank co-conspirator and my hot wife Irina Moises for all her help and support in this and all my other projects.

My agent Keith Urbahn told me that it was the first time he had ever gotten a book proposal by text. And yet he got it sold in a day. What a stud—and a veteran too! Thanks, Keith!

And thanks to everyone at Regnery, especially my editor Tony Daniel.

As always, a lot of other people supported me and contributed to this, consciously or otherwise, by kicking around ideas with me. These included Larry O'Connor, Hugh Hewitt, Duane Paterson, Bill Wenger, Michael Walsh, Cam Edwards, Glenn Reynolds, Liz Sheld, Matt Betley, John Cardillo, Jesse Kelly, Ned Ryun, Dan Bongino, Buck Sexton, Seb Gorka, David Limbaugh, Tony Katz, Ace, Liz Sheld, Jack Posobiec, Samantha Nerove, Jim Hanson, Tim Pool, Jerry Hendrix, Dave Reaboi, and many others. Thanks!

There are others as well, and they know who they are! Your secret is safe with me!

And a huge thanks to the crew at Townhall.com for letting me explore my ideas before a vast audience.

Thank you also Twitter and Gettr followers, and thank you to those who have supported my writing all along—you rock!

And, as always, thank you Andrew Breitbart. You made this possible. Andrew, if you were still here, we might not be in this situation, but what you did us shows us the way out of it. Cheers!

KAS

ABOUT THE AUTHOR

Kurt Schlichter is a senior columnist for Townhall.com. He is also a Los Angeles trial lawyer admitted in California, Texas, and Washington, D.C., and a retired United States Army Infantry colonel.

A social media activist (@KurtSchlichter) with over 400,000 followers on Twitter and 340,000 followers on GETTR, Kurt was personally recruited to write conservative commentary by Andrew Breitbart.

Kurt is a news source, an on-screen commentator on networks such as Fox and Newsmax, and a guest on, and frequent guest host of, nationally syndicated radio programs talking about political, military, and legal issues.

He is the author of *The 21 Biggest Lies about Donald Trump and You* (2020), the *USA Today* bestseller *Militant Normals: How Regular Americans Are Rebelling against the Elite to Reclaim Our Democracy* (2018), as well as *Conservative Insurgency: The Struggle to Take America Back 2013–2041* (2014). He is also the author of the Amazon bestselling conservative action novels *People's Republic* (2016), *Indian Country* (2017), *Wildfire* (2018), *Collapse* (2019), *Crisis* (2020), and *The Split* (2021).

Kurt served as a U.S. Army infantry officer on active duty and in the California Army National Guard, retiring at the rank of full colonel. He commanded the 1st Squadron, 18th Cavalry Regiment (Reconnaissance-Surveillance-Target Acquisition) and is a veteran of both the Persian Gulf War and Operation Enduring Freedom (Kosovo). He also served on the streets with the 3-160th Infantry

Battalion during the Los Angeles riots. Kurt graduated from the Army's Combined Arms and Services Staff School, the Command and General Staff College, and the United States Army War College, where he received a master's degree in strategic studies.

Kurt lives with his wife Irina and his monstrous dogs Bitey and Barkey in the Los Angeles area. Kurt enjoys sarcasm and red meat.

His favorite caliber is .45.